Dilemmas of European Democracy

Dilemmas of European Democracy

New Perspectives on Democratic Politics in the European Union

Edited by
NIKLAS BREMBERG AND LUDVIG NORMAN

EDINBURGH
University Press

Edinburgh University Press is one of the leading university presses in the UK. We publish academic books and journals in our selected subject areas across the humanities and social sciences, combining cutting-edge scholarship with high editorial and production values to produce academic works of lasting importance. For more information visit our website: edinburghuniversitypress.com

© editorial matter and organisation Niklas Bremberg and Ludvig Norman, 2023
© the chapters their several authors, 2023

Edinburgh University Press Ltd
The Tun – Holyrood Road
12(2f) Jackson's Entry
Edinburgh EH8 8PJ

Typeset in 10/13 Giovanni by
IDSUK (DataConnection) Ltd, and
printed and bound by CPI Group (UK) Ltd, Croydon, CR0 4YY

A CIP record for this book is available from the British Library

ISBN 978-1-3995-1193-3 (hardback)
ISBN 978-1-3995-1195-7 (webready PDF)
ISBN 978-1-3995-1196-4 (epub)

The right of Niklas Bremberg and Ludvig Norman to be identified as the editors of this work has been asserted in accordance with the Copyright, Designs and Patents Act 1988, and the Copyright and Related Rights Regulations 2003 (SI No. 2498).

CONTENTS

Notes on the Contributors / vii

INTRODUCTION / Democratic Dilemmas of Europe's Political Order / 1
Niklas Bremberg and Ludvig Norman

ONE / Representation without a Demos? A Very European
Democratic Dilemma / 28
Christopher Lord

TWO / Beyond the Nation-State: Multilevel Democracy in Europe / 56
Michael Keating

THREE / Dilemmas of Deliberative Democracy in the European Union:
Why (Not) and How (Not)? / 76
Firat Cengiz

FOUR / Dilemmas of EU Citizenship: The Persistent Divide
between Economic and Political Integration / 99
Sandra Seubert

FIVE / European Capitalism without European Democracy?
Democratic Dilemmas and Markets in the European Union / 121
Kathleen R. McNamara

SIX / Beyond Democratic Minimalism: How Democratic Contestation
Can Support European Integration / 144
Joseph Lacey

SEVEN / Europe's Democratic Dilemmas in Historical Perspective / 169
Sheri Berman

EIGHT / The European Union's Main Democratic Deficits in
Comparative Perspective / 181
R. Daniel Kelemen

CONCLUSION / The Dilemmatic Perspective on European Democracy / 195
Niklas Bremberg and Ludvig Norman

Index / 213

NOTES ON THE CONTRIBUTORS

Sheri Berman is Professor of Political Science at Barnard College, Columbia University. Her research interests include the development of democracy and dictatorship, European politics and history, and fascism, populism, and the history of the left. Her most recent book is *Democracy and Dictatorship in Europe: From the Ancien régime to the Present Day* (Cambridge University Press, 2019).

Niklas Bremberg is Associate Professor at the Department of Political Science, Stockholm University and Senior Research Fellow at the Swedish Institute of International Affairs. His research focuses on the foreign and security policy of the European Union, international security, and secessionism and European integration. He is the co-author with Richard Gillespie of the book *Catalonia, Scotland and the EU: Visions of Independence and Integration* (Routledge, 2022) and has co-authored with August Danielson, Elsa Hedling and Anna Michalski the book *The Everyday Making of EU Foreign and Security Policy: Practices, Socialization and the Management of Dissent* (Edward Elgar, 2022). Previous articles have appeared in *European Journal of International Relations*, *Journal of Common Market Studies*, *Journal of European Integration*, *Journal of International Relations and Development*, *WIREs Climate Change* and *European Security*.

Firat Cengiz is Senior Lecturer in Law at the Liverpool Law School, University of Liverpool. Her research interests include European governance, particularly from a deliberative perspective. She also teaches and researches law and gender and the law and regulation of blockchain and cryptocurrencies. Previous articles have appeared in *Journal of Common Market Studies*, *European Law Review* and *Parliamentary Affairs*.

Michael Keating is Professor Emeritus of Politics at the University of Aberdeen. He has published widely on territorial politics and nationalism in Europe and on public policy and decentralisation. His most recent book is *State and Nation in the United Kingdom: The Fractured Union* (Oxford University Press, 2021).

R. Daniel Kelemen is Professor of Political Science and Law and Chair of the Department of Political Science at Rutgers University. Kelemen's research focuses on politics and law in the European Union. He is the author or editor of six books, and author of over one hundred articles and book chapters. His book *Eurolegalism: The Transformation of Law and Regulation in the European Union* (Harvard University Press, 2011) won the Best Book Award from the European Union Studies Association. Prior to Rutgers, Kelemen was Fellow in Politics, Lincoln College, University of Oxford. He was educated at the University of California, Berkeley (AB in Sociology) and Stanford University (PhD in Political Science).

Joseph Lacey is Associate Professor of Political Theory at the School of Politics and International Relations, University College Dublin. His research interests include European Union politics, including political problems relating to the existence of linguistically divided public spheres, the democratic deficit debate, referendums, the electoral design of the European Parliament and the problem of democratic backsliding. Many of these themes are brought together in the monograph *Centripetal Democracy: Democratic Legitimacy and Political Identity in Belgium, Switzerland and the European Union* (Oxford University Press, 2017).

Christopher Lord is professor at ARENA, The Centre for European Studies at the University of Oslo. He has written several books and articles on democracy, legitimacy and the European Union. He has also worked on Brexit and differentiated integration.

Kathleen R. McNamara is Professor of Government and Foreign Service at Georgetown University, where she co-directs the Global Political Economy Project. She is the author of *The Politics of Everyday Europe: Constructing Authority in the European Union* (Oxford University Press, 2015) and *The Currency of Ideas: Monetary Politics in the European Union* (Cornell University Press, 1998) as well as numerous articles. Her current research examines the EU's geoeconomic shift and emerging activist market policies.

Ludvig Norman is Associate Professor at the Department of Political Science, Stockholm University and Senior Fellow at the Institute of European Studies at UC Berkeley. His research focuses on the institutions of the European

Union, democratic theory and social science methodology. He is the co-editor with Richard Ned Lebow of the book *Robustness and Fragility of Political Orders* (Cambridge University Press, 2022) and has authored the book *The Mechanisms of Institutional Conflict in the European Union* (Routledge, 2016). Previous articles have appeared in *Democratization*, *Political Studies*, *European Journal of International Relations*, *European Journal of Social Theory*, *Journal of Common Market Studies*, *Journal of European Public Policy* and *Cooperation and Conflict*.

Sandra Seubert is Professor of Political Theory at Goethe University Frankfurt am Main. Her research interests cover transformations of citizenship, transnational democracy and European integration from a citizen-centred perspective. She has been co-coordinator in the collaborative EU Project *Barriers towards EU citizenship* and has co-edited the volume *Reconsidering EU Citizenship: Contradictions and Constraints* (Edward Elgar, 2018).

INTRODUCTION

Democratic Dilemmas of Europe's Political Order

Niklas Bremberg and Ludvig Norman

The European political order has an ambivalent relationship with democracy. Democratic concerns have been part of the discussions on European cooperation since its inception in the aftermath of the Second World War. In the early days of postwar reconstruction, however, transnational cooperation built around democratic principles was often viewed with suspicion by Western European political elites (Holland 1996). Lessons from the breakdown in democracy and fascist rule in the interwar years as well as the looming threat of Soviet communism, made them wary of the weaknesses they perceived to be inherent to democracy (Berman 2019; Müller 2013). Democratic concerns re-emerged later on as political elites, and gradually European citizens, found themselves in a setting where the institutions of the European Community and later the European Union (EU) had gained considerable influence over politics in the member states. This triggered wide-ranging debates – both academic and non-academic, especially after the end of the Cold War – regarding the genuine possibility that the European political order might operate according to something resembling robust democratic principles. How such principles can and should be applied beyond the nation-state remains an issue of key concern for citizens, politicians and academics.

Our volume adds to long-standing discussions on how democracy might be transposed to a European political order with the EU at its centre. We take a previously less explored perspective on these issues by placing the multi-dimensional character of democracy front and centre. The democratic dilemmas in plural referred to in the book's title signifies a shift in analytical perspective from discussions on democracy as a unified concept, where the main dilemma has been identified as one between democracy realised at the national level or at the supranational level. We instead choose a disaggregated view on European democracy, taking a step back to consider different dimensions of democratic politics and the tensions and trade-offs that the application of these aspects to the European political order entails. The contributors to this volume engage in focused discussions on democracy's different dimensions such as representation, democratic contestation and the notion of citizenship in relation to the EU. A central point of the book is that this disaggregated perspective on democracy opens up the discussion of more specific dilemmas that have as of yet not been treated in the context of a collected set of texts.

What does a focus on democratic dilemmas mean in the context of discussions on democracy in Europe and the EU? How does such a focus provide a new outlook on these debates and why is it important? Part of the answer to these questions have to do with our basic conception of democracy in this setting. We start from the contention that any effort to democratise a political order like the EU presents actors with dilemmas between different democratic values. We see the contested nature of democratic politics – of what democratic politics is and what it requires – as a necessary precondition for democracy itself and put forward our dilemmatic perspective to bring this notion into theoretical discussion on European democracy. Furthermore, when considering different dimensions of democracy, it quickly becomes apparent that there is little consensus on what concepts such as representation, deliberation or contestation imply in terms of the concrete arrangements necessary to realise the democratic ideals on which they are based.

Our perspective places tensions and trade-offs inherent to any democratic arrangements front and centre, adding to what we see as the often incomplete picture of what is at stake when bringing democratic notions to bear beyond the confines of the European nation-state. In this context, we do not necessarily perceive democratic dilemmas as situations in which we are forced to choose between undesirable outcomes. Rather, democracy ultimately rests on the understanding that any particular choice aimed at altering the status quo will entail trade-offs regarding which democratic values are emphasised, and how those values are operationalised in concrete institutional arrangements. On this basis we also think it is important to ask questions regarding the more specific dilemmas that come to light as we consider the constituent part of democratic politics.

Theoretically, the shift towards democratic dilemmas that we propose here offers an alternative to how discussions on EU democracy have unfolded in recent decades. In this sense, the contributions to this volume collectively offer a counter-position to what we refer to as 'grand theory' approaches to European democracy. These approaches came to dominate discussions as questions related to EU democracy gained momentum in the early 1990s, in particular after the entry into force of the Treaty on European Union (TEU) in 1993 (cf. Diez and Wiener 2019). They were broadly mapped on competing perspectives of the character of the EU as either an intergovernmental cooperative arrangement or an emerging transnational political order with supranational competences and powers. These perspectives were partly associated with normative theorisation, which drew from them the implication that there was a need (or not) to rethink democracy in the EU. Early debates were driven by the observation that the growing influence of supranational decision-making on EU member states was not being matched by sufficiently strong democratic mechanisms at the European level (Eriksen and Fossum 2000; Weiler et al. 1995;). These debates were in large part shaped by competing interpretations of the EU's 'democratic deficit', understood as the increasingly asymmetrical relationship between the influence of the EU on member states and the (in)ability of the citizens in those member states to hold policymakers accountable (Bellamy and Castiglione 2000; Follesdal and Hix 2006). The implication of this notion is often assumed to be that mechanisms for representation, participation and accountability need to be introduced at the European level. Others share the general diagnosis that there is a democratic deficit but are more sceptical about the possibility of remedying the situation by strengthening supranational democracy in the EU. Instead, they argue that the EU has been part and parcel of a more general trend of depoliticisation in member states and the subsequent 'hollowing out' of national democracies (Bickerton 2012; Mair 2013). Seen from this perspective, reproducing a failing national institutional architecture at the European level is not likely to provide solutions. Instead, shortcomings at both the national and the supranational level need to be addressed, preferably by organising politics around more explicit political cleavages thus allowing choices between more clearly defined alternatives than those currently on offer.

Those on the other side of these debates question the very existence of a democratic deficit. Intergovernmentalists argue that, in a similar way to other functional international organisations, opportunities for political representation, participation and accountability in the EU reside firmly at the member state level (Bickerton et al. 2015; Majone 1998; Moravcsik 2008). The political authority of the EU is delegated from its member states and decision-making rests on the legal principles enshrined in the EU treaties. As the withdrawal of the United Kingdom from the EU clearly shows, these powers can be reclaimed if member state governments so decide.

Seen from this perspective, Brexit can be said to have strengthened the democratic legitimacy of the EU, albeit it might, at the same time, have weakened the EU in political and economic terms. From the intergovernmentalist perspective, the introduction of EU citizenship and the European Parliament's increasing influence over the EU policymaking process are of lesser importance. In fact, supranational democracy in this view is neither necessary nor desirable. As with any international cooperative arrangement that states may be involved in, the important point in terms of democracy is that citizens hold their national representatives accountable for how they conduct themselves in the context of these international arrangements. As long as national principals retain control over the agents to which tasks at the international level are delegated, the notion of a democratic deficit leads in the wrong direction. If anything, attempts to mimic national democratic institutions at the supranational level is likely to make mechanisms of accountability more diffuse.

A more recent addition to the grand theory debates focuses on the notion of the European demos, or rather, the absence thereof and what the implications of that general condition may be for European democracy. Discussions in this literature take as their starting points that democracy, first, requires a common identity and sense of togetherness generated by shared values or cultural and linguistic ties and that, second, the European political order lacks such a common demos in any meaningful sense. A key set of social conditions that would make such a democracy function are thus absent in the EU. The notion that a common European demos could emerge from attempts to politicise European politics along the left–right political spectrum is seen as a risky wager (Cheneval and Schimmelfennig 2013). The EU should instead rely on the already deeply entrenched multiple *demoï* of Europe to ground its democratic aspirations and adjust its institutional framework accordingly. Although they emerge from a different set of debates than those that inform the intergovernmentalist perspective, they tend in practice to end up with similar positions on how to approach democratic politics in Europe (Bellamy 2016, 2019; cf. Wolkenstein 2020). The main difference lies in the argument that rather than member state governments, the fundamental building blocks of European democracy should be the *demoï*, or peoples, of Europe (Nicolaïdis 2013). It is in these *demoï* that any legitimate forms of European democracy need to be based.

These grand theory perspectives on what EU democracy is and should be are informative in terms of establishing a set of well-defined analytical and normative positions. They have helped make partial sense of an emerging and increasingly complex European political order and can be used to assess the viability of particular institutional arrangements. It is also clear that the discussions throughout this book owe a great deal to these theoretical starting points. Tensions between politics at the national and supranational levels have dominated debates on EU democracy and these theories remain important as models for capturing key political dynamics in Europe. Consequently, even as we consider a more disaggregated view of democracy, allowing our contributors to engage with specific dimensions of democratic politics, we expect the national–supranational binary to reappear but perhaps in a new guise, along with dilemmas that have previously received less attention in the existing literature.

Our main point of contention with the grand theory debates on EU democracy is that the enactment of democracy in a regional political order such as the EU gives rise to a much broader variety of tensions and trade-offs than these theories acknowledge. Part of the problem is that proponents of competing perspectives in these debates tend to concentrate their respective scholarly gazes on the specific aspects of Europe's political order that map most closely on to their favoured positions. Thus, depending on which aspect of the EU is being emphasised, different criteria are established for thinking about which democratic mechanisms need to be in place. Perspectives that assume that the EU is best understood as an international organisation created to regulate a common market will use different democratic benchmarks from those that see it as an emerging transnational political order that, at its core, transforms the conditions for democratic politics in Europe. Scholars have thus tended to focus alternately on the political behaviour of directly elected Members of the European Parliament (MEPs) (Hix 2008), the ability of unelected experts in the European Commission to achieve pareto efficient outcomes (Majone 1998), the bargaining dynamics and large-scale treaty changes involving member state governments in the European Council (Moravcsik 1999), or to what extent the EU's constitutional order could be reformed more clearly according to the principles of a 'demoïcratic polity' (Cheneval and Schimmelfennig 2013).

The perspective that we advance in this book, and which serve as the framework for the book's contributors, does not discount the potential value of grand theories of EU democracy, such as democratic intergovernmentalism or European demoicracy, as a basis for further analysis and debate. However, we see parallels with recent discussions on the role of grand theories of European integration in EU studies, and especially the notion that such theories – be they intergovernmentalism, neofunctionalism or post-functionalism – in reality deal with different aspects of the EU, and therefore focus on different theoretical and empirical puzzles (Hooghe and Marks 2019). We believe that the tendency to pitch the key dilemma of European democracy as one between national and supranational democracy is far less informative than it might seem at first glance. Instead, we seek to establish a perspective that allows researchers to discuss in a more open-ended, and hopefully more productive, way democratic dilemmas that have received less attention in previous discussions on democracy beyond the European nation-state. Our dilemmatic approach to democracy in Europe's political order can thus be said to share theoretical concerns with the literature on norm contestation, particularly the notion that the practice of contestation forms an integral part of any democratic political system (Wiener 2014). We do not, however, seek to advance a particular democratic model applied to the European political order. Our framework rather provides space for our contributors to explore normative concerns highlighted by the analytical focus on democratic dilemmas in ways that enable discussion on previously underexplored aspects of European democracy.

Rethinking Dilemmas in EU Democracy

Rather than posing our questions by foregrounding the state, people or institutions, our approach takes as its starting point a set of democratic concepts or themes that we argue capture key aspects of democracy and democratic politics. Our contributors discuss different aspects of democracy that have previously often been dealt with in separate literatures on European politics, but which are brought together here by a more sustained focus on the democratic dilemmas that come to the surface once these aspects are considered in relation to the EU. The room for individual citizens to participate in and deliberate on EU politics, for sub-state entities to claim democratic rights, or the various tensions between democratic logics and those that pertain to the market are examples of issues that come into focus by a shift away from treating the tensions between national and supranational politics as the exclusive starting point for theoretical discussion (cf. Neyer and Wiener 2010). We are confident that approaching these discussions from the point of view of the multiple dimensions of democratic politics, rather than from a fixed set of reference points regarding the locus of democracy, will pave the way for new thinking about these issues, since doing so invites us to ask new questions. What happens when we explore democratic dilemmas in the EU from the point of view of concepts such as representation, citizenship, sovereignty, democratic contestation, deliberation or markets? How are democratic dilemmas and the trade-offs they give rise to usually understood in discussions on these concepts in the framework of the EU? Are there reasons to rethinking these, and if so, how?

We think that there are many benefits with our approach to analysing EU democracy. First, it offers a way to identify and study how conflicting democratic conceptions intersect at the EU level, paving the way for renewed perspectives on EU democracy. It brings the types of trade-offs inherent in the democratisation of any political order front and centre, and takes this as a starting point for the analysis of particular democratic aspects. Second, it allows for a more graded and nuanced notion of EU democracy, which could enable us to identify problems that have not been properly explored thus far, and to develop ways in which such problems can be addressed. Third, and relatedly, in leaving the notion of a clearly resolvable 'democratic deficit' aside, our focus on dilemmas helps to steer discussions towards more acutely felt trade-offs, the solutions to which are likely to remain preliminary. This corresponds to a position on democracy that allows for continued discussion on its forms. We contend that this is particularly important for an emergent and evolving political order such as the one centred on the EU, its institutions and its legal framework.

While often contested, the EU remains a political project with broadly defined democratic aspirations, which means that it is dependent on democratic legitimisation and cannot rest only on functionalist or utilitarian means of legitimacy (Majone 1998; Scharpf 1999). The TEU stipulates that the EU is 'founded on the values of respect for human dignity, freedom, democracy, equality, the rule of law and respect for human rights' (Art. 2 TEU). The Provisions on Democratic Principles for the EU also stipulate that the functioning of the EU shall be based on representative democracy (Art. 10 TEU). The treaty further tasks the EU's institutions with ensuring a degree of participation in order to 'give citizens and representative associations the opportunity to make known and publicly exchange their views in all areas of Union action' (Art. 11 TEU), while also acknowledging an important role for political parties at the European level. To be sure, declaratory statements such as these ones can be said to portray a highly idealised image of the EU, but we believe there are good reasons to take these aspirations seriously.

That said, these commitments to democratic concepts as they are laid out in the treaties provide few clues as to how they should be understood or frame an institutional architecture in which the relations between these different principles remain fundamentally unclear. Uncertainties and disagreements regarding how to implement democratic procedures in the emergent European political order are no less evident in academic debates; and some have argued there might be more significant democratic challenges to be dealt with at the national level. Problems with autocratisation and democratic backsliding among some member states (Kelemen 2017), or, more generally, the inability of member states to fully adapt to how the EU has reshaped the scope of democratic politics at its core (Schmidt 2006) remain key. However, this must not lead to the conclusion that discussions on the democratic qualities of the European political order and its institutions are superfluous. Rather, as we contend below, it should be acknowledged that these issues are intimately intertwined. As noted above, theorists, politicians and citizens disagree on what applying democratic principles to an organisation such as the EU might mean. While some identify democracy as necessarily anchored in state-bound political communities, others argue that actors beyond the state can interact in ways that live up to ideals of democratic legitimacy. We think that an advantage of our perspective is that it allows for a continuing discussion on what EU democracy can and should mean.

Our approach helps to bring together discussions on several overarching themes that, we argue, cut to the core of contemporary discussions on democracy in the EU. The themes that the book's contributors engage with advance our understanding of Europe's democratic dilemmas, even though they by no means exhaust the study of democratic politics in contemporary Europe. Other themes such as accountability, civil society and bureaucracy could also serve to highlight different democratic dilemmas, but we nonetheless contend that the themes chosen for this volume speak to fundamental issues of concern to European democracy, especially as the contributors use them to rethink important aspects of long-standing debates in this field of study.

From its inception, European integration brought difficult questions to the fore related to democratic representation. The shift of an increasing number of policy issues beyond the European nation-state complicated the already thorny issue of representation as it played out in the context of individual states. The institutional answers to these questions have resulted in various avenues for political representation in the EU that involve a multiplicity of procedures, which alternately identify member states, citizens or 'stakeholders' as their primary subjects. Citizens are represented in the European Parliament by MEPs elected through a popular vote. Member state governments are represented in the Council by national ministers. In the context of particular policy processes, the EU often relies on representation by different stakeholders, whether in the form corporate interests, regional associations or civil society organisations and other non-governmental organisations (NGOs). The question of whether and, if so, how such compound representation arrangements strengthen or detract from the procedural legitimacy of the EU is far from settled (Lord and Pollack 2010).

In the popular and academic debate, strengthening the role of the directly elected European Parliament has often been made synonymous with moves to democratise EU decision-making. Such equivalence is not necessarily warranted, however, which again betrays the limitations of directly transposing national experiences to the European level. The European Commission and the European Parliament have increasingly pushed for the establishment of a transnational system of political parties in Europe to consolidate a European political space (Norman 2021). In this context, proposals have also been put forward for transnational electoral lists to strengthen Europe-wide political debate and, by implication, EU democracy. National parliaments have, by contrast, often remained sceptical about such initiatives, commonly taking the view that both political parties and representative democracy should reside primarily at the national level. A focus on the concept of representation, discussing the basis on which representative arrangements beyond the state can be justified, therefore helps to highlight some of the fundamental democratic dilemmas associated with the European political order. Christopher Lord's chapter in this volume deals specifically with these dilemmas.

Discussions on representation invariably bring discussions on the primary subjects of democratic politics to the surface. Can a state-centric understanding of sovereignty be maintained, or does it need to be rethought in the light of how the order diffuses political power in new ways? Democracy tied to state institutions has been seen as one of its fundamental preconditions and some believe it needs to remain there to ensure its continued survival even in a highly intertwined polity like the EU (Bellamy 2016). In contrast, shifts in the locus of sovereignty have prompted some scholars to describe the EU as a 'post-sovereign' political system; or a system where state sovereignty is becoming increasingly obsolete (Keating 2001). As developments in recent years have indicated, actors tied to the state but also to political units at sub-state levels have sought to reassert their sovereignty, raising questions about where the most appropriate reference points for the EU's representative system lie (Bremberg and Gillespie 2022). The implications of strengthening the position of some of these actors over others remain uncertain, in similar ways to those associated with combining different avenues for political representation. Michael Keating's chapter, in particular, elaborates on these implications in the light of the concept of 'rescaling' European democracy and shifts our perspective towards new reference points for the organisation of democratic politics.

The introduction of an EU citizenship has also opened up ambiguities regarding how to understand the role of citizens and their involvement in EU decision-making, as well as the rights and duties that this evolving notion of citizenship implies. Even though these rights are dependent on national citizenship, there are currently elements in the legal order of the EU that suggest that individuals are recognised as subject to EU law beyond the rights and duties conferred on them by regulations governing the function of the internal market. It has even been suggested, linked to a series of rulings by the Court of Justice of the European Union (CJEU), that EU citizenship 'exists in the Treaties as one thing, and it exists in the jurisprudence of the CJEU as something considerably more far-reaching' (Kenealy 2014: 591). Within particular polities, democratic citizenship has served to protect the universality of rights regardless of social status. EU citizenship, however, relies on slightly different tenets. The question arises whether these different conceptions merely complement each other or exist in tension. Again, understanding how these different conceptions relate to each other will require further exploration to appreciate how they affect the democratic credentials of the polity in which they exist. Sandra Seubert takes on this task by discussing EU citizenship and the tensions that have arisen as a consequence of its introduction.

The theme of participation and deliberative mechanisms raises an additional set of related but distinct questions in relation to democracy in the EU. The 'deliberative turn' in democratic theory rests on the assumption that people's opportunity to participate in effective deliberation on collective decisions is what ultimately grants democratic legitimacy to any given political system (Dryzek 2002). People might of course choose not to participate in deliberative processes, but not having the right and means to do so is a different matter. However, there are persistent tensions between notions of representation and deliberation even in well-established European democracies. For example, national parliaments can be said to represent their citizens in quite different ways depending on electoral and party systems, which to a large extent shape the nature of deliberation by elected representatives. The question of the extent to which democratic deliberation among citizens can work beyond more delimited settings is particularly relevant in a political order that involves some 450 million people, such as the EU. How should we think about participation and deliberation in relation to the different aspects of an EU policy process that comprises elite bargaining among national representatives in the European Council, the political dynamics of the European Parliament and the expertise provided by the European Commission? In the light of recent debates on deliberative democracy: are there new ways to assess and discuss initiatives to make EU policymaking more responsive to EU citizens? Firat Cengiz adds to the discussions in this volume by addressing these questions. A focus on dilemmas between representation and deliberation might help to advance debates on EU democracy beyond the tendency to reify the current political status quo, and thus further tease out what is at stake in the democratic dilemmas of Europe's political order.

Democratic contestation is another theme that opens up new perspectives on long-standing questions about democracy in the context of European integration. The notion that democratic politics necessarily rest on opportunities for meaningful political contestation is more or less taken for granted in most European countries today. However, academic debates on the issue have often relied on the view that more far-reaching democratic contestation would risk fundamentally undermining the stability of the European political project (Bartolini 2005; Mair 2007). The fact that citizens in the EU have voted against further European integration when offered a chance to do so in popular referendums on EU treaty reform, combined with the rise of Eurosceptic parties, has been taken as an indication that such worries are not unwarranted. At the same time, however, popular support for EU membership is still high in many EU member states, despite a succession of crises (Eurobarometer 2021). These contradictions raise the question, discussed in Joseph Lacey's contribution to this volume, of whether democratic contestation can be a means to further strengthen popular support for the EU and perhaps even foster a deeper sense of political community.

The nature of the relationship between the market and democracy is yet another theme that is situated at the core of the debates on the emergent political order in Europe. The intimate links between the birth of capitalism and the rise of European nation-states suggest to some observers that state capacity to create and regulate markets and enforce property rights was essential not only to the capitalist mode of production and economic growth, but also to the birth of modern democracies (Tilly 1992). The market is not, of course, a democratic concept. However, the intimate entanglement between democratic politics and market institutions in the EU makes this theme crucial. EU member states have put in place market regulations at the supranational level and 'constitutionalised' certain economic policies as a result. By the same token, they have given up a great deal of control over their economic and financial policies. The fact that these developments have not been matched by the creation of redistributive arrangements at the same level in Europe suggests to some observers that the delicate postwar settlement of embedded liberalism and democratic capitalism is now being severely undermined (Streeck 2014). Neither renationalising regulatory competences back to the member states nor strengthening democratic control over these aspects of the work of the EU institutions seems to be on the table. A renewed discussion on the relationship between the market and democracy that is not exclusively confined to the institutional reforms introduced following the euro crisis therefore seems to be of fundamental importance. Kathleen McNamara's contribution to this volume precisely serves this purpose by expanding perspectives on the relation between democracy and the market that allow us to see this relationship, and the dilemmas it produces, in a new light.

Our engagement with these themes and concepts aims to highlight and discuss the democratic dilemmas they give rise to in the European context. While we do not foresee being able to resolve these dilemmas in any final sense, many of the authors suggest tentative ways in which the trade-offs they give rise to can be handled. The contributors to this volume proceed in a more open-ended way than is often the case with academic discussions, with the aim of offering fresh insights into EU democracy and highlighting new ways to understand the tensions and trade-offs inherent in the application of democratic concepts to the European political order. Collectively, they show how different aspects of the EU's bricolage of democratic practices can be strengthened. We hope this will provide a better assessment of the EU's democratic dimensions and help to identify how they can be further developed and strengthened.

European Democracy beyond Crisis Politics

The contributions to this volume can be read as an exercise in applied democratic theory. The authors address conceptual and theoretical questions and not empirical ones. That said, these theoretical discussions are, throughout, firmly anchored to the contemporary state of the European political order and the various challenges it faces. We thus think it is important that we also situate our volume against the backdrop of the political developments that have unfolded in the past decade. We consider what we see as general conditions that are important when considering questions of European democracy, including shifting support for the EU, processes of autocratisation and the questioning of the nation-state. In doing so, this book helps us to move beyond the notion of 'crisis' as the most relevant reference point for discussing democratic politics in Europe and it rejects the pervasive perspective in studies on European politics which suggests that the EU should primarily be understood as a polity constantly embroiled in crisis.

It is of course true that the EU has been faced with a range of crises in recent decades. The global economic and financial crisis unleashed on Europe in 2008 and how that challenged and reshaped European democracy has been documented in a now substantial literature (Cramme and Hobolt 2015; Demetriou 2014; Garben et al. 2019; Kriesi 2017; Ryner 2015; Schmidt 2020). This literature has highlighted the challenges posed by differences among EU member states brought to light by how the crisis hit countries to differing degrees. The crisis also fomented institutional change that for many meant a step away from more open-ended democratic ambitions and towards more technocratic forms of governance. Since then, the UK has left, the EU member states have demonstrated an inability to agree on a common policy on migration and the EU has instead increasingly operated, at least temporarily, through border closures. The COVID-19 pandemic once again brought the cleavages among EU member states to the fore. Worsening and more frequently occurring natural disasters linked to climate change are also likely to have an impact on the conditions for European cooperation as they affect different EU member states and regions of Europe to different degrees. The pandemic also reignited questions of how multiple crises might affect the democratic qualities of the EU and the extent to which EU decision-making is increasingly driven by an emergency logic characterised by speed and limited transparency (Rhinard 2019; White 2015; Wolff and Ladi 2020). We do not doubt that new and perhaps even graver challenges could lie ahead. As we worked to finalise this volume, Russia initiated a full-scale invasion of Ukraine and the EU has responded with far-reaching sanctions on Russia as well as commitments to extend economic and military support to Ukraine. The President of the Russian Federation, Vladimir Putin, on his part has made unprecedented gestures regarding the use of nuclear weapons, and European countries highly dependent on Russian gas have scrambled to deal with soaring energy costs. Europe once again finds itself faced with the possibility of interstate conflict on a scale not seen since the Second World War. Apart from the direct possibility of a large-scale humanitarian catastrophe, the conflict is likely to have far-reaching consequences for the EU. These events and developments clearly present themselves as acute challenges and are set to reinforce the EU's crisis mode. High-level meetings between European heads of government and foreign ministers often seem to make the detail of democratic procedures redundant.

Even in this context, however, we think that it is important to resist viewing the EU through the exclusive lens of crisis. This is because it tends to impose limitations on democratic theorisation and unduly restricts the analytical lens to immediate challenges and risks, thereby reproducing a narrow perspective on the European political order that tends to favour a position in defence of the status quo and side-line more general theorisation of conditions for democratisation of the European political order. Apart from the irrefutable magnitude of events like the euro crisis, Brexit, the climate crisis or Russia's war against Ukraine, we also suspect that the predominant academic focus on crisis relies, in part, on a slightly problematic reading of the past, especially where the EU is concerned. The notion of a Union in crisis invokes an implicit contrast with some often-undefined period of harmony where European democracy, or European cooperation more generally, stood unchallenged. It might be the case that the decade immediately after the end of the Cold War set the tone for an understanding of the European political order as not only stable, but also expanding, and able to push not just itself but other parts of the world in a more democratic direction. The reference point taken in contemporary discussion is seldom the economic stagnation of the 1970s and early 1980s, or the fact that many of the Central European EU member states that are now experiencing increasing autocratisation were at that time fully fledged single party autocracies under Soviet tutelage. The triumphalist perspectives on the 1990s also tend to stay silent about the devastating civil wars unfolding on the EU's doorstep in the Balkans. Croatia is now a full member of the EU and other Balkan countries have been given candidate status. If we extend our historical gaze further, as Sheri Berman does in her contribution to this volume, we see that European postwar cooperation was also, of course, at its very inception borne out of the crisis of the twentieth century, brought about by fascist rule, unprecedented warfare and genocide on the European continent. Our point here is not to diminish or trivialise attempts to make sense of shifts and developments in the European political order as a result of various defining events in recent times. However, we think that continuing to pitch discussions on EU democracy in terms of crisis, or post-crisis, adds very little to our ability to understand and provide new perspectives on these issues. Rather, it risks stymying discussions on the democratic qualities of the EU, postponing them to some undefined future point in time when current crises have been dealt with.

This volume instead emphasises the need to think about democratic politics as part of the everyday reproduction of the political order (Adler-Nissen 2014; Kauppi 2018; McNamara 2015). We seek to re-engage with the theoretical groundwork required for further debate on institutional and political reform that could help the EU to move in a more democratic direction. Rather than subsuming these discussions under the rubric of 'crisis', we anchor our discussions in the contemporary political environment by considering the fundamental challenges that the EU will continue to face as a political project for the foreseeable future. This is a position from which we argue our theories will be better equipped to identify both the limits and the possibilities of democracy in the EU.

EU Support, Autocratisation and Questioning the Nation-State

We highlight three long-term aspects or broadly defined conditions that we identify as particularly important when considering democracy in

Europe's emerging political order, and which serve as a general background to the discussions in this book: shifts in popular (dis)satisfaction with the organisation of the EU, challenges to the rules and norms related to liberal democracy in EU member states, and conflicting views on popular and state sovereignty in contemporary Europe.

The first condition is linked to the ebb and flow of popular dissatisfaction with the organisation of the EU. This is a complicated set of trends that has involved anti-system contestation from the political left as well as the right. Prevalent criticisms of the EU, in particular from the right, emphasise the importance of national sovereignty. In some cases, most evidently the UK, this led to demands to pull out of the EU altogether and has in many other cases led to calls to drastically reduce the scope of EU competences and decision-making powers. Criticism from the left tends to be more focused on the specific ways in which the European project is in its very constitution intertwined with the capitalist market economy, and how this is perceived to fuel rather than assuage socio-economic inequalities.

Popular dissatisfaction with the EU has at times highlighted the discrepancies between the views of citizens and those of political elites. From this perspective, the EU has found itself in what some have referred to as a state of disequilibrium between large swaths of its citizenry with increasingly Eurosceptic attitudes, on the one hand, and an integrationist-minded political elite, on the other (Hodson and Puetter 2019). This is an imbalance that negatively affects the conditions for developing EU democracy as member state governments are faced with the difficult choice of either ignoring the preferences of parts of the European citizenry or accepting policymaking gridlock and breakdown at the European level (de Vries 2014; Hix 2018; Moravcsik 2008). Historically, the EU has tended to venture along the former of these paths when faced with explicit opposition. The decision to press forward with wide-ranging treaty reform throughout the 2000s, despite the negative results of the referendums on the Constitutional Treaty in France, the Netherlands and Ireland, is one of the most glaring examples of this tendency. This dynamic seems to only have been strengthened in the EU's response to the euro crisis.

These developments emerged in tandem with heightened anti-system pressures on the EU as an organisation, and widespread perceptions that the EU was being governed by hegemonic powers, be they based in Brussels, Luxembourg or Frankfurt. The dividing lines between southern and northern European states were highlighted by the euro crisis and further on by the uneven burdens being shouldered in terms of the management of migration flows and the reception of refugees. Negotiations in 2020 on the economic recovery packages designed to mitigate the economic fallout from the COVID-19 pandemic served to reignite these political conflicts, as the positions of member states mapped out the familiar divisions between northern creditor states and countries more dependent on support. These broad power dynamics, fuelled by uneven economic development in different European states, are likely to remain an enduring condition that shape discussions on EU democracy.

Recent opinion polls, however, have indicated that European citizens have become somewhat more satisfied with and rather less sceptical about the EU (Eurobarometer 2021). There are also signs that the populist far-right has in many member states abandoned 'hard' Eurosceptic positions and demands to pull out of the project (de Vries 2018). In the run-up to the 2019 elections to the European Parliament, there were indications that Eurosceptic far-right parties were coordinating to a greater degree than previously. The typical strategy of these political actors has long been to use the European political arena exclusively as a platform to amplify their rhetoric in relation to national audiences rather than to engage in serious attempts to shape EU policy. However, these parties are increasingly considering the possibility that their growing electoral support, as well as their support among some leaders in the European Council, could yield genuine impact on policy outcomes. The prospect of working within the EU institutions with the goal of reshaping the political order in Europe, rather than attacking it from the outside, is becoming increasingly attractive for these actors. Opinions on the EU are thus shifting, partly as a result of the gradual change in disposition towards the EU among the far-right.

Contrary to the expectations of many, it seems that the EU has emerged more stable from a decade of crises, bolstered by higher levels of public support than was previously the case. How to interpret these trends, however, is not a straightforward task. Whether they should be taken primarily as a sign of strengthened support for the European project or rather as a sign of a more fundamental lack of confidence in national governments in Europe is far from self-evident. What they do seem to signal is a heightened level of contestation and politicisation regarding the shape and form of the European political order. A broader acceptance of the polity in general might help shift ingrained debates on the extent to which the European political order can be opened up to more far-reaching democratic contestation on substantive policies. As noted above, the largely functionalist beginnings of postwar European cooperation were built on the notion that mass democracy was a perilous thing, and its mechanisms easily corrupted and used for sinister ends (Norman 2022). Positions in the debates that unfolded half a century later regarding the possibility of democratising the EU expressed similar ideas, warning against the dangers of more far-reaching mechanisms for democratic contestation at the EU level (Bartolini 2005; Mair 2007; Scharpf 1999). Maybe the surprisingly stable support for the EU in the present setting provides reasons to rethink those positions.

A second and related condition concerns the anti-system pressures related to the increasing challenges in the past decade to the fundamental democratic principles and practices on which European cooperation and integration are supposed to rest. The dismantling of liberal democratic institutions in Poland and Hungary are the most unambiguous manifestations of these developments. Similar tendencies are in evidence in other Central and Eastern European member states such as Romania and Slovenia. The purportedly democratic EU is now faced with a situation in which it harbours member states that are increasingly authoritarian, which creates a fundamental challenge to its further democratisation (Kelemen 2020). The EU places strict conditions on candidate countries to adhere to democratic principles before they accede but has proved incapable to deal with member states that are veering in an authoritarian direction. It appears that a considerable proportion of the European electorate as well as some political leaders have developed a cavalier attitude to liberal democratic institutions. However, the success of far-right populists in Austria, Belgium, Denmark, France, Italy, the Netherlands, Spain, Sweden and elsewhere tells us that this is a problem to which Western European countries are certainly not immune. Some argue that these developments should be interpreted under the general heading of Euroscepticism (Treib 2021). We agree that they often overlap but we also think that it is important to treat the authoritarian turn in Europe as a distinct trend, in both its content and its implications for EU democracy (White 2020). These developments raise difficult questions regarding the democratisation of a political order where some of its constituent units are moving in the opposite direction.

The emergence of sharply drawn fault lines related to fundamental values has implications for the basis on which deliberation can function, and the extent to which civil society might participate in EU politics. The conditions necessary for harnessing the potentially positive effects of deliberative practices on the EU's democratic qualities might appear lacking (Dryzek 1999; Eriksen and Fossum 2018). Nonetheless, Firat Cengiz argues in her chapter that there are still ways in which such practices can be applied to EU policymaking. However, the emergence of a common political identity in the Habermasian sense, one that could potentially support a pan-European political debate and politicisation on substantive issues, seems still far away (Habermas 2015). The political cleavages that the European far-right is mobilising around are not necessarily those that were expected to create a European political space from which a common European political identity could grow. The rise of authoritarian governments in some member states underlines the formidable obstacles to such a project, at the same time as it seems to suggest that a very different, and distinctively less democratic, kind of European political order could emerge from current conditions.

There are also possible knock-on effects associated with how increasingly beleaguered political elites work to safeguard the liberal democratic status quo. The possible effects of such efforts are analogous to what is implied by the exclusive focus on crisis. Reactions to anti-system actors among those who want to safeguard core democratic institutions also give rise to dilemmas between democratisation and efforts to keep anti-system actors at bay. How leaders deal with such trade-offs could have serious implications for European democracy. As political elites in Europe seek ways to protect existing institutions from assaults by perceived anti-democratic challengers, more effective mechanisms for political representation, participation and contestation are often placed on the back-burner. Discussions tend instead to veer towards more restrictive procedures and decreasing confidence in the principle of self-government (Kelemen 2020; Müller 2015). At the supranational level, specifically in the European Parliament, increased support for far-right political parties in European elections has prompted the political mainstream to form coalitions, establish *cordons sanitaires* and alter procedural rules with the aim of diminishing the influence of such parties. Recent discussions on the EU's long-term budget, as well the COVID-19 relief fund, have also been shaped by demands to make access to EU funds conditional on member states' adherence to the rule of law. The CJEU's judgment in this direction further strengthens the ability to put pressure on member states (CJEU 2022). Our aim here is not to evaluate the feasibility or normative dimensions of such protective measures. Indeed, as Kelemen notes, the continued flow of EU funds to Hungary and Poland has helped to solidify the autocratic trend in these member states, fuelling corruption and clientelist relations that help to bolster these governments (Kelemen 2020). Conditioning funds on respect for democratic institutions and the rule of law might thus be an important tool for counteracting these developments. Whether effective or not, this suggests a dilemma with potentially far-reaching implications for EU democracy: between the perceived need to protect the EU from anti-system forces, on the one hand, and to respond to calls for more democratic, open and inclusive decision-making procedures, on the other (Norman 2021). The heightened salience of this dilemma is likely to shape policymakers' perceptions of what democratising the EU might mean, and what constitute the conditions for such efforts. One possible worry is that the institutional reforms that would provide more opportunities for citizen participation and more robust mechanisms for democratic contestation might be seen as less attractive or even harmful in this context.

A third overlapping but we argue distinct development with implications for EU democracy concerns sub-state political entities such as Scotland, Catalonia and Flanders, which are increasingly challenging existing member states as the natural point of reference for democratic representation in the EU (Bremberg 2020). The notion of a Europe of peoples that conforms more or less to the member states represented in the Council and the Commission excludes important sub-state divisions, and this has implications for the democratic functioning of the EU. The resurgence of nationalism at the regional level poses new challenges for thinking about EU democracy in the sense that EU member states are being contested as the natural reference point when thinking about sovereignty, political community and deliberation. It also undermines the idea of a Europe-wide political identity based on a dual allegiance to the currently existing member states and the European political project as a whole.

The difficulties of dealing with the resurgence of these sub-state political identities within the framework of the EU came to the fore in the Spanish constitutional crisis of 2017, set off by the illegal referendum on the independence of Catalonia from Spain. Regardless of what one thinks about the legitimacy of Catalan independence claims, this crisis shed light on an inherent tension at the heart of the EU as an emerging polity with democratic aspirations – that the member states are seen as the ultimate masters of the fundamental treaties at the same time as the EU is meant to bring the peoples of Europe closer together. Even though it could be argued that the challenge posed by Catalan secessionism for debates on EU democracy is different to those posed by increasingly authoritarian governments in Hungary and Poland, both sets of challenges can be said to present a similar kind of problem for the notion that EU democracy stops at the borders of the member states. Discussions on what representation and sovereignty might mean in the context of discussions on EU democracy need to consider developments through which the state is increasingly being questioned as the taken for granted point of reference. These broadly defined conditions, in various ways, supply a background to the contributing chapters to this volume. They tie their discussions to existing debates that revolve around core democratic themes, and each offers ways in which to rethink the tensions and trade-offs that arise once they are discussed in the context of the European political order.

Structure of the Book

Christopher Lord's chapter (Chapter 1) centres on the key concept of representation and departs from the observation that it is a concept around which much of existing debates on EU democracy revolves. The 'meta-dilemma' he uses as a starting point is one that dovetails with a key motivation of this book, namely the observed tensions between the EU's far-reaching legislative power and its failure to live up to fundamental democratic criteria. However, the chapter challenges a key aspect of recent debates on democracy relating to the issue of representation. His engagement with representation helps to question common assumptions underpinning these discussions, and in particular the notion that supranational democratic arrangements require a common demos. The chapter argues that there are good reasons to develop the Union's own system of representation even without such a demos. It does so by taking an original perspective on democratic legitimacy to argue how representation in the EU needs to be rethought, and how its implementation gives rise to dilemmas that have not been sufficiently explored in existing debates. These dilemmas are tied to the externalities generated by an interconnected world which pushes politicians to consider the balance between dealing with issues in the context of the nation-state or through supranational representative institutions. An in-depth discussion of these trade-offs, arising as a result of the interconnectedness of contemporary European states, helps to demonstrate that we need to rethink what the democratic duties of national democratic systems require in terms of representative arrangements at the EU level. This provides a new perspective on how to evaluate supranational representative arrangements, even for those that see democratic legitimacy as firmly tied to the level of member states. Lord's chapter thus demonstrates the continued salience of the dilemma between national and supranational arrangements in the EU while highlighting the ways in which it needs to be reconceptualised.

In Michael Keating's view (Chapter 2) we need to more fundamentally rethink the state-centric basis for European democracy, and his perspective also prompts a more radical questioning of the notion that European democracy should use the dichotomy between national and supranational levels as its primary reference point. Keating develops this argument with the help of the concept of rescaling. He uses the concept to highlight political spaces which scholarly discussions on European democracy have neglected and which have not been mirrored in the institutional arrangements of the EU. Rather than the notion of multilevel governance, Keating instead explores the notion of multilevel democracy and advances the argument that representation and accountability must be reconceptualised in a more pluralist mode. The core of the dilemma he explores is summarised as 'the need for an institutional framework for democracy covering all its dimensions in a world where spheres of public action, political identities and political representation are shifting and unstable' (Keating this volume). The European political order is understood by Keating as plurinational, often characterised by a striking mismatch between the territorial units where political power is concentrated and the multiple settings where political interests and democratic claims are formulated. We are thus faced here with a set of rarely discussed dilemmas regarding the ways in which the democratic impulses from such more diverse settings can be accommodated in existing and new institutional arrangements. Keating also underlines the key point in this context that democracy cannot be reduced to the revealed preferences of citizens through elections but needs invariably to include also deliberative arrangements where members of societies may participate and find compromises to issues of common concern. Trying to balance such deliberative arrangements with territorially based notions of representation give rise to a host of dilemmas for those aiming to more fully democratise European politics.

Firat Cengiz (Chapter 3) turns our focus to a set of questions overlapping those raised by Keating in discussing how EU democracy can be reimagined in a more inclusive direction. She adds to this perspective by focusing more squarely on the possible role for deliberative arrangements to achieve such inclusive participatory goals and goes on to discuss the dilemmas that may arise when such concrete arrangements are introduced. A key dilemma that comes to the fore in her discussion is that while deliberation is a 'potentially promising method of giving alienated citizens a voice in large, diverse, and polarised societies, it is also more challenging to implement in societies with these qualities' (Cengiz this volume). The challenge highlighted by the formulation of this dilemma ties into long-standing discussions on deliberative democracy as a method geared towards achieving compromise and consensus. Cengiz's discussions proceed by focusing on how deliberative arrangements, apart from dilemmas associated to the basic social and political conditions they require, can also be expected to give rise to particular dilemmas related to the balance between deliberative arrangements and formal representative procedures in a multilevel system such as the EU. The chapter uses the discussion on such tensions to explore new ways to understand the potential role of deliberative democratic tools for EU democracy. The chapter offers some preliminary proposals regarding the incorporation of deliberative democracy at different points of the EU's decision-making processes, as well as pointing to some possible pitfalls of such arrangements.

Sandra Seubert's contribution (Chapter 4) takes a democratic dimension as its entry point that further shifts our attention towards the implications of EU democracy for individuals by focusing on the notion of democratic citizenship. Citizenship is a notion intimately tied to the recognition of individual rights, including democratic ones. Seubert's discussion brings to light how the introduction of competing notions of citizenship in the EU give rise to unresolved dilemmas at the European level. The chapter offers a key contribution by analysing EU citizenship as primarily an 'economic citizenship' which, Seubert argues, threatens to hollow out rights-based conceptions. By tracing the conflicting political and economic logics at the heart of these conceptions this chapter reflects on the recent dynamics in the development of a European citizenship regime. It argues that the normative surplus of EU citizenship lies in its potential of transcending the state-centred logic of European integration, a potential that has not been sufficiently discussed in public political discourse. Here again, we are presented with a different facet of democratic politics that is made visible by the shift in perspective from the conventional focus in discussions that take the national–supranational binary as its starting point. By wavering between a self-standing and complementary status, EU citizenship's political determination remains uncertain. In particular regarding the normative dimension of citizenship and its connection to democratic self-determination, the EU citizenship regime is currently stuck in a limbo of unresolved tensions.

Themes relating to the tensions between market logics and democratic logics are given a more general treatment by Kathleen McNamara (Chapter 5). McNamara argues that democratic norms and practices have always existed in a dilemmatic relationship with the workings of modern capitalist markets, but perhaps never more so than in the case of the EU. It is often argued that the EU is dominated by market rationales leaving concerns with democracy in the background. However, McNamara challenges the clear-cut nature of the market–democracy binary and as such highlights new aspects of this dilemma. She demonstrates how market logics and democratic politics are interlaced in more complex ways than usually acknowledged through a discussion that situates contemporary politics within a broader historical trajectory of the tensions between capitalism and democracy. By highlighting the specifics of these tensions, and how they have played out in the context of national political systems, the chapter brings trade-offs associated with strengthening democracy in various spaces to the fore and discusses how a more democratic capitalism may be devised for the European political order.

Joseph Lacey (Chapter 6) ties his discussion to a set of debates that speaks to a core dilemma for democracy in the EU, and one which has become increasingly salient against the background of increasing polarisation in many countries: the extent to which the EU can and should accommodate higher levels of democratic contestation. In addressing these questions, Lacey argues that the costs of trading-off democratic contestation to serve problem-solving effectiveness may be far greater than they first appear. The chapter challenges the standard rendition of the dilemma related to democratic contestation in EU studies which regards real democratic contestation as problematic in an environment characterised by far-reaching scepticism from anti-system actors. Lacey draws our attention to the impacts of depoliticisation on the ability of the system to defend itself against critique, especially from anti-system actors. In the absence of democratic contestation about the EU, citizens are more likely to maintain ambivalent attitudes towards this political system. In periods of crisis that implicate the EU, citizens' ambivalent attitudes can be easily exploited by political entrepreneurs who colourfully and vigorously make the case against European integration. Shifting our understanding of dilemmas related to democratic contestation in the EU reveals opportunities for exploring how democracy's contestatory aspects may serve to strengthen the political order.

The discussions that are raised by the contributors to this volume are placed in a wider context by two reflective chapters. Sheri Berman's (Chapter 7) reflections on EU democracy offers a historical perspective on the broad conditions for European democracy and its evolution, while also highlighting the developments that provide clues to its current fragilities. In tune with McNamara's conclusions on markets and democracy, Berman highlights the need for considering the type of interventionist regulatory systems that enabled European nation-states in the postwar era to find a balance between the market and democratic politics in a way that served as a protection against its more damaging side effects and paved the way for stable democratic systems. In a second reflection chapter, Daniel Kelemen (Chapter 8) questions one of the key premises for the discussions of this volume, namely the need to further strengthen the collective democratic arrangements in Europe. To make this point, Kelemen takes a comparative perspective and argues that the oft-assumed democratic shortcomings of the EU in fact stack up rather well against similar systems. This concerns both current public support for the system, at times higher than the confidence placed in national politicians, and the ways in which Europeans engage in politics at the EU level, evidenced for instance by the considerable levels of participation in European elections. Instead, Kelemen argues, we should turn our attention to the way in which current institutional arrangements in the EU not only allow democratic backsliding in its member states, but also facilitate the continued dismantling of democratic institutions, most prominently including Poland and Hungary, by largely unconditional access to EU funds.

In the book's concluding chapter, these discussions as well as those offered by the book's contributors are drawn together to set out directions for future research on democracy in Europe's political order from the perspective of our dilemmatic approach. Key benefits with this perspective are highlighted with the help of the respective contributions to our volume. In these concluding discussions we also highlight a range of questions that our volume provokes and which future projects would do well to explore further.

References

Adler-Nissen, Rebecca (2014) *Opting out of the European Union: Diplomacy, Sovereignty and European Integration*. Cambridge: Cambridge University Press.

Bartolini, Stefano (2005) *Restructuring Europe: Centre Formation, System Building, and Political Structuring Between the Nation State and the European Union*. Oxford: Oxford University Press.

Bellamy, Richard (2016) A European Republic of Sovereign States: Sovereignty, Republicanism and the European Union. *European Journal of Political Theory*, 16(2): 188–209.

Bellamy, Richard (2019) *A Republican Theory of States*. Cambridge: Cambridge University Press.

Bellamy, Richard and Castiglione, Dario (2000) Democracy, Sovereignty and the Constitution of the European Union: The Republican Alternative to Liberalism. In Bankowski, Z. and Scott, A. (eds) *The European Union and its Order*. Oxford: Blackwell, pp. 170–90.

Berman, Sheri (2019) *Democracy and Dictatorship in Europe: From the Ancien Régime to the Present Day*. Oxford: Oxford University Press.

Bickerton, Christopher J. (2012) *European Integration: From Nation-States to Member States*. Oxford: Oxford University Press.

Bickerton, Christopher J., Hodson, Dermot and Puetter, Uwe (eds) (2015) *The New Intergovernmentalism: States and Supranational Actors in the Post-Maastricht Era*. Oxford: Oxford University Press.

Bremberg, Niklas (2020) The Dream of the Nation-State: Is Regional Secessionism a Threat to European Integration? In Bakardjieva Engelbrekt, A., Leijon, K., Michalski, A. and Oxelheim, L. (eds) *The European Union and the Return of the Nation-State*. Cham: Palgrave, pp. 241–67.

Bremberg, Niklas and Gillespie, Richard (2022) *Catalonia, Scotland and the EU: Visions of Independence and Integration*. London: Routledge

Cheneval, Francis and Schimmelfennig, Frank (2013) The Case for Demoïcracy in the European Union. *JCMS: Journal of Common Market Studies*, 51(2): 334–50.

Court of Justice of the European Union (2022) Judgments in Cases C-156/21 Hungary v Parliament and Council, and C-157/21 Poland v Parliament and

Council. Press release, no.28/2022. Luxembourg, 16 February, <https://curia.europa.eu/jcms/upload/docs/application/pdf/2022-02/cp220028en.pdf> (last accessed 13 September 2022).

Cramme, Olaf and Hobolt, Sara Binzer (eds) (2015) *Democratic Politics in a European Union under Stress*. Oxford: Oxford University Press.

Demetriou, Kyriakos N. (ed.) (2014) *The European Union in Crisis: Explorations in Representation and Democratic Legitimacy*. Dordrecht: Springer.

De Vries, Catherine E. (2014) Rethinking Electoral Democracy in Europe. In Cramme, O. and Hobolt, S. (eds) (2015) *Democratic Politics in a European Union under Stress*. Oxford: Oxford University Press, pp. 217–35.

De Vries, Catherine E. (2018) *Euroscepticism and the Future of European Integration*. Oxford: Oxford University Press.

Diez, Thomas and Wiener, Antje (2019) Introducing the Mosaic of Integration Theory. In Wiener, A. Börzel, T. and Risse, T. (eds) *European Integration Theory*. Oxford: Oxford University Press, pp. 1–26.

Dryzek, John S. (1999) Transnational Democracy. *The Journal of Political Philosophy*, 7(1): 30–51.

Dryzek, John S. (2002) *Deliberative Democracy and Beyond: Liberals, Critics, Contestations*. Oxford: Oxford University Press.

Eriksen, Erik and Fossum, Jan-Erik (eds) (2000) *Democracy in the European Union: Integration Through Deliberation?* London: Routledge

Eriksen, Erik and Fossum, Jan-Erik (2018) Deliberation Constrained: An Increasingly Segmented European Union. In Bechtiger, A., Dryzek, J., Mansbridge, J. and Warren, M. (eds) *The Oxford Handbook of Deliberative Democracy*. Oxford: Oxford University Press, pp. 842–55.

Eurobarometer (2021) Public Opinion in the EU. Standard Eurobarometer 94. Winter 2020–2021, <https://europa.eu/eurobarometer/surveys/detail/2355> (last accessed 9 June 2021).

Follesdal, Andreas and Hix, Simon (2006) Why There is a Democratic Deficit in the EU. *Journal of Common Market Studies*, 44(3): 533–62.

Garben, Sacha, Govaere, Inge and Nemitz, Paul (2019) *Critical Reflections on Constitutional Democracy in the European Union*. Oxford: Hart Publishing.

Habermas, Jürgen (2015) Democracy in Europe: Why the Development of the EU into a Transnational Democracy Is Necessary and How It Is Possible. *European Law Journal*, 21(4): 546–57.

Hix, Simon (2008) *What's Wrong with the European Union and How to Fix it*. Malden: Polity Press.

Hix, Simon (2018) When Optimism Fails: Liberal Intergovernmentalism and Citizen Representation. *Journal of Common Market Studies*, 56(7): 1595–1613.

Hodson, Dermot and Puetter, Uwe (2019) The European Union in Disequilibrium: New Intergovernmentalism, Post Functionalism and Integration Theory in the Post-Maastricht Period. *Journal of European Public Policy*, 26(8): 1153–71.

Holland, Martin (1996) Jean Monnet and the Federal Functionalist Approach to the European Union. In Murray, P. and Rich, P. (eds) *Visions of European Unity*. Boulder: Westview Press.

Hooghe, Liesbeth and Marks, Gary (2019) Grand Theories of Integration in the Twenty-First Century. *Journal of European Public Policy*, 26(8): 1113–33.
Kauppi, Niilo (2018) *Toward a Reflexive Political Sociology of the European Union: Fields, Intellectuals and Politicians*. Cham: Palgrave Macmillan.
Keating, Michael (2001) *Plurinational Democracy: Stateless Nations in a Post-Sovereignty Era*. Oxford: Oxford University Press.
Kelemen, Daniel (2017) Europe's other Democratic Deficit: National Authoritarianism in Europe's Democratic Union. *Government and Opposition*, 52(2): 211–38.
Kelemen, Daniel (2020) The European Union's Authoritarian Equilibrium. *Journal of European Public Policy*, 27(3): 481–99.
Kenealy, Daniel (2014) How Do You Solve a Problem like Scotland? A Proposal Regarding 'Internal Enlargement'. *Journal of European Integration*, 36(6): 585–600.
Kreuder-Sonnen, Christian (2018) An Authoritarian Turn in Europe and European Studies? *Journal of European Public Policy*, 25(3): 442–64.
Kriesi, Hanspetter (2017) The Implications of the Euro Crisis for Democracy. *Journal of European Public Policy*, 25(1): 59–82.
Lord, Christopher and Pollak, Johannes (2010) The EU's Many Representative Modes: Colliding? Cohering? *Journal of European Public Policy*, 17(1): 117–36.
Mair, Peter (2007) Political Opposition and the European Union. *Government and Opposition*, 42(1): 1–17.
Mair, Peter (2013) *Ruling the Void: The Hollowing of Western Democracy*. London: Verso.
McNamara, Kathleen R. (2015) *The Politics of Everyday Europe: Constructing Authority in the European Union*. Oxford: Oxford University Press.
Majone, Giandomenico (1998) Europe's 'Democratic Deficit': The Question of Standards. *European Law Journal*, 4(1): 5–28.
Moravcsik, Andrew (1999) *The Choice for Europe: Social Purpose and State Power from Messina to Maastricht*. London: Routledge.
Moravcsik, Andrew (2008) The Myth of Europe's 'Democratic Deficit'. *Intereconomics: Journal of European Economic Policy*, 43(6): 331–40.
Müller, Jan-Werner (2013) *Contesting Democracy: Political Ideas in Twentieth-Century Europe*. New Haven: Yale University Press.
Müller, Jan-Werner (2015) Should the EU Protect Democracy and the Rule of Law inside Member States? *European Law Journal*, 21(2): 141–60.
Neyer, Jürgen and Wiener, Antje (2010) *Political Theory of the European Union*. Oxford: Oxford University Press.
Nicolaïdis, Kalypso (2013) European Demoicracy and its Crisis. *Journal of Common Market Studies*, 51(2): 351–69.
Norman, Ludvig (2021) To Democratize or to Protect? How the Response to Anti-System Parties Reshapes the EU's Transnational Party System. *Journal of Common Market Studies*, 59(3): 721–37.
Norman, Ludvig (2022) Democracy's Fragility and the European Political Order: Functionalism, Militant Democracy, and Crisis. In Lebow, R. N. and Norman, L. (eds) *Robustness and Fragility of Political Orders*. Cambridge: Cambridge University Press, pp. 176–201.

Rhinard, Mark (2019) The Crisification of Policy Making in the European Union. *Journal of Common Market Studies*, 57(3): 616–33.

Ryner, Magnus (2015) Europe's Ordo-Liberal Iron Cage: Critical Political Economy, the Euro Area Crisis and its Management. *Journal of European Public Policy*, 22(2): 275–94.

Sánchez-Cuenca, Ignacio (2017) From a Deficit of Democracy to a Technocratic Order: The Post-Crisis Debate on Europe. *Annual Review of Political Science*, 20: 351–69.

Scharpf, Fritz (1999) *Governing in Europe: Effective and Democratic?* Oxford: Oxford University Press.

Schmidt, Vivien (2006) *Democracy in Europe: The EU and National Polities*. Oxford: Oxford University Press.

Schmidt, Vivien (2020) *Europe's Crisis of Legitimacy*. Oxford: Oxford University Press.

Streeck, Wolfgang (2014) *Buying Time: The Delayed Crisis of Democratic Capitalism*. London: Verso Books.

Tilly, Charles (1992) *Coercion, Capital, and European States, AD 990-1992*. Oxford: Blackwell.

Treib Oliver (2021) Euroscepticism Is Here to Stay: What Cleavage Theory Can Teach Us about the 2019 Elections. *Journal of European Public Policy*, 28(2): 174–89.

Weiler, Joseph H. H., Haltern, Ulrich, R. and Mayer, Franz (1995) European Democracy and Its Critique. *West European Politics*, 18(3): 4–39.

White, Jonathan (2015) Emergency Europe. *Political Studies*, 63(2): 300–18.

White, Jonathan (2020) Europeanizing Ideologies. *Journal of European Public Policy*, 27(9): 1287–1306.

Wiener, Antje (2014) *A Theory of Contestation*. Heidelberg: Springer.

Wolff, Sarah and Ladi, Stella (2020) European Union Responses to the Covid-19 Pandemic: Adaptability in Time of Permanent Crisis. *Journal of European Integration*, 42(8): 1025–40.

Wolkenstein, Fabio (2020) The Revival of Democratic Intergovernmentalism, First Principles and the Case for a Contest Based Account of Democracy in the European Union. *Political Studies*, 68(2): 408–25.

ONE

Representation without a Demos? A Very European Democratic Dilemma

Christopher Lord

This volume identifies many dilemmas in applying democratic politics to the European Union. But, maybe, there is a meta-dilemma: an overarching dilemma of which all other dilemmas are instances. If so, that dilemma would probably be as follows. The European Union (EU) cannot do without some kind of democratic politics. No body that is a source of shared law-making can do that if individuals are to be free and equal in the control of all their own laws. Yet, the Union does not satisfy conditions for democratic politics very well. That, in turn, suggests sub-dilemmas and intersecting dilemmas. Sub-dilemmas, since each dimension of democratic politics is difficult to reproduce at the Union level in its own way. Intersecting dilemmas where difficulties in making the Union democratic are not 'free-standing'. Rather, they interact with dilemmas in combining the interconnectedness of member state democracies with the internal autonomy of each of those democracies. Still, dilemmas are hardly uncommon to democratic politics. The institutional design of many democratic systems owes as much to democratic dilemmas as to democratic ideals. But more or less cunning institutional designs obviously require understanding of the dilemmas to which they are supposed to respond. This chapter argues that one dimension of European Union politics along which democratic dilemmas have not been very well understood is that of representation itself.

Much of the democratic deficit debate is really about representation. For those who coined the term, the democratic deficit consisted of taking powers away from national systems of representation without developing corresponding systems of representation at the Union level (Marquand 1979: 64). For some of those who doubt the Union is in democratic deficit or even that it makes much sense to suppose it might be, the problem is also one of democratic representation (Majone 2005), albeit, in their view, it has been one huge mistake of institutional design even to have attempted a form of European Union with representative institutions and politics of its own. According to that argument, the EU lacks conditions for democracy. It especially lacks a demos; or, in other words, a public that sees itself as a democratic people. Hence, majorities of voters or representatives at the Union level are understood as having limited authority to decide or bind without the agreement of all member state democracies, which are the real democratic political communities in Europe. Hence also, the Union's painstaking, and sometimes painful, procedures for building consensus between its member state democracies even where qualified majority voting (QMV) is possible. Hence, finally, limits to how far the Union can develop democratic institutions and politics through its own system of representation complete with European Union elections, a European Union Parliament and European Union parties.

But does the absence of a European Union demos really preclude the development of a Union with its own system of representation? I argue that it does not. Obligations national demoi owe their own publics – and obligations citizens of national demoi owe their national co-citizens – are enough on their own to justify representative institutions specific to the European Union. So why has that possibility not been fully understood before? I suspect the answer lies in a misapplication to the EU and its member democracies of the concept of a democratic political community or demos. It is unfortunate that so much of the debate about demos, democracy and how people should be represented in decisions of the European Union has focused on identity. Democratic political community is more than shared identity. It is also a relationship of mutual obligation (Miller 2007: 124). That obviously includes the obligations of democracy itself. But it also includes any obligations to secure justice, rights and non-domination that are all mutually required by one another and by their relationship to democracy. However – without managing externalities between themselves – Europe's highly interconnected democracies are likely to struggle to meet those most basic obligations to their own publics to secure rights, justice, welfare and democracy itself. Their citizens will also find it difficult to use their own national democracies to do those things that define democracies as democracies: namely, accord one another rights and obligations, and control their own laws as equals. Externalities can, therefore, corrode national democratic political communities as sources of democratically defined mutual obligation. Democracies may need to work together to manage some kinds of externality if they are to meet the very obligations that justify them as democratic states and define them as democratic political communities. By demonstrating all that, we can also identify forms of representation beyond the state that can be justified and even required by democracy within the state.

I make my argument by identifying what I call an indirect legitimacy dilemma. Below I set out reasons of feasibility, value and right for why any form of European Union – and, therefore, any exercise of Union powers by representative bodies – is likely to depend on some degree of indirect legitimation, or, in other words, legitimation by member state democracies. Yet indirect legitimacy requires more than consent. It also requires a form of European Union that can be justified by the obligations of member state democracies to their own publics. As the previous paragraph suggests, just such a justification might be provided by a need to manage externalities between member state democracies if the latter are to meet their own obligations to their own publics. However, I will also show how working together to manage externalities seems simultaneously to require control by national democracies and control over national democracies. That is what I call the indirect legitimacy dilemma.

For sure, it does not necessarily follow that the kind of European Union we have right now – or even any kind of European Union – is the only or best means of managing externalities between European democracies. Nor are the obligations that democracies owe their own publics – as opposed to more cosmopolitan obligations – their only obligations. Nor is it even impossible that the Union might develop new forms of political association and legitimation that transcend any need for legitimation by member state democracies. I merely argue that, notwithstanding all the foregoing, managing externalities – in ways needed for member state democracies to meet their own core obligations to their own publics to secure rights, justice and democracy itself – can be sufficient to justify some form of European Union. What is of special interest and importance is that it can justify some form of European Union with its own system of representation. The justification for supranational forms of representation can come from the needs and obligations of the democratic state itself and the very dilemmas national democracies have in reconciling their interconnectedness with their internal autonomy.

Of course, obvious questions follow. What obligations do member state democracies owe their own publics? What is meant by externalities between democracies and why is managing them so important to obligations democracies owe their own publics? When would doing all that be sufficient justification for a particular kind of European Union? How, then, should the membership, powers, institutions and procedures of any

European Union be configured if it is to be justified as a means of managing externalities between member democracies in ways that help them to meet their own obligations to their own publics? Who should decide those questions and how?

Although those are difficult questions, we might think that resolving them is quite straightforward, given the key distinction between legitimation by outcomes and legitimation by inputs and procedures. At first sight, all that has been said so far might seem to suggest an output standard of indirect legitimacy. To say that the Union should be understood as indirectly legitimate where it can manage externalities in ways needed for its member democracies to meet obligations to their own publics to provide rights, justice, security, welfare and democracy, is to set a standard the EU can only meet by producing certain outcomes. It might likewise be incoherent to believe that certain outcomes for rights, justice, welfare and democracy itself justify the democratic state without also accepting those same democracies would be justified, and even required, to seek means of managing externalities between themselves where that is needed to deliver the outcomes and obligations that justify them as democracies in the first place.

Yet member states also have procedural obligations to their own democracies. Indeed, they only have obligations to secure outcomes in so far as they have procedural obligations. Their publics must be able to define as equals any outcomes and obligations their democracies should secure and how. That might suggest that all the questions raised so far can have the same easy answer: they should be decided by the procedures of each member state democracy. But that cannot be an adequate solution where the problem is one of externalities between democracies. As we will see, if one democracy has an interest in imposing negative externalities or free riding on positive externalities then so will the voters and representatives who employ the procedures of that democracy.

That is why I said indirect legitimacy seems to require both control by national democracies and some control over national democracies. Without subjecting themselves somewhat to shared constraints, highly interconnected national democracies may be unable to manage externalities between themselves in ways needed to deliver outcomes that are no less obligations they owe their own publics than any procedural obligations to ensure their citizens are able to control all their own policies and laws as equals. Bind themselves too little and member state democracies may do too little to meet obligations to their own publics. Bind themselves more closely and they may face the difficulty of how to represent their publics in a form of shared rule-making aimed at managing externalities that must be capable of binding national demoi even in the absence of a shared demos. Member state democracies either have a problem of obligations or one of representation.

But maybe forms of representation at the EU level can themselves contribute to resolving the dilemma? Maybe, as suggested earlier, representative institutions and politics at the EU level do not require a European demos where they can be justified as helping national demoi meet dilemmas in securing their own legitimacy. This chapter demonstrates that possibility has important implications for how we should think about democracy and the EU and for the wider themes of this volume. It shows just how far democracy and democratic deficits at the national and European levels are mutually implicated, not dichotomous. It demonstrates the importance of basing explanations, evaluations and prescriptions for any democratic deficit(s) on dilemmas and trade-offs, not just democratic ideals. How far democratic representation at the Union level falls short of ideals and how well it deals with dilemmas in meeting those ideals are both important lines of enquiry.

Understanding that is an important contribution to the argument of this volume that the distinction between national and supranational forms is not always helpful. Supranational forms of representation, I will argue, can even be an answer to dilemmas in legitimating the Union indirectly through its member state democracies.

The chapter proceeds as follows. The first section discusses arguments of others that the absence of a European demos precludes the development of a full system of representative democracy at the Union. The next section expands on the dilemma involved in legitimating the Union via its member democracies. The following section argues that, in so far as they can help with that dilemma, representative institutions and politics at the Union level can be justified by obligations national demoi owe their own citizens, even in the absence of a shared demos at the European level. The conclusion briefly discusses implications for wider crises in representation, within and beyond the state, and within and beyond the Union.

Folly or Innovation? The EU's Experiment with Representation beyond the State

It might be supposed that representation within and beyond the democratic state should be two different things. There should be a simple dichotomy between how actors should combine to provide a system of representation in single democratic states and how publics should be represented in any rule-making beyond the state. Representation within democratic states requires the 'full range' of actors needed to deliver democratic politics: namely, citizens, voters, parties, parliaments, media and civil society. In contrast, democratic publics are normally represented in rule-making beyond the state by the elected governments of their democratic states. Experts, bureaucrats, diplomats and elected representatives give some variety to the actors who participate in rule-making beyond the state on behalf of democracies. Yet those actors mostly have the single underlying characteristic that the legitimacy of their participation in any decisions, power, coordination or rule-making beyond their democratic states follows from their appointment by national governments. Actor combinations needed to justify rule-making within democracies seem more complex than those needed to justify any shared rule-making by many democracies. A glorious technicolour of different, autonomous and often self-organised actors is needed for representation within democratic states. A monochrome of actors designated by elected national governments may be enough to legitimise and represent democratic peoples in joint rule-making by several democracies.

Yet, the European Union has more composite elements that arguably approach a 'system of representation'. It has a supranational parliament directly elected by the represented themselves. That Parliament has significant co-decision over laws, budgets and the political leadership of the Commission. The EU has its own forms of party representation in which national parties are constrained by European parties as well as vice versa. Many civil society actors and stakeholders represent their views directly to EU institutions.

Indeed, one of the strongest examples of how the Union performs differently across different dimensions of democracy in ways that reflect the underlying dilemma of a political order that needs to be democratic even though it cannot easily meet the conditions for democracy, is that the EU is arguably good at representing many views in its decisions for the same reasons as it is bad at political competition and accountability. When the views, votes and vetoes of so many actors are represented in Union decisions it is easier to attribute those decisions to 'everyone' than 'anyone'. And even where the Union represents many individual views in its decisions it is less clear that it has developed a system of democratic representation; or, in other words, a form of democratic politics that structures choice, competition, control, deliberation and opinion formation in ways relevant to the exercise of the Union's own powers and not just the politics of its member states (Reif and Schmitt 1980). It is hard to organise choice, competition and control of Union decisions around the election of representatives at any one level when the procedures and practices for making those decisions aim at the highest level of agreement within and between multiple categories of representatives. Nor is there any obvious way out of that dilemma. The EU is constrained to aim at the highest level of agreement between representatives of member states whose active cooperation is needed for implementation on the ground; and even between representatives of affected interests whose willingness to share information is crucial to EU regulation (Greenwood 1997: 18). Hence, it can be questioned how far the Union's attempt at its own system of representation through European elections, parties and a European Parliament can really produce anything so very different to bargaining between governments or interests (Bartolini 2005: 329–30).

For some (Majone 2005) the idea that the European Union could develop its own form of democratic representation beyond the state was always more of a folly than an act of originality. It was, in their view, a mistake to have ever believed that the Union belongs to that category of political system capable of developing a system of democratic representation of its own.

Worse than a mistake, it risks domination. To attempt a democratic politics at the Union level peopled by Euro-citizens, Euro-parties, a European Parliament and Euro-media participating, aggregating, compromising and deliberating together to make binding decisions may, as seen, be to assume what is in question: namely, that a shared democracy at the Union level can confer legitimacy or even be legitimate at all. Without democratic authority or democratic political community of its own, the decision-rules that form the core of what the Union takes to be its representative system – qualified majority in a Council representing national democracies and co-decision with a Parliament representing citizens – may themselves be an imposition. They may be a source of democratic deficit rather than a solution to it. Or at least they would be if the Union did not sensibly qualify its pretensions to have developed an ambitious and original form of representation beyond the state by seeking after all to align its policy and law with what its member state democracies represent to be their preferences. Hence, on that understanding, the real work of legitimating the Union is not done by its Potemkin village of shared representative politics at the Union level. Rather it depends on what Peter Lindseth (2010: 14) calls 'national legitimating mechanisms' and especially the representation of national democracies through the intimate participation of their own elected governments in Union decisions.

An Indirect Legitimacy Dilemma

Indeed, a need for the EU to forego representative institutions and politics beyond the state and concentrate, instead, on 'reconnecting' (Bellamy 2019) the Union to national systems of representation might seem to follow from a more general need to legitimate the Union via its member state democracies.

I take direct legitimacy to be the idea that the EU can be legitimated autonomously of member states; and indirect legitimacy to be the idea that its legitimacy can be conferred, derived or even borrowed from its member state democracies. Yet, whatever act or attribute of member state democracies also legitimates the Union, I assume indirect legitimacy cannot remove a need for Union laws to be legitimate with individuals as free and equal citizens. Citizens must be free to control all their own public policies and laws as equals if they are, indeed, to be, free and equal. Direct and indirect legitimacy can only differ on how individuals should control the Union: as equal citizens of the EU; or as equal members of their own member state democracies; or some combination of the two (Habermas 2012).

Maybe any concept of the European Union presupposes its legitimacy depends to some degree on its member state democracies. Even a fully federal Union would be one in which the legitimacy of making law together and the legitimacy of making law apart presuppose and constrain one another. At least the following arguments are part of any full understanding of why member democracies remain important to the Union's legitimacy.

First, are arguments of feasibility. Consider the long and demanding set of conditions that may be needed for representative democracy to work. They might include: a) freedoms of speech and association; b) free and fair elections; c) appointment of leading legislature and executive positions by popular vote; d) a form of political competition that allows voters to control the political system; e) a civil society in which all groups have equal opportunity to organise to influence the polity; f) a public sphere in which all opinions have equal access to public debate; and g) a defined demos with agreement on who should have votes and voice in the making of decisions binding on all.

Achieving all those conditions simultaneously may be hard for the EU, given that it is a multi-state, non-state political system that operates from beyond the state. The capacity of the state to concentrate power, resources and legal enforcement has historically been useful in all kinds of ways to democracy: in ensuring that the decisions of democratic majorities are carried out; in guaranteeing rights needed for democracy; in drawing the boundaries of defined political communities; and in motivating voters and elites to participate in democratic political competition for the control of states which manifestly affect their needs and values. Key ingredients and infrastructures of democratic representation – parties, organised interests, social movements, parliaments and elections – have only developed patchily beyond the state. Nowhere are those elements so fully and evenly developed beyond the state that they fit together to form a complete system of representation in the same way as their equivalents within the state.

Second, are arguments of value. Any need for beyond-state bodies to draw legitimacy from democratic states may be more than a second-best solution in an imperfect world where it is hard to reproduce conditions for democracy beyond the state. Citizens may value existing democratic states and communities. As Habermas has argued (2001, 2012), citizens may value, and seek to preserve, the achievements of a democratic–constitutional–welfare state in which each of those hyphenated terms depends on the other.

Third, are arguments of right. Even universal rights need specification, application and interpretation (Miller 2007). It may be that people can only determine for themselves as equals how rights are to be specified, applied and interpreted through procedures that require democratic states and forms of political community associated with democratic states (Bellamy 2019: 42–4). The no-demos argument may even understate the difficulty. There may also be a no-*kratos* problem in so far as democracy requires stateness (Mikalsen 2017), which the European Union does not have.

What, though, is needed if the Union is to be legitimated by its member state democracies? The normal answer is their consent. Yet, consent can be wrongly given or wrongly withheld where it does not correspond to other obligations (Estlund 2008). Hence, any indirect legitimation of any European Union by its member democracies needs to be consistent with their obligations and not just their consent.

But can we really demonstrate that member state democracies might need some forms of European Union to meet core obligations that justify their own powers as democratic states? Yes, very much so. National democracies and their citizens may be systematically less likely to meet their obligations to their publics and co-citizens without some form of European Union (though not necessarily the European Union we now have) to manage externalities between themselves.

The problem of externalities is familiar. Externalities are uncompensated harms or benefits that are not reflected in rewards to those who produce them (Laffont 2008). Simply summarised, externalities are negative where actors do not pay the full cost of harms they impose on others. They are positive where actors do not receive the full benefits of their own actions. Negative externalities will be over-produced. Public goods – which function as 'very strong' positive 'externalities' (Begg et al. 1984: 352) – will be under-produced. So, too little will be done to clean up climate change (a positive externality) and too much to create climate change (a negative externality). Too little will be done to provide stable systems of human security and economic exchange (positive externalities) and too much to create financial risks that put entire economic systems at risk (negative externalities). It is also worth noting that much cooperation between democracies to provide collective goods is functionally equivalent to cooperation to manage inter-democracy externalities. Foremost amongst choices that can only be made collectively if they are to be made at all are choices over externalities, whether those are choices to provide positive externalities or to limit negative externalities.

The need to provide collective goods and manage externalities has long been understood as a core justification for political authority. David Hume (1978: 538–9) famously remarked that 'political society easily remedies' the 'difficulty' that individuals will seek to 'free' themselves of the 'trouble and expense' of providing some goods by laying 'the whole burden on others'. Thus, political authority can solve the free-rider problem that otherwise constrains the elimination of negative externalities and the provision of positive externalities. The result is that 'bridges are built, ramparts raised, canals formed, fleets equipped and armies disciplined everywhere under the care of government' (ibid).

Still, useful though building bridges and lighthouses might be, it might be objected that only the most fundamental obligations to secure justice and enforce rights so that the freedom of each is compatible with the freedom of all (Kant 1970: 133–4) can justify anything as morally problematic (Beetham 2013: 3) as the exercise of political power by some people over others. There are two answers. First, even where it is just a matter of welfare or utility, the role of public authority in providing collective goods and regulating externalities is crucial to life chances and to sustaining all kinds of systems on which the quality of life depends.

Second, providing collective goods and managing externalities is, in any case, something that needs to be done in the course of securing rights justice and democracy itself (Lord 2015, 2017). Take the very example of externalities between democracies. Closely interconnected democracies, such as those of the European Union, may struggle to provide their own publics with rights against polluters, monopolists, tax-evaders, terrorists, traffickers, discriminators or spreaders of slanders and hate if the sources of those forms of arbitrary domination (Pettit 1997) are located in other states.

Those externalities may then make it hard to provide justice in the Rawlsian (2003: 8–10) sense of how well 'political and social' institutions, laws and practices all 'hang together as one' more or less 'fair system of co-operation'. As Laura Valentini (2011: 208) puts it: 'We can no longer assume that each state is uniquely responsible for securing domestic social justice. States' ability to do so depends on what happens beyond their borders.' If externalities mean that some 'goods' and 'bads' are systematically under- or over-produced between democracies, it will be hard for actors within any one democracy to coordinate on any concept of justice that involves those 'goods' and 'bads'.

If, finally, it is an ideal of democracy that citizens should be able to 'define the terms of their living together as equals' (Bohman 2007: 2), democracies may need means of managing inter-state externalities if their citizens are to have much chance of influencing choices in matters as vital to the 'terms of their living together' as protection against pandemics; as providing security without arms racing; as providing financial systems without systemic risks; or fighting climate change. Indeed, if their decisions can be overwhelmed by the negative externalities of others or undermined by the free riding of others on their provision of positive externalities, publics may struggle to use their own democracies to accord one another rights and obligations or to control their own laws as equals. They will find it difficult to use their national democracies to do those things that define them as democracies.

Yet, politics, democracy, institutions and law are often misaligned with the externalities they are supposed to manage. Political authority to provide positive externalities and eliminate negative externalities has historically been accumulated by states. However, under conditions of interdependence, states may become a part of the problem. Interdependence increases their ability to impose negative externalities on other states and decreases their ability to provide their own citizens with public goods (Collignon 2003: 88). Ulrich Beck (2000: 31, 39) wrote of a 'world risk society' in which 'highly developed societies' are running up against the limits of how far they can 'externalise' risks to one another.

Democracy may even make things worse. If any one national democracy has an interest in imposing harms on its neighbours or in free riding on the efforts of others to maintain economic, ecological or security systems, then its own electorate and parliament will also have an interest in behaving in those ways (Lord 2015). If voters are purely self-regarding, electoral competition within any one democratic state may only be in 'equilibrium' (where those competing for power have done everything possible to win votes) at precisely the point that maximises negative externalities and free riding between democracies (Grant and Keohane 2005).

We can now set out the full extent of the dilemma we briefly sketched in the introduction. We have said that the EU depends on some element of indirect legitimation. We have also said that indirect legitimacy depends in part on helping member state democracies manage externalities between themselves in ways needed for them to deliver their own obligations to their own publics to secure rights, justice, welfare, freedom from arbitrary domination and democracy itself. However, as well as securing those outcomes, democracies plainly also have procedural obligations to ensure their publics have full control of their own policies and laws as equals. So, as seen, input conditions for indirect legitimacy would seem to require control by national democracies. Yet, output conditions for indirect legitimacy would seem to require enough power over national democracies to manage externalities between democracies in ways needed to secure the obligations within democracies that justify acting together in the first place. The solution is, presumably, some element of self-binding where citizens and their representatives control as equals the means by which their democracies bind themselves to means of managing inter-democracy externalities. That might include powers to scrutinise, revise, recall or exit, all on the assumption, none the less, that – as long as a democracy remains a part of any framework for managing externalities – it binds itself to rules and meta-rules it has itself agreed. But, note that the idea of self-binding constitutes the dilemma as much as it resolves it. Democracies can even gain autonomy by tying their hands to the mast in the sense that allows them to make choices over the management of externalities they would otherwise be unable to make. But they also lose some autonomy. Tying their hands they may have to do if they are to deal with externalities between themselves.

Representation within and beyond the State: Towards a Democratic Reconnect

Can different ways of providing indirect legitimacy by representing member state democracies in Union decisions help with the dilemma identified in the last section? This section considers three possibilities. All are ways of representing member state democracies in Union decisions over the management of externalities. But they differ in how far they involve shared representative practices or institutions; or a shared representative politics which structures choice, competition, contestation, control and deliberation in ways relevant to the Union's own powers and not just the politics of its member states.

One possibility is that it is sufficient to represent national democracies by their own elected governments in inter-state bargaining over the management of externalities. A second possibility is that bargaining between elected governments cannot be enough without shared norms, rules and practices of representation. Yet those things can be largely pieced together from national systems of representation. A third possibility is that combining the management of inter-democracy externalities with continued legitimation and control by national democracies may itself benefit from, and even require, shared representative institutions and politics at the European level.

Possibility 1. Cooperation without Shared Norms or Institutions of Representation

Why might it be enough to represent even highly interconnected democracies in inter-state bargaining by their own elected governments over externalities, without any shared norms, rules, institutions or authority, still less shared systems or agreed practices of representation? Since providing certain kinds of collective good and removing externalities is Pareto-improving, democracies may often be able to coordinate on solutions each can justify in their own way. The conditions where that is possible – low transaction costs in monitoring and enforcing agreements (Coase 1960) – are also more likely to hold where externalities are between states rather than individuals. Whilst managing diffuse externalities between millions of individuals may be difficult, groups of states such as the EU 27 may be sufficiently few to monitor one another without that requiring much by way of a shared institutional authority. Contrary to the view that bargaining is purely strategic and without normative value, bargaining together without agreeing shared norms over the management of inter-democracy externalities can itself have the special normative quality of allowing each democracy to cooperate for its own reasons of value (Buchanan and Tullock 1962). Acting together, whilst deciding norms and values apart, may be especially appealing in the case of cooperation between democracies. After all, as the EU itself illustrates, conditions for democracy – such as political competition, high levels of voter participation, a well-formed public sphere and political community – seem easier to achieve within states than beyond them.

There are, however, at least two difficulties with the idea that it can be enough to represent publics in bargaining between their own elected governments over the management of externalities. First, the conditions for managing externalities by bargaining alone may break down. What if the transaction costs of reaching and monitoring agreements are too high for democracies to achieve very much by just bargaining between themselves over the provision of collective goods and the management of externalities? Democracies will then have to choose: do they leave collective goods underprovided and externalities untreated? Or do they agree and bind themselves together to shared norms and even shared institutions that might help to construct, monitor and enforce the means of providing collective goods and manage externalities?

A second difficulty, however, would arise even if things go well and democracies really can do all they need to do to provide collective goods and manage externalities by bargaining alone. Even where bargaining allows each democracy to reach optimal agreements as determined by its own norms, values and democratic procedures, it will only do that subject to some distribution of power. Bargaining will likely follow distributions of power between democracies in the absence of any agreed values, rights, norms, rules or institutions. The obvious question is whether a bargain based on some distribution of power between democratic states can have much resemblance – either as process or outcome – to what is required for democracies to meet their obligations to their own publics, or their citizens to meet their obligations to their co-citizens. How far the costs of avoiding an inter-democracy externality fall on its producer or its victim will depend on how easily the democracy representing the one or the other can live with the default of non-agreement. Publics may feel that some collective goods and externalities are of such fundamental importance that they should be provided or avoided as a matter of right and not as a matter of what can be bargained with other democratic states. They will not expect to have to bargain for compensation, to split differences, to divide remedies between victim and perpetrator, or even to negotiate over who should be understood as the victim and perpetrator. Rather, democracies might expect a clearly defined right – and a right to be able to live with the certainty of having clearly defined rights – not to have certain negative externalities imposed upon them and not to have others frustrate their own efforts to provide positive externalities they believe are essential to their rights or well-being. Rather than leaving things to bargaining on the assumption that is the best way of making their own decisions on questions of right, value and obligation, national democracies might get far closer to meeting their obligations to their own publics by developing shared obligations with other democracies over the management externalities.

Possibility 2. Cooperation through Shared Norms and Practices Based in National Systems of Representation

Whilst, though shared obligations, norms and practices may be needed to manage inter-democracy externalities, those things could be pieced together from national systems of representation, without requiring anything that would amount to shared representative institutions or politics. The EU suggests at least the following ways in which the shared management of externalities between democracies might be reconciled after all with continued legitimation and control by national systems of representation (Lindseth 2010).

   1. Member state democracies are thoroughly represented by their own elected governments in Union decisions from conception to implementation. Voting in the Council of Ministers demonstrates how far the Union strives for the agreement of all its member

states to all its decisions, even where qualified majority voting in possible (Mattila and Lane 2001). Once made, Union decisions are often further adapted in real time to what member states are willing and able to implement on the ground (Sabel and Zeitlin 2010). For sure, the close participation of member states in Union decisions is also consistent with the idea that it is enough to represent publics in bargaining between their elected governments over the management of externalities. However, points 2-5 which follow suggest that the intimate participation of governments in Union decisions is important for reasons of representation and not just bargaining.

2. In building agreement, member state governments are governed by norms of justification, communication and shared learning which are more typical of representation than bargaining. That connects, in turn, to the shared management of externalities. Christian Joerges and Jürgen Neyer (1997) have argued that the Union's whole institutional design and system of law puts multiple requirements on member states to justify the external effects of their preferences, proposals or behaviours. Representatives of any one member democracy can question any of the others about negative externalities; about free riding on positive externalities; and about cooperation to deal with either difficulty. That can even be understood as partially addressing the 'constitutional defect' in the democratic state (Joerges 2006) that gives affected outsiders no representation in its decisions. Deliberation on externalities can also help member state democracies to feel their way towards constructing shared obligations out of their mutually affected individual obligations to their own publics.

3. Their representation in Union decisions gives member state democracies a distinctive mix of collective and individual control (Lindseth 2010: 12). Elected national governments have shared oversight and collective control. As just seen, they even have high levels of individual control, given that the Council only resorts to QMV after other means of reaching agreement have been exhausted. Moreover, that reticence is structurally required. The Union needs to aim at the highest possible agreement between member democracies if it is also to aim at their closest possible cooperation in implementation. Yet, the individual control of member states is not so complete that the Union is altogether blocked from managing externalities from which a few members benefit at the expense of the rest. Formally, QMV gives vetoes

to combinations of governments, working in multiple and variable blocking minorities, not to single governments. Informally, a need to manage externalities can itself be the basis for a norm that justifies giving up on the accommodation of all member states and resorting to QMV after all. Accommodating opportunities to externalise harms or to free ride cannot, logically, be a part of any process of building the highest possible agreement between member democracies, since those are preferences that can only be had at the expense of other members. On the other hand, knowledge that QMV can be used – but only after a deliberation on joint management of externalities – might be expected to encourage compromise. Rather than being outvoted, member states might find it better to continue searching for solutions where everyone can minimise negative externalities and maximise positive externalities to their mutual advantage. After all, managing externalities ought, as said, to be Pareto-improving. A mixture of QMV as the formal voting rule and a practice of attempting to reach the highest level of agreement seems to provide a high level of control by each member state democracy without removing all possibility of sufficient control over national democracies to manage externalities.

4. The same factors can reconcile national parliamentary oversight with the need to avoid vetoes by individual national representative institutions over the shared management of externalities between democracies. National parliaments can be demanding in their scrutiny – perhaps even more demanding than they are right now – in the knowledge that the Union needs to aim at the highest possible level of agreement to secure the active cooperation of each of its member state democracies. Yet pressure from national parliaments on their governments to adopt positions that would create negative externalities or free ride on the provision of positive externalities by other member state democracies would plainly be a move away from any search for the highest possible level of agreement between national democracies. National parliaments, no less than national governments, need to be aware that deliberation at the European level aimed at removing negative externalities and at cooperating over the provision of positive externalities requires reciprocity. Lindseth (2010: 26, 224) also suggests how oversight by national parliaments can be effective without that blocking individual decisions at the Union level aimed at managing externalities between member state democracies.

Even on domestic matters, scrutiny does not primarily work through powers to block decisions. Rather, it works by exposing inadequate justifications and weakening the credibility of insufficiently justified policies. Hence, national parliamentary scrutiny of Union law-making – and of the contributions of national governments to Union decisions – can be a part of the domestic politics of member states without that undermining attempts to manage externalities between member states. It is enough that national parliamentarians can demand justifications and that national governments need to maintain their general reputations within wider processes of democratic choice, competition and control. National parliaments can scrutinise single decisions aimed at managing inter-democracy externalities without having veto powers over them.

5. As well as having individual rights of scrutiny, national systems of representation can also have powers of control over Union decisions that they can only use together. An interesting innovation here has been the Early Warning Mechanism (EWM; Cooper 2015). The EWM allows national parliaments to challenge proposals on the grounds of subsidiarity. But they can only do that jointly and not individually. So the power is not one single national parliaments can easily use to block proposals to manage externalities between member democracies. Yet it is a power that encourages national parliaments to 'Europeanise' their arguments enough to persuade one another to act together in using the EWM. Some (Bellamy 2019; Chalmers 2013) see the EWM as suggesting a more general model for filling the democratic deficit. Why not give national systems of representation more general powers of veto or initiative that go beyond the restriction of the EWM to questions of subsidiarity and proportionality? Those would be powers national parliaments can only use jointly and not individually. Searching out sources of mutual gain from minimising negative externalities and maximising positive externalities would be one way of acting jointly. Deliberation and communication within a supranational parliament is not the only way in which elected representatives from all member democracies can justify to one another their positions on laws they make together through the Union. Mechanisms that encourage deliberation and communication between national parliaments can have the same effect without that creating individual vetoes that undermine ways of legislating together to manage externalities.

Perhaps, though, the Achilles heel in the foregoing argument already comes at point 1 above. Collective oversight by national executives (Lindseth 2010: 12) is precisely what others see as executive domination of Union decisions to the exclusion of public contestation, debate or parliamentary supervision. It risks substituting technocratic management of problems between states for democratic politics within states (Habermas, 2012, 2015). Optimism that national parliaments can then scrutinise how their national governments contribute to decisions on inter-democracy externalities arguably gets power relationships the wrong way around. In many systems, governments control their parliaments. National executives may even practise forms of 'reverse agency' (Bohman, 2007: 7). Instead of supervising international bodies on behalf of their publics, governments may use international bodies to take decisions in ways their own publics and parliaments find hard to control. Hence, Habermas's complaint that euro-crisis decisions were dominated by a 'self-authorising European Council ... confined to heads of governments' who – far from being supervised by national parliaments – undertook to 'organise majorities in their own national parliaments under threat of sanctions' (2012: viii) for failing to deliver those majorities. Joe Weiler (1997: 274) noted long ago that the Council's participation in legislation reconstitutes the executive branch of each member state as part of the legislature at the European level. Inter-state management of externalities risks executive domination within democracies as well as any democracy-on-democracy domination that may follow from any asymmetries of bargaining power that are not softened by institutions or norms.

The close involvement of national governments in Union decisions is a part of what needs justification, and not just a part of what can provide representation and legitimacy. The Union changes the very statehood of its member state democracies. To be a member state of the EU is to be a different kind of state (Bickerton 2012). Even the core powers (Genschel and Jachtenfuchs 2014) of member states are exercised in ways that are shaped by their membership of the Union. The EU changes the way in which its member states rule, even where it does not itself rule. Elected national governments become a part of a power relationship that did not exist before in which those governments a) meet at least some of their obligations to their own publics by b) managing externalities between themselves with the help of c) policies and laws they agree with other members states within the institutions and procedures of the Union, all d) with a commitment to enforce those decisions on their own individual citizens. What needs legitimation, then, is not just the Union itself. Rather, it is the entire structure of power relations shaped by Union membership. That includes those powers and practices of member states that are reconfigured by membership: notably, the huge empowerment of national executives through their active everyday participation in Union decisions; and their making of some of the rules by which they coerce their publics through a process of shared law-making that is quite different in its powers, procedures and participants to law-making within single democracies.

Possibility 3. Cooperation and Control by Member State Democracies Supported by Representative Institutions and Representative Politics at the Union Level

If the intimate participation of national governments in EU decisions is not enough and even a risk of executive domination, then indirect legitimation presumably requires legitimation by the wider democratic politics of each member state. But does that just take us back to the indirect legitimacy dilemma and the seeming contradiction of attempting to internalise to the democratic politics of each member state the control of decisions aimed at managing externalities between them? Didn't we say that, if a member democracy has an interest in imposing negative externalities or free riding on the provision of positive externalities by others, its voters and parliaments are also likely to have a like interest? So, seeking to control inter-democracy externalities through each national democracy might seem like putting the sharks in charge of the swimming pool.

As said, the solution is presumably to find ways in which democracies can – through their membership of the Union – bind themselves to managing externalities whilst maintaining some control over the means by which they bind themselves. Here, an important – and, I think, underappreciated – feature of the Union is that its member state governments do not even pretend to a monopoly of representation of their own publics in Union institutions. Instead, they have shared powers over the Union's law-making, its budgets and the appointment of the political leadership of the Commission with a European Parliament (EP) their publics themselves elect. Yet the EP is itself a dual system of representation. For sure, it is primarily organised into European party groups which bring together at the Union level the mainly left–right ideologies and party families found in most member states. However, the practices of the EP mean that it is also a representation of its 200 or so national party delegations (Ringe 2010). The groups depend on the disciplines of the national party delegations for their own cohesion. They attempt to decide voting instructions by a consensus of the national party delegations. Sure, conflicts between national party delegations and party groups are rare. But, where they do occur, Members of the European Parliament are four times more likely to vote with their national parties than their European party groups (Hix et al. 2007: 193). Elected in member states and comprised of national party delegations as well as European party groups, the EP needs to be included in any complete account of how national democracies are represented in EU law-making. That point was not lost on the German Federal Constitutional Court (GFCC) in its ruling on the Lisbon Treaty: 'as seats are allocated to the Member States, the EP remains a representation of the Member States . . . designed as a representation of peoples' (GFCC, 2009: paras 280–4). (See also Lord and Pollak 2013.)

So, important powers are shared between national governments and a European Parliament. The EP is directly elected, but in the member states. The EP is composed of European party groups, but they have to build compromise between national party delegations. How might all that help member state democracies bind themselves to ways of managing externalities whilst retaining control over those means of binding themselves?

First, a directly elected EP can simply help in the discovery of externalities and, therefore, of opportunities for Pareto-improving cooperations between member state democracies. Here I take it that a shared commitment to the maximum autonomy of each member democracy compatible with the autonomy of all those democracies does not just constrain. It also enables. It does not just have a 'downside' in requiring members to bind and constrain themselves in many tiresome ways if they are to deliver their own obligations to their own publics under conditions of externalities. It also provides an opportunity to identify ways of managing externalities to the mutual advantage of member democracies. It enlarges the autonomy of each member democracy in making choices over the joint management of externalities that it would otherwise find it hard to make at all. Shared forms of representation can help to make people(s) aware of themselves as mutually affected by externalities (Dewey 1954: 35). Especially helpful may be forms of representation that involve debate between political parties, given their competing understandings of how markets, security policies and ecological problems create externalities and with what implications for values of fairness, non-domination or democracy. A supranational parliament can also help member democracies to overcome a huge problem in achieving the optimal management of externalities. It is hard to discover what everyone is prepared to pay to eliminate negative externalities and provide positive externalities where anyone has incentives to overstate the costs and understate the benefits of cooperation (Cornes and Sandler 1986: 114). In the case of a cooperation between democracies, that problem often takes the form of governments overstating the domestic political costs to themselves of shared commitments to manage externalities. A directly elected European Parliament reduces that risk. As seen, it has the effect of directly including national parties of opposition in any EU law-making aimed at managing externalities. Extensive co-decision of laws between the Council and EP – and the EP's practice of building the largest possible majorities – means that representatives of national parties of opposition are included in most compromises on most legislation. National party delegations in the EP must at least take a position, even if it is only to abstain on legislation. Hence, the views of national parties of opposition can be directly tested and even accommodated. That limits scope for governments to misrepresent dangers of domestic opposition to legislation aimed at managing externalities.

Second, a form of parliamentary representation at the European level that is also to some degree a representation of national democracies can contribute to the 'norming of laws' aimed at managing externalities. By that I mean the specification of the rights and values that should guide and constrain what would otherwise be technical rules. If politics and parliamentary representation are useful to discovering solutions to externalities, they are even more important to legitimating any laws aimed at regulating them. The very argument that managing externalities between democracies might be needed for the deeply normative tasks of securing obligations, values and rights within and across those democracies, implies that confining any shared law-making to executive actors may be a category error. There is likely to be reasonable disagreement over the definition and management of externalities. Whether and how political authority should be used to manage externalities are political and moral choices and judgements (Claassen 2016: 554; Kumm 2016; Shapiro 2003: 63–4). Nor is it obvious that political authority should deal with all externalities. An imperfect world in which many more minor externalities go unmanaged may be preferable to one in which political authorities aim at the optimal internalisation of externalities. Such a political authority would need to be perfectionist, technocratic and interfering, and not just occasionally but continually. Preferences 'drift' and people continually discover new ways of externalising costs or free riding on benefits.

Yet, the specification of the exact obligations, values and rights that laws should secure and respect requires a specifically parliamentary form of representation. Here I assume what Habermas (1996: 171) calls the 'parliamentary principle'. Only parliamentary deliberation ensures a) representatives elected on a basis of one person, one vote can b) test justifications for laws during the process of law-making itself within c) a public forum where all views can be tested in relation to one another (Mill 1972), all d) by an institution that can subsequently scrutinise, control and even sanction the application of those laws. Unless the Union is prepared to pass laws through national parliaments, and transfer powers to censure the Commission to some combination of national parliaments, it is hard to see how the requirements in a–d could be met in full without a directly elected European Parliament. Then, there are the justificatory and deliberative requirements of shared law-making. Not only does democracy require that all those who are subject to laws should be able to control the authoring, amendment and administration of those laws as equals. It also requires that all those who author laws should be able to justify them in public debate. That creates special challenges where laws are jointly made by democracies with the aim of managing externalities between themselves. The externalities which justify those laws will often originate in one democracy and be experienced in another. And, in so far as they are the shared laws of a shared polity, their authorship will be the shared responsibility of the Union's participating democracies. All those subject to them will also have rights to justification of each of those laws. A directly elected European Parliament – which is also to some degree a representation of national democracies and through which EU laws must pass between conception and legislation – is an additional way in which any norms, rights and values that shape Union law can be deliberated across the national and European levels without that either abstracting from national concerns or reducing the justification of laws aimed at managing externalities between national democracies to the preoccupations of single national parliaments. For sure, it might not be impossible to arrange forms of inter-parliamentary deliberation in which national parliaments can represent their concerns about externalities to one another (Bohman 2007). But, I will argue in a moment that even deliberations of Union matters within and between national parliaments would benefit from a directly elected European Parliament in overcoming asymmetries of information.

Third, as some of the above suggests, a directly elected EP can contribute more to the representation of other possible majorities within member state democracies than governing ones. Majorities are not the people. Indeed, they are only majorities at one particular moment, at one level of aggregation, and according to just one method of counting votes (Rosanvallon 2008). A directly elected EP – rather than, say, a European Assembly formed out of national parliaments – means that opinion within each national democracy is more likely to be represented differently in the EP, the (European) Council and its own parliament. Only parties of government get access to the Council. In contrast, representatives of national parties of opposition are structurally likely to form the larger part of an elected EP – and to be more numerous in the EP than in their own national parliaments – so long as the

EP is elected in somewhat second-order contests that do not coincide with most national electoral cycles (Bardi 1994). That, ironically, is one advantage of second-order elections.

Fourth, a directly elected European Parliament can also help to safeguard against collusion by member state governments to evade rules on managing externalities their own national democracies have agreed. Recall the Council decision in 2003 to suspend the Stability and Growth Pact aimed at limiting fiscal externalities within a shared monetary union. As the European Central Bank's chief economist put it, 'potential transgressors' may not be the best people 'to pass judgement on actual transgressors' (Issing 2008: 199). Governments can help one another to avoid political inconvenience or embarrassment. National democracies seeking to manage externalities between themselves may need, therefore, to avoid giving the club of governments monopolies over rule changes. In the case of the EU, one solution is to require co-decision of rule changes with a European Parliament whose strong representation of national parties of opposition gives it no obvious interest in changes motivated only by the political convenience of some governments.

Fifth, a European Parliament can help to overcome asymmetries of information in ways needed for national publics and parliaments to participate effectively in the democratic oversight of EU decisions and of the contributions of their own governments to those decisions. A huge problem in any democratic oversight is asymmetries of information that favour the very executive bodies that publics and parliaments need to oversee (Krehbiel 1991). Scrutinising Union decisions requires expertise specific to the institutions and policies of the Union. Expertise in scrutinising Union policies may be a capability that needs to be cultivated over time (March and Olsen 1995). The Union may also depend on an experimental form of decision-making in which 'actors have to learn what problem they are solving, and what solution they are seeking, through the very process of problem solving' (Sabel and Zeitlin 2010: 11). Hence, oversight may need to be continuously updated, as EU policies aimed at managing externalities – as well as justifications for those policies – evolve in response to experience with the policies themselves. There is also an opportunity cost for national representative institutions. Time spent monitoring Union decisions is time not spent following domestic decisions. In contrast, a directly elected European Parliament, specialised, and full-time in following EU decisions, can itself be a positive externality in providing information and scrutiny from which national democracies cannot be excluded and to which they can be structurally linked through the high overlap between national party delegations in the EP and parties in national parliaments (Crum and Fossum 2009).

Conclusion

The European Union has attempted to construct its own system of democratic representation beyond the state. Critics see that as a mistake. The EU, in their view, lacks the conditions for democracy. It especially lacks a demos or, in other words, a public that sees itself as a democratic people with a collectively binding authority. We should, however, take seriously the converse possibility that national democracies may themselves experience legitimacy difficulties without some form of representation within some form of European Union. Without a form of European Union that can manage externalities between member state democracies, national demoi may struggle to secure outcomes needed to meet their own obligations to their own publics. Yet, member state democracies must also meet their procedural obligations to ensure their own publics can control Union laws as equals. So, they seem to face a dilemma. They can only achieve their procedural obligations where their publics can control Union laws aimed at managing externalities. However, they can only secure outcomes that deliver their most basic obligations – to secure rights, justice, welfare and democracy itself – by accepting some constraints on how far their democracies can control Union laws aimed at managing externalities.

The way out of that dilemma, I have argued, is for citizens of each member state democracy to have equal control over those means by which their own democracy binds itself to shared means of managing externalities at the European level. Up to a point that can be achieved by the close representation and participation of national democracies in the exercise of Union powers. But that solution will itself need safeguards against executive domination and democracy-on-democracy domination. It will also require member state democracies to agree rights, justice and standards of non-domination that they cannot achieve by bargaining alone. Given those challenges, a system of representation specific to the Union – and additional to the representation of national governments in its decisions – can help member state democracies, first, to identify externalities; second, to justify and deliberate norms and laws for managing those externalities in a public parliamentary process that includes more than governing majorities; third, to avoid collusion between governments in evading rules their own national democracies have themselves agreed to manage externalities; fourth, to overcome asymmetries of information that inhibit national publics and parliaments in their own oversight of Union decisions aimed at managing externalities; and, fifth, to link cooperation at the Union level to political choice and competition at the national level, especially that between government and opposition. A directly elected EP gives national parties of opposition representation they would not otherwise have in a Union institution, and, indeed, representation at the Union level in the EU's legislative procedures.

Dilemmas created by externalities are acute in the case of member state democracies of the EU. But they are also a wider problem for contemporary democracy. Externalities have exposed incapacities in the representative state (Warren 2010). On the other hand, cooperations between governments to manage externalities may themselves fuel populist critiques of representative democracy. 'Representatives', in the view of many populists, are turned into unrepresentative and unaccountable elites by the very process of representation. What could be a better example than governments cooperating together beyond the state in ways their publics find hard to control or even observe? Yet, inter-democracy externalities and collective action problems are unlikely to go away. Nor is the technical nature of those externalities likely to stop requiring forms of representation that mix the expert with the political. Nor are popular and participatory forms of democracy likely to substitute for expertise or, indeed, replace representative democracy itself (Plotke 1997). A post-populist rethinking of representative democracy and of the relationship between representation within and beyond the state is, therefore, needed. That rethinking will need to solve problems of identity, demos and democratic political community in ways that go well beyond the questions of externalities considered here. But, equally, demoi whose own concepts of democratic community do not allow them to cooperate effectively over the management of inter-state externalities will fail to solve problems of climate change, pandemics, systemic risk in banking systems, tax evasion or cross-border crime (see especially Mansbridge 2014); and, with those failures, they will also fail to meet their own obligations to their own publics to secure rights, justice, non-domination and democracy itself.

References

Bardi, L. (1994) Transnational Trends in European Parties and the 1994 Election of the European Parliament. *Party Politics*, 2(1): 99–114.

Bartolini, Stefano (2005) *Restructuring Europe: Centre Formation, System Building and Political Structuring between the Nation State and the European Union*. Oxford: Oxford University Press.

Beck, Ulrich (2000) *What is Globalization?* Cambridge: Polity.

Beetham, David (2013) *The Legitimation of Power*. Basingstoke: Palgrave.

Begg, David, Fischer, Stanley and Dornbusch, Rudiger (1984) *Economics*. Maidenhead: McGraw Hill.

Bellamy, Richard (2019) *A Republican Europe of Sovereign States. Cosmopolitan Statism, Republican Intergovernmentalism and Demoicratic Reconnection of the EU*. Cambridge: Cambridge University Press.

Bickerton, Christopher (2012) *European Integration. From Nation States to Member States*. Oxford: Oxford University Press.
Bohman, J. (2007) *Democracy across Borders from Demos to Demoi*. Cambridge, MA: MIT Press.
Buchanan, James and Tullock, Gordon (1962) *The Calculus of Consent. Logical Foundations of Constitutional Democracy*. Ann Arbor: University of Michigan Press.
Chalmers, Damian (2013) *Democratic Self-Government in Europe: Domestic Solutions to the EU Legitimacy Crisis*. London: Policy Network Paper.
Claassen, Rutger (2016) Externalities as a Basis for Regulation: A Philosophical View. *Journal of Institutional Economics*, 12(3): 541–63.
Coase, Ronald (1960) The Problem of Social Cost. *Journal of Law and Economics*, 3(1): 1–44.
Collignon, Stefan (2003) *The European Republic: Reflection on the Political Economy of a Future Constitution*. London: The Federal Trust.
Cooper, Ian (2015) A Yellow Card for the Striker: National Parliaments and the Defeat of EU Legislation on the Right to Strike. *Journal of European Public Policy*, 22(10): 1406–25.
Cornes, Richard and Sandler, Todd (1986) *The Theory of Externalities, Public Goods and Club Goods*. Cambridge: Cambridge University Press.
Crum, Ben and Fossum, John-Erik (2009) The Multilevel Parliamentary Field: A Framework for Theorising Representative Democracy in the EU. *European Political Science Review*, 1(2): 249–71.
Dewey, John [1927] (1954) *The Public and its Problems*. Athens: Ohio University Press.
Estlund, David (2008) *Democratic Authority: A Philosophical Framework*. Princeton: Princeton University Press.
Genschel, Philipp and Jachtenfuchs, Markus (eds) (2014) *Beyond the Regulatory Polity? The European Integration of Core State Powers*. Oxford: Oxford University Press.
German Federal Constitutional Court (GFCC) (2009) Judgement of the Second Senate of 30 June 2009, 2 BE 2/08, <http://www.bundesverfassungsgericht.de/SharedDocs/Entscheidungen/EN/2009/06> (last accessed 10 February 2016).
Grant, Ruth and Keohane, Robert (2005) Accountability and Abuses of Power in World Politics. *American Political Science Review*, 99(1): 29–43.
Greenwood, Justin (1997) *Representing Interests in the European Union*. Basingstoke: Macmillan.
Habermas, Jürgen (1996) *Between Facts and Norms*. Cambridge: Polity.
Habermas, Jürgen (2001) *The Postnational Constellation*. Cambridge, MA: MIT Press.
Habermas, Jürgen (2012) *The Crisis of the European Union: A Response*. Cambridge: Polity.
Habermas, Jürgen (2015) *The Lure of Technocracy*. Cambridge: Polity.
Hix, Simon, Noury, Abdul and Roland, Gérard (2007) *Democratic Politics in the European Parliament*. Cambridge: Cambridge University Press.
Hume, David [1739] (1978) *A Treatise on Human Nature*. Oxford: Clarendon Press.
Issing, Otmar (2008) *The Birth of the Euro*. Cambridge: Cambridge University Press.
Joerges, Christian (2006) Deliberative Political Processes Revisited: What Have We Learnt about the Legitimacy of Supranational Decision-Making? *Journal of Common Market Studies*, 44(4): 779–802.

Joerges, Christian and Neyer, Jürgen (1997) From Intergovernmental Bargaining to Deliberative Political Processes: The Constitutionalisation of Comitology. *European Law Journal*, 3(3): 273-99.

Kant, Immanuel [1797] (1970) The Metaphysics of Morals. In Reiss, H. (ed.) *Kant. Political Writings*, Cambridge: Cambridge University Press.

Krehbiel, Keith (1991) *Information and Legislative Organisation*. Ann Arbor: University of Michigan Press.

Kumm, Mattias (2016) Sovereignty and the Right to be Left Alone: Subsidiarity, Justice-Sensitive Externalities, and the Proper Domain of Consent Required in International Law. *Law and Contemporary Problems*, 79(2): 238.

Laffont, Jean-Jacques (2008) Externalities. In Durlauf, S. and Blume, L. (eds) *The New Palgrave Dictionary of Economics*, London: Palgrave.

Lindseth, Peter (2010) *Power and Legitimacy: Reconciling Europe and the Nation State*. Oxford: Oxford University Press.

Lord, Christopher (2015) Utopia or Dystopia? Towards a Normative Analysis of Differentiated Integration. *Journal of European Public Policy*, 22(6): 783-98.

Lord, Christopher (2017), An Indirect Legitimacy Argument for a Directly Elected European Parliament. *European Journal of Political Research*, 56(3): 512-28.

Lord, Christopher and Pollak, Johannes (2013) Unequal but Democratic? Equality According to Karlsruhe. *Journal of European Public Policy*, 20(2): 190-205.

Majone, Giandomenico (2005) *Dilemmas of European Integration. The Ambiguities and Pitfalls of Integration by Stealth*. Oxford: Oxford University Press.

Mansbridge, Jane (2014) What is Politics For? *Perspectives on Politics*, 12(1): 8-17.

March, James and Olsen, Johan (1995) *Democratic Governance*. New York: Free Press.

Marquand, David (1979) *Parliament for Europe*. London: Jonathan Cape.

Mattila, Mikko and Lane, Jan-Erik (2001) Why Unanimity in the Council? A Roll-Call Analysis of Council Voting. *European Union Politics*, 2(1): 73-97.

Mikalsen, Kjartan (2017) No Cosmopolitan Morality without State Sovereignty. *Philosophy and Social Criticism*, 43(10): 1072-94.

Mill, John Stuart [1861] (1972) *Utilitarianism, On Liberty and Considerations on Representative Government*. London: Dent.

Miller, David (2007) *National Responsibility and Global Justice*. Oxford: Oxford University Press.

Pettit, Phillip (1997) *Republicanism: A Theory of Freedom and Government*. Oxford: Oxford University Press.

Plotke, David (1997) Representation is Democracy. *Constellations*, 4(1): 19-34.

Rawls, John (2003) *Justice as Fairness: A Restatement*. Cambridge, MA: Belknap Press of University of Harvard Press.

Reif, Karl-Heinz and Schmitt, Hermann (1980) Nine Second-Order National Elections: A Conceptual Framework for the Analysis of European Election Results. *European Journal of Political Research*, (1): 3-45.

Ringe, Nils (2010) *Who Decides and How? Preferences, Uncertainty and Policy Choice in the European Parliament*. Oxford: Oxford University Press.

Rosanvallon, Pierre (2008) *La Légitimité Démocratique : Impartialité, Reflexivité, Proximité*. Paris: Seuil.

Sabel, Charles and Zeitlin, Jonathan (eds) (2010) *Experimentalist Governance in the European Union: Towards a New Architecture*. Oxford: Oxford University Press, pp. 1–27.

Shapiro, Ian (2003) *The Moral Foundations of Politics*. New Haven: Yale University Press.

Valentini, Laura (2011) Coercion and Global Justice. *American Political Science Review*, 105(1): 205–20.

Warren, Mark (2010) Beyond the Self-Legislation Model of Democracy. *Ethics and Global Politics*, 3(1): 47–54.

Weiler, Joseph (1997) Legitimacy and Democracy of EU Governance. In Edwards, G. and Pijpers, A. (eds) *The Politics of European Union Treaty Reform*. London: Pinter, pp. 249–87.

TWO

Beyond the Nation-State: Multilevel Democracy in Europe

Michael Keating

The Democratic Challenge

Democracy can be defined as rule by the people, but that begs the questions of who are the people and what do they rule. As emphasised in the introduction to this volume, there is no single, grand theory of democracy but rather a series of democratic dilemmas. Since the emergence of democracy in modern Europe, these have been subordinated to a concept of the people rooted in the unitary nation, and a conception of rule reliant on the territorial, sovereign state. The two are linked in the concept of the nation-state, whereby the national people realises its ambitions. This actually represents an ideal type, or aspiration, as the European political order has always been more complex than that. The model is under stress, as a process of rescaling has taken functional systems, identities and political imaginations to new spatial levels, above, below and across the states. Rescaling is sometimes presented as a response to technical necessities and the search for Pareto-optimal solutions to social and economic problems. This can lead to a reinforcement of tendencies to depoliticisation, a neglect of distributive issues and a consequent loss of democratic engagement in policy. Yet these tendencies are countered by new challenges from losers and a repoliticisation and a search for new democratic spaces. There are campaigns for self-determination and, at the limit, secession, in Scotland, Catalonia and elsewhere. In several states, a new regional or 'meso' level of government has emerged while others have older federal traditions. Cities and metropolitan regions have become important sites for democratic exchange. In other cases, the nation-state remains the dominant focus for democratic self-expression.

The debate about the democratisation of the European Union (EU) has largely been confined to two territorial levels: that of the EU itself as an emerging polity; and that of the member states. The contribution of this chapter is to take a larger view of territory, encompassing the sub-state as well as the supranational level, linked in a common problematic of democratisation beyond the state. The argument is that, if government and regulation are operating at multiple and changing levels, democracy must keep pace with that.

Democracy and the Nation-State

Three conceptions of democracy are relevant to our theme. The first is based in ontological individualism and sees democracy as a vehicle for realising the policy preferences of individual citizens in a manner analogous to the ideal market. This may include aggregating individual preferences into broader programmes. The second moves beyond the individualist ontology and brings in more collective perspectives. Democracy, in this view, entails deliberation about interests but also about ideas, which may take in broader conceptions of justice and equity. Preferences are not fixed and the broader social interest is not merely the aggregation of individual desires but includes ideas of social cohesion. The third conception sees democracy as a means of confronting inequalities of power in society, including, but not limited to, structural inequalities of wealth. The assumption is that unregulated markets (even the mythical 'perfect' market) will not enable everyone to participate equally in public life but that there are inbuilt obstacles. Political power and representative institutions are instruments available to the economically powerless to realise their individual and collective ambitions. The latter two conceptions imply that democracy is more than the counting of revealed preferences but requires mechanism for deliberation These three conceptions are not mutually exclusive. Any democratic system will contain elements of more than one and there will inevitably be comprise among them.

The privileged framework for realising democracy in modern times has been the territorially bounded sovereign nation-state. It is the nation that, since the nineteenth century, has defined the demos. This in turn allowed state sovereignty to be rooted in popular consent. The nation provided a shared identity, which fostered trust and allowed a democratic political culture and deliberation, a common communicative sphere and the acceptance by political movements of regular electoral defeats. The functional capacity of the nation-state gave sovereignty meaning by enabling the people to achieve substantive economic and social objectives. The territorial delimitation of the nation-state served to define the political community, both including some and excluding others. Borders also served to turn politics and interest articulation inwards, encouraging social compromises, economic management and welfare provision, which in turn strengthened the nation and underpinned state legitimacy (Bartolini 2005). Following the Second World War, active policies of spatial management sought to integrate national economies, while welfare states were essentially national. Electoral politics also took on a national form (Lipset and Rokkan 1967; Caramani 2004). Although spatial differences never disappeared, politics, and hence democracy, appeared to be essentially national.

This is a powerful theory but rests on a stylised or ideal-typical model of the nation-state, disguising a series of dilemmas. It remains heavily influenced by classical modernist historiography, sociology and political science, with its teleology of modernisation as a process of functional differentiation and territorial integration (Durkheim 1964), leading to the unitary and bounded polity. In practice, territorial closure was never complete and historic cleavages remained, within and across states (Rokkan 1999). Nor was territorial politics merely a legacy of state-formation and incomplete modernisation. It is reproduced in industrial and post-industrial society (Keating 1988, 1998). In the nineteenth century, as nation-states emerged and consolidated, rival nation-building projects emerged across large parts of Europe, both in the central empires and in large states like the United Kingdom and Spain. Successive waves of state transformation have subsequently provoked territorialised responses, questioning the foundations of the demos and boundaries.

Spatial Rescaling

Spatial rescaling refers to the migration of functional systems, identities and politics to new territorial levels (Keating 2013). Economic restructuring has escaped the national frame. It is a global phenomenon but also an intensely local one as testified by the literature on globalisation and on local and regional economies. Now states are resigned to the need to manage within transnational and global parameters, while uploading the task of market-making and (for some) monetary policy, to the European level. Policies of spatial economic integration have given way to an ethos of territorial competition as cities and regions find their place within the global and European division of labour. Welfare states remain largely national but new challenges to social cohesion have often arisen at the local level, creating the need for more differentiated approaches (Ferrera 2005). The creation of the European single market has posed challenges to social cohesion, which have politicised the issue and spurred demands for democratisation of the European economic regime to secure a stronger social dimension. It has also raised questions of territorial cohesion (a term now incorporated in the treaties) as market integration has an uneven impact on state and sub-state spaces.

Governments respond to rescaling by seeking ways to master and regulate functional systems that have escaped their functional and territorial reach. One strategy for mastering rescaling on the part of states has been to construct new systems for policymaking in both Europe and sub-state regions in a technocratic and depoliticised mode, shifting functions spatially upwards and downwards and away from representative towards non-elected bodies. Such is the design of European monetary policy, as well as various regulatory bodies. Regional development policies of European states from the 1960s were based on technocratic principles in which regions and localities were the objects rather than subjects for policy. Such depoliticisation (itself a political strategy) has been justified on the grounds that economic management and development should serve the market, with compensation for losers addressed elsewhere, usually by national welfare states. European spatial development policies and funds have always been framed by an economic logic, as a means of promoting the single market and overcoming market imperfections, although in practice, they have served as a form of social compensation and also serve a political purpose in sustaining support for the European project in struggling regions (Piattoni and Polverari 2016).

There is an element of functional determinism in many academic accounts of these processes, as though inexorable forces were dictating the scale of public action. Ohmae (1995) presents a purely functionalist approach while Hooghe and Marks (2009) see it as one side of a process, the other element of which is determined by identities. At best, however, functional explanations for rescaling provide reasons, but reasons are not causes. Reasons, moreover, are normatively charged and only make sense in relation to particular policy objectives so that a neoliberal may have different ideas about ideal structures from a social democrat. Rescaling, like the much-contested concept of globalisation, should therefore be seen as a site of contestation and political argument rather than an ineluctable force. This has often been obscured by the resort to the concept of 'governance', a notoriously imprecise term but which serves to present policymaking as a mode of agreement among multiple 'actors' on optimum policy solutions, downplaying the other side of politics, which focuses on differing interests, the uneven distribution of power and competition over objectives.

The simultaneous reconfiguration of territorial and functional systems, and political authority, has been widely described as multilevel governance (Hooghe and Marks 2001; Bache and Flinders 2004; Piattoni 2010). The concept is notoriously difficult to operationalise. One weakness is the ontological foundation. Any organisation or system can be broken down into sub-units; in this sense it may be no more than a warning against reification. A whole generation of work did this with the supposedly monolithic French unitary state, now seen as a constellation of actors (Dupuy and Thoenig 1985). The danger is that the analysis, drawing largely on organisational theory, is then reduced to the study of socially unembedded actors and their interactions. It is unable to address normative issues about the constitution of democratic spaces or the mobilisation of political power against structural inequality. In fact, one school of thought, identifying it in some way with participation, seems to present it as democracy-enhancing (Piattoni 2010). Another identifies it with corporate governance and negotiated order, excluding popular participation and deliberation (Smismans 2008). This is similar to Fossum's (2020) concept of segments, which may have an inbuilt cognitive bias to particular definitions of problems and solutions and to the argument about policy communities, which have also been analysed at multiple scales, including the emerging meso or regional scale (Keating 2013). The European Commission, for its part, has seized on 'governance' and 'multilevel governance' as normative, legitimating concepts in spite (indeed, because) of these ambiguities. It thus provides a justification for depoliticisation.

The danger is that, as functional systems, political mobilisation and institutions rescale at different levels and paces, the outcome is a dislocation of functional systems, territory and political institutions and a potential fragmentation of political space. Spaces of political representation and democratic deliberation may not correspond to functional spaces in which power is mobilised and decisions are taken. Spaces of economic regulation may not correspond to those of social solidarity and welfare so that national social compromises may be undermined as states are forced to deal with the social consequences of decisions taken elsewhere (Bartolini 2005). What is at stake in this new politics is not merely the policies to be pursued within the polity but the shape of the polity itself. Drawing the boundaries around policy-making systems will necessarily include some people and exclude others and will influence the resources available. This is as true of the boundaries of the European Union as for those of regions and cities. The drift of functions to new spatial levels can reinforce a functional 'segmentation' in which policies are drawn into closed systems, with a limited range of actors and shared assumptions (Batora and Fossum 2020; Fossum 2020).

To understand the emergence of new territorial spaces, above or below the state, it is not enough to examine formal institutions. We must, rather, examine how they are imagined and conceptually structured and given meaning (Keating 2017). One conception is as a sphere of economic competition and markets. The danger here is of a reification of regions as economic units themselves, in competition with others in global markets (Bristow 2005, 2010). Similarly, one conception of the EU is as a sphere of market competition but also a competitive unit in global markets. By definition, competition produces winners and losers and so exacerbates inequalities both between regions in Europe and within them as they prioritise economic development in the narrow sense. This in turn gives rise to demand for market correction and social cohesion. A rival conception is of the region, or Europe, as a space of social solidarity, a corrective to global economic forces. Territories are also spaces of identity, which means that they form the basis for individual attachment and meaning as well as defining the community that underpins collective endeavour in political, social, cultural and economic domains (Keating et al. 2003). The framework for the construction and reconstruction of these political communities is frequently Europe rather than the nation-state.

The new spaces, far from being sites of unanimity, are then contested in multiple ways: as to their boundaries; their purpose (economic, social, environmental); the balance of power within them; and their institutionalisation. Unlike the old (ideal-type) nation-state, these are weakly bounded territories, which do not have the ability to 'cage' social relations (Mann 1993) and so incentivise political compromise. Social and economic interests have multiple opportunities for 'partial exit'. Yet politics will out and the losers of policy decisions will mobilise. Rescaling thus potentially delinks the definition of the demos from the scales where collective action is required and from territory. It poses multiple challenges for democracy as traditionally conceived. Where democracy is seen as the satisfaction of individual preferences, it raises the question of the level at which those preferences should be aggregated. In so far as democracy entails deliberation and compromise, then the boundaries of the relevant community need to be set. If democracy requires that democratic choices be realised in effective public action, then those spaces need to be linked to policy capacity. There is a common dilemma – the need for an institutional framework for democracy covering all its dimensions in a world where spheres of public action, political identities and political representation are shifting and unstable. This raises both analytical questions about the nature, causes and consequences of rescaling, and normative questions about the effects on democracy as well as social cohesion. Analytical arguments frequently shade into normative arguments, whose assumptions are not always made explicit.

Depoliticisation is inevitably challenged as social groups losing out from rescaling have sought to repoliticise the process and to obtain representative and accountable institutions to manage it. Technocratic, top-down regional and urban development policies were challenged because they often disrupted existing production systems, displaced populations and distributed benefits unevenly (Keating 1988). They may also have undermined community values and cultures. The technocratic vision of Europe has similarly been challenged both by those advocating a stronger social dimension and those pushing for a market liberal vision. If political parties remain largely (but not entirely) state-based, social movements have mobilised at both European and local levels – often in response to economic change and the consequent social repercussions. Environmentalism, with its slogan of 'think global, act local', is the most obvious example, but there are others (Della Porta 2013). Territory itself has become an object of political competition as leaders seek to defend their local spaces from adverse changes or seek a new place in the global division of labour.

Rescaling is not a single, uniform process undermining one spatial hierarchy and replacing it with another. Rather the elements are mixed in differing proportions in different places, producing a variety of forms of territorial politics. In some cases, like the Nordic countries, the national framework remains the key. In others, there are strong movements for territorial autonomy and in a few, limiting cases, demands for secession. This all brings into question the national state as the privileged level at which to arrive at democratic decisions and give them effect. It is not only the substance of policy decisions that are at stake but the level at which they should be made. Rescaling is thus a complex process, which does not produce a new ontology of groups or a clearly defined spatial hierarchy to replace the old one. This poses twin challenges to democratic theory and practice: how to democratise the new spaces in the three dimensions; and how to determine democratically what the boundaries of the new spaces should be.

Institutional Responses: From Governance to Government

We are faced, then with a combination of spatial rescaling and functional transformation, and of top-down impulses to rationalise and bottom-up pressures for politicisation and democratisation The historical response to all this has been the establishment of multifunctional levels of territorial administration and government, as in nineteenth-century Europe. If governance is seen (as in some of its meanings) as a system of self-regulating, non-hierarchical modes of cooperation, then what we are seeing is a move from governance to government. So the European Union has expanded its functional reach and has acquired and strengthened democratic and representative elements like the European Parliament. This has stopped short of creating a European state, but that was never the intention. At the substate level, notable moves have been the establishment of new territorial levels of government and their subsequent legitimation by direct election (Hooghe et al. 2016). These include provincial-scale regions, metropolitan regions, reformed local government and the recognition of cultural and historical demands in territories with a strong sense of identity, sometimes articulated in the form of nationalism. Germany and Austria have established federal systems, while over time Belgium has been converted into a federation based both on territorial regions and language-based communities. Spain and Italy have set up regions with legislative powers, more than local government but less than full federalism. Regions in France occupy an intermediate level between central and local government and are mainly concerned with spatial planning and investment. In the United Kingdom, Scotland, Wales and Northern Ireland have legislative assemblies with extensive powers. England, by contrast, has experimented with a whole gamut of territorial arrangements at the meso level. Regional planning machinery and non-elected councils have been established and abolished twice, metropolitan regions have been set up and abolished and then reinvented. Unlike in other countries, none of these matured into a stable form of regional government and the only proposal for that was rejected in a referendum in the north-east of England in 2004. Elsewhere, county governments have been consolidated and expanded or weaker regional institutions have been put in place, as in Poland.

The management of the new spaces may take a variety of forms, including corporatist intermediation, participative government or electoral competition. Yet, however institutionalised, these new spaces, above, below and across states, are never bounded as tightly as the old nation-state. Participants, especially the holders of mobile capital, will be able to engage in partial exit (Bartolini 2005) and venue-shopping for the place where they have most advantage. Nor are the spaces 'given' as were the old nation-states. On the contrary, where the boundaries are drawn will, to a degree, determine who is included and excluded and the internal balance of power. This has long been a central feature of urban politics, where the drawing of boundaries has been highly contentious.

From the 1980s onwards, there was a succession of efforts to fix and codify the emerging sub-state spaces at a European scale. The European Commission produced standard regions (*Nomenclature des unités territoriales statistiques* (NUTS)) for statistical purposes, although they were all contained within national boundaries. It developed an anti-disparity policy, using structural funds and produced new spatial planning frameworks. The Maastricht Treaty created the Committee of the Regions, with consultative powers equivalent to the Social and Economic Committee. The concept of Europe of the Regions, vaguely defined as it was, pointed to new forms of three-level politics or even regions somehow bypassing the member states. The experience of this concept illustrates the difficulty of fixing a new spatial scale, given the heterogeneity of sub-state spaces. There are regions with a strong sense of identity, or 'stateless nations' such as Scotland or Catalonia (Keating 2001). There are strongly institutionalised regions embedded in national systems of government, like the German Länder. There are decentralised regions in Italy and Spain and functionally limited regions in France. These coexist with big cities and smaller localities. There were tensions within the European of the regions movement as some larger entities created a movement of Regions with Legislative Powers. Others insisted on their differentiated status as historical or self-determining entities. The European framework has continued to provide a vital reference point for sub-state governments and movements but there is no single territorial hierarchy emerging; instead there is a variety of experiences as regions are constructed in different ways and given differing meanings.

Rescaling and Democracy

There have been various efforts to reconnect new spatial scales of action beyond the nation-state with democracy. One mode of analysis is predicated on an ontological and methodological individualism and the conception of democracy based upon the satisfaction of individual preferences. Tiebout (1956) presented a parsimonious theory suggesting that preferences could be realised by sorting people into smaller jurisdictions, either by moving the people or moving the boundaries so as to arrive at communities in which citizens share the same preferences. This was later elaborated by public choice theorists, who relax the assumption that there will be bounded communities at all. Some advocate multiple, single-purpose agencies with varied territorial reaches, so as to allow like-minded individuals to pursue their own goals (Frey 2003). This might satisfy one element of democracy, meeting individual preferences, but it does not take into account the broader meaning, as deliberation in a shared space. The question of power is dealt with by assuming that competing agencies will prevent dominance or hegemony, but this is dependent on assumptions about perfect markets, not on capitalist markets as they actually exist. Nor does public choice handle the issue of social solidarity and redistribution well, reducing them to individual preferences rather than the contestation over values and interests within shared political space. It depends on a stylised view of the world that largely ignores structural inequalities.

Various strategies have been used to move away from the individualist ontology and bring in collective entities and communities. Some functional determinists derive new units directly from economic change. Ohmae (1995) sees nation-states as giving way to 'regional states' seeking their own place in the global division of labour. The argument is then made for a neoliberal policy strategy, albeit combined with a form of neo-mercantilism in the pursuit of a united regional interest. Some political theorists, on the other hand, see the main issue as being the maintenance of community cultures in the face of assimilationist pressures. Kymlicka (1995, 2007) questions purely state-based approaches, points to the existence of unassimilated groups and, drawing on ideas about recognition and self-determination being part of democracy, argues for giving them political autonomy. Indeed, he argues that so strong are these ideas that, in Europe at least, all such groups have gained territorial autonomy (Kymlicka 2007). 'Post-functional' approaches (Hooghe and Marks 2016) accept a degree of functional determinism but argue that it comes up against strongly held community identities. These, however, often gloss over the complexity of identity itself and the way it is negotiated collectively and individually and invested with different meanings.

Another approach is to delink democracy from territory. Some forms of public choice theory effectively do this by providing for non-territorial forms of provision. The old Austro-Marxist idea of National Cultural Autonomy has been revived as a way of dealing with diversity within territories (Nimni 2005). That combined territorial federalism with the ability of groups to provide services on a non-territorial basis. Some elements of this can be found in Belgium, where the territorial governments and language communities do not entirely correspond, notably in Brussels. Government, however, is intrinsically territorial. Much of it concerns the management of space or the provision of services across territory. Territorial boundaries define the application of jurisdiction and partly define who is included and excluded. Citizenship based on territory can minimise (if not eliminate) the use of invidious distinctions based on ascriptive criteria to accord citizenship.

Alesina and Spolaore (2003) combine economic determinism with cultural reductionism. They argue that the size of 'nations'[1] is determined

---

[1] They concede that this really means states but stick with 'nation' nonetheless.

by the external economic environment. In protectionist eras, large states are needed to secure extensive internal markets. In times of free trade, such large states are not necessary and therefore do not come into being or survive.[2] This allows for the emergence of ethnically 'homogeneous' states in which citizens are likely to share policy preferences, thus fostering democratic responsiveness. This extends the Tiebout argument by adding the assumption that co-ethnics will share the same views about substantive policy issues.

None of these approaches resolves the dilemma of democratisation and rescaling. They all tend to assume that, if we take issues to the right level, political consensus will prevail and democracy will thereby be realised. Economic determinism assumes that people should be subject to market forces, rather than being able to organise collectively to tame and confront them. Approaches based on recognition of cultures and identities have not, for the most part, recognised that these are socially constructed and reproduced in multiple ways; this includes state-based identities. They do not form a stable substratum of meaning but are themselves rescaling all the time so forming a weak ontological foundation for claims and rights. Ethnicity and homogeneity are contested concepts, both analytically and normatively. Some very small places (like Northern Ireland) are divided societies. In any case, ethnic homogeneity (whatever it means) does not entail agreement on substantive policy issues. Democracy cannot be reduced to unanimity. On the contrary, it entails deliberation on rival conceptions of the public good, along with a large dose of social compromise. Ethnic sorting, celebrated by Alesina and Spolaore, can work against social cohesion as well as being generally ethically unacceptable. Both Ohmae and Alesina and Spolaore define away the third element, the need to mobilise political power against structural inequalities. Marko (2020) is on stronger ground in recognising all this and arguing that recognition and democratisation may mean moving away from old concepts and ontological categories as they change and develop.

The problem remains, that shifting ontologies and scales of action make it difficult to formulate a prescription for democracy that works across European space. There are places, such as Scotland, Catalonia or the Basque Country, where historic identities have been refashioned to underpin modern systems of action and institutionalisation, although questions of self-determination are still unresolved. In other cases, regions are constructed

---

[2] It is not true, historically, that small states have emerged at times of free trade; the interwar years after the fragmentation of the central empires were marked by protectionism.

around themes of development or social inclusion as well as democratic deliberation (Keating 2013). Elsewhere, cities have emerged as spaces of democratic engagement. In other parts of Europe, territorial institutions are weaker, as is the capacity for democratic engagement and collective action.

Some political theorists have sought to resolve the dilemmas of democratising the European order by questioning the requirement for a single demos while preserving the advantages of functional action on different levels. One such proposal is demoicracy (Cheneval and Nicolaïdes 2017). This is defined succinctly by Nicolaïdes (2014) as a 'third way' between statist and Europe-wide conceptions of democracy: 'Demoicracy identifies the EU as a union with two normative subjects: states and citizens. Pursuing the common good of Europe, therefore, means protecting and promoting the values and interests of both states as self-governing collectives and citizens as autonomous individuals.' Cheneval and Schimmelfennig (2013) similarly recommend a European order that combines representation of citizens and of member states. This builds on a tradition of federalism as well as older conceptions of representation of territories and groups within states and on intergovernmental theories of European integration. Demoicracy scholars, however, take the argument a step further. They focus on 'peoples' not states or other governmental units. They also recognise that these are socially constructed. This does not mean that they are artificial or ephemeral; they are, rather a 'social fact' (Cheneval and Nicolaïdes 2012). They thus avoid both the individualism underlying Alesina and Spoloare and the collectivism of Kymlicka and anchor their theories in normative principles.

Bellamy (2019) extends the proposal in a slightly different direction, taking the various strands of democracy into an argument for a 'republican association of sovereign states'. While not straying into functional determinism, he notes that there are tasks that states can better achieve by cooperation. These include not merely economic management and social policy but also democratic consolidation. The burden of citizenship and democracy, however, will be borne by the nation-state. This is not a thin conception of democracy and citizenship such as that presented by public choice scholars or economic determinists but a deep sense of commitment based on civic values. It also includes the element of social solidarity, based on shared identity and destiny.

These approaches offer a deeper and richer understanding of democracy than some of the others, yet they still rely on the traditional ontology of the nation-state as one of the building blocks at a time when democratic forms of expression cannot all be fitted into that procrustean form. It is true that Eurobarometer surveys show that citizens in aggregate identify more with their national state than with Europe but that in itself is not proof that this is the appropriate level for democratic deliberation and will formation. There are plurinational states in which not only do multiple national identities coexist, but the very meaning of identity is contested – the United Kingdom, Spain and Belgium for example. Deeper surveys, probing multiple levels of attachment, show a variety of configurations of attachment to the state, the sub-state or region and Europe. Surveys have shown that support for Brexit does not correlate with British identity but with a sub-state identity (with England), while Scottish identity is being reconstructed around, among other, things, pro-European themes (Keating 2021). More broadly, democratic challenges arise at multiple levels below the state. Cheneval and Schimmelfennig (2013) recognise the problem of how to fit national minorities into this but do not develop the point. Bellamy (2019) locates the demoi in 'states and their regions' but the argument is elaborated exclusively in relation to states.

The argument also rests upon the idea of two-level games, in which the national will can be determined at state level, then taken into the intergovernmental arena for bargaining. National governments, in turn, can be held responsible for the outcomes. In practice, policymaking does not end with the Council of the EU but continues through implementation, feedback and adjustment, which operate at multiple levels.

More fundamentally, the nation-state is a historically contingent political form, which poses the same ontological and normative questions that attend the analysis of emerging political entities and spaces themselves. The nation-state is not axiomatically legitimate and morally unimpugnable; as Renan (1882) reminded us, some brutal things were done to create it. Nation-states may have served as the instruments of social welfare but they have equally been available for its weakening. Challenges to the state may represent democratising impulses linked to new conceptions of authority, based on the division rather than the unification of sovereign power.

Multilevel Democracy

Another approach (Keating 2001) emphasises is that not only are nations (or peoples or demoi) multiple, but the very definition of those categories is contested. The idea that each nation can have its own territorial state is illusory, not merely because there are too many nations and too few possible states, but because the meaning of those terms is multiple and changing. Rescaling has changed the relationships among self-conscious peoples, territory and functional capacity in ways that defy straightforward categorisation. The plurinational perspective recognises that some of these have been so constructed as to qualify as demoi in their own right even if they have not established their own sovereign states. Jennings (1956) long ago argued that the principle of self-determination made no sense because, before the people could self-determine, someone had to determine who are the people. Rescaling, by undermining the old ontological certainties, might seem to have made this problem worse, but it is not intractable. Peoplehood is obviously not an objective category, to be resolved by science, but nor is it purely subjective because, for me to belong a community, others must also do so. It is, rather, a relational or inter-subjective category. So Catalonia is a meaningful entity in the way that Padania, the creation of the old Lega Nord, was not. That is not because one is natural and the other artificial, but because of how they have been constructed and gained social acceptance. Such demoi are never homogeneous or clearly bounded, but this is not to say that they do not exist or should not be taken seriously. Nor is it to say that any claim to be a demos or for the drawing of new boundaries is democratically legitimate. Forms of community building and boundary-drawing based on racism, xenophobia and exclusion are not compatible with the democratic mission; this would include manifestations such as the Vlaams Belang or the Lega Nord.

This does not mean that emerging demoi at the sub-state or suprastate level should simply displace the nation-state framework. It is to recognise, rather, the need to democratise all the relevant political spaces. Some of these may be constructed using the vocabulary of nationhood, but that in itself does not give them an axiomatically superior status (Marko 2020). Democratic practice is equally important at the regional level, if that is where power is exercised and functions undertaken, and in the local and neighbourhood arenas. Democratic control, moreover, cannot be confined to just one level, whether that be the state, the sub-state or suprastate level or it risks being divorced from power and effectiveness.

The various arenas, moreover, need to be connected, or else power holders can merely delegate responsibility to new levels while constraining the real choices that can be made. This is why the European level is important for the quality of sub-state democracy, if not in the old 'Europe of the Regions' format. Supranational regulation is not just an imposition on lower levels but a vital mechanism to protect democratic spaces from market pressures and venue-shopping by powerful interests. There is a well-rehearsed danger of a 'race to the bottom' in tax levels and regulation as cities and regions compete to attract mobile investment. This is a common feature of US states and cities, with their open boundaries, which make it easier for holders of capital to move, while the power of labour is constrained. The consequence is the widespread practice of giving incentive packages to investors, diverting tax revenues away from social expenditures. It is less of an issue in Europe, where such practices are constrained by EU competition policies. Labour movements, while weakened everywhere in Europe, were learning to act within regional policy communities to compensate partially for their loss of influence in state-level corporatist arrangements. Our study of the rescaling of interest articulation found that environmental groups were adept at operating at multiple levels (Keating and Wilson 2014). It is these forms of mobilisation that may prevent the new territorial spaces becoming the site of segmented policy systems with an inbuilt bias to particular interests.

Modern understandings of territory similarly complicate the ontological question while at the same time providing new ways of transcending it. Traditional conceptions of territory are topological, referring to lines on the map enclosing spaces and demarcating them from each other. Modern conceptions are more sociological, referring to the relation of social processes to space, so yielding new combinations (Keating 2013). So the global cityregions perspective focuses on the way that global restructuring and investment patterns impact on localities (Scott 1998; Sassen 2000). Borders are seen not as sharp divisions between distinct social and political systems but as locations in their own right, generating new political challenges. This is by no means new. Braudel (1986) takes the case of Gascony, which is certainly a place but has been imagined in multiple different ways over time. The same is true of the Basque Country (Euskadi, Euskal Herria, Vasconia . . .). This is not to say that territory is meaningless or lacking any ontological value. On the contrary, territory has become a key element in political competition, by setting the bounds of political community, which are no longer exhausted by the nation-state. It has also become a theme in political mobilisation as politicians and political parties pose as defenders of their territory against competitors in other places in 'competitive regionalism'.

The concept of sovereignty has, in the modern age, been tied closely to democracy, as the means by which the (national) demos can control its fate. In its traditional format, it is unitary and indivisible. In a multilevel Europe, however, it can never be absolute and must always be shared. Sovereignty has to do with the foundation of legitimate authority but this becomes an empty principle if it is divorced from the capacity to act. Indeed, states can enhance their capacity by sharing authority, as in the European Union; whether this amounts to shared sovereignty is perhaps a question of semantics. Brexit has shown how the recovery of formal sovereignty may entail a loss of capacity to operate in an interdependent world. Claims to sovereignty by sub-state actors, for their part, are increasingly placed within a European context. Sovereignty, in these new understandings, is less a thing, belonging to a single entity, but rather a set of relationships (Loughlin 2003). The 'post-sovereignty' perspective (MacCormick 1999; Keating 2001) does not assert that sovereignty has disappeared but rather that is not unitary and can be shared and divided, and derived from multiple sources. This is a new term, although it is also familiar from historical experiences before the rise of the nation-state.

The argument for allowing bottom-up constructions of political communities and for the reshaping of the sovereign order might appear to be an endorsement of the idea of secession. In fact, it rather works in the opposite direction, as secession entails the replacement of one sovereign polity with another, recreating the old problems at a new scale. Indeed, it is to misconstrue what has actually been happening across European political space. In spite of the alarmism expressed in some quarters, there is only one serious secessionist challenge in the EU presently, in Catalonia, and only two more in Western Europe, Scotland and Northern Ireland There may be secessionist potential in Flanders and Corsica, but public support is just not there. In Walker's (2019) account, most sub-state nationalisms have moved from 'teleological nationalism' founded on the sovereign state, to a 'reflexive nationalism', adapted to changing opportunities, especially the realities of divided sovereignty in Europe. At the limit, if there is a serious democratic will to establish a new state by breaking with an existing one, then there is no reason to disqualify it on the grounds that the new state should meet criteria not applied to existing states, but cases such as that are rare in established democracies.

UK withdrawal from the European Union (Brexit) represents a very different instance of secession and sovereignty, a claim in the name of democracy to 'take back control'. This was an extreme instance of reclaiming national sovereignty. Initially focused on restoring the sovereignty of Parliament, this transmuted into a claim for popular sovereignty embodied in the referendum of 2016 which, it was claimed, provided a binding mandate for leaving the EU. It subsequently morphed into a restoration of executive supremacy, with efforts to bypass Parliament and new powers for ministers to act by statutory instrument. At the same time, there are efforts to scale back judicial review of executive decisions on the ground that it is only government that possesses the democratic mandate. Brexit, however, has been accompanied by no measures to reinforce internal democratic procedures within the United Kingdom. It has, rather, entailed a recentralisation of the polity as a 'unitary state' as Brexit has been predicated on a unitary people or demos (Keating 2021). In fact, two of the constituent parts of the UK voted to remain. Nationalists in Scotland and Northern Ireland have taken this as a mandate to remain in the EU, which necessarily entails leaving the British union.

Democracy, to return to our initial argument, is about creating spaces for deliberation, common purpose and compromise, and linking these to effective capacity for action in the face of other forms of power. Rescaling has dispersed power and constrained states' capacity, creating new spaces and arenas for contestation. The consequent fragmentation of political space has posed a serious challenge to the traditional nation-state-based model of democracy. On the other hand, it opens up the possibility of new spaces of democracy, confronting new forms of power with new forms of representation and political mobilisation. Yet efforts to democratise the European Union remain in thrall to the model of the nation-state. They tend to argue that the EU must become more state-like, albeit on federal lines; or that the democratic heavy lifting must be done by the member states. The focus is on the EU as an institution rather than the broader process of rescaling of power, function and authority. At the sub-state level, there is a variety of experiences but efforts to link those with EU institutions have disappointed early enthusiasts for a Europe of the Regions.

There is no simple fix to the democratic dilemmas arising from rescaling (some of which are actually long-standing). Democratising the European polity involves much more than restoring the classic model of polity in which demos, sovereignty, representation and functional capacity coexist within the same territorial boundaries, whether of the European Union, its member states or new secessionist polities. Instead, a multiplicity of democratic spaces has emerged, linked, more or less loosely, to functional capacity. There is no new spatial fix to replace the old ontological certainties of the nation-state. Rather, we are in an era in which not only substantive issues of public policy are contested but so is the spatial and institutional framework in which they are contested and resolved. Fundamental issues like economic growth, social solidarity or environmental sustainability can rarely be addressed at one level alone and decisions taken at one level have repercussions on others. This is not a question with a clear answer but a democratic dilemma, previously obscured by the hegemonic power of the nation-state in defining political order and democratic norms. There is not a simple institutional fix but rather a series of dilemmas and compromises as issues of rescaling and boundaries become part of political contestation and not merely a neutral framework within which democratic politics takes place.

References

Alesina, Alberto and Spolaore, Enrico (2003) *The Size of Nations*. Cambridge, MA: MIT Press.

Bache, Ian and Flinders, Matthew (eds) (2004) *Multi-Level Governance*. Oxford: Oxford University Press.

Bartolini, Stefano (2005) *Restructuring Europe. Centre Formation, System Building, and Political Structuring between the Nation State and the European Union*. Oxford: Oxford University Press.

Batora, Josef and Fossum, John Erik (2020) Introduction. In Batora, Josef and Fossum, John Erik (eds) *Towards a Segmented European Political Order. The European Union's Post-Crises Conundrum*. London: Routledge.

Bellamy, Richard (2019) *A Republican Europe of Sovereign States. Cosmopolitan Statism, Republican Intergovernmentalism and Demoicratic Reconnection of the EU*. Cambridge: Cambridge University Press.

Braudel, Fernand (1986) *L'identité de la France. Espace et Histoire*. Paris: Arthaud-Flammarion.

Bristow, Gillian (2005) Everyone's a 'Winner': Problematising the Discourse of Regional Competitiveness. *Journal of Economic Geography*, 5(3): 285–304.

Bristow, Gillian (2010) *Critical Reflections on Regional Competitiveness*. London: Routledge.

Caramani, Daniele (2004) *The Nationalization of Politics. The Formation of National Electorates and Party Systems in Western Europe*. Cambridge: Cambridge University Press.

Cheneval, Francis and Schimmelfennig, Frank (2013) The Case for Demoicracy in the European Union. *Journal of Common Market Studies*, 51(2): 334–50.

Cheneval, Francis and Nicolaïdes, Kalypso (2017) The Social Construction of Demoicracy in the European Union. *European Journal of Political Theory*, 16(2): 1–26

Della Porta, Donatella (2013) *Can Democracy Be Saved? Participation, Deliberation and Social Movements*. Cambridge: Polity.

Dupuy, François and Thoenig, Jean-Claude (1985) *L'Administration en Miettes*. Paris: Fayard.

Durkheim, Emile (1964) *The Division of Labour in Society*. New York: Free Press.

Ferrera, Maurizio (2005) *The New Boundaries of Welfare*. Oxford: Oxford University Press.

Fossum, John Erik (2020) The Institutional Make-Up of Europe's Segmented Political Order. In Batora, Josef and Fossum, John Erik (eds) *Towards a Segmented European Political Order. The European Union's Post-Crises Conundrum*. London: Routledge.

Frey, Bruno (2003) Functional, Overlapping, Competing Jurisdictions: Redrawing the Geographic Boundaries of Administration. *European Journal of Law Reform*, V(3–4): 543–55.

Hooghe, Liesbet and Marks, Gary (2001) *Multilevel Governance and European Integration*. Lanham: Rowman & Littlefield.

Hooghe, Liesbet and Marks, Gary (2009) Does Efficiency Shape the Territorial Structure of Government? *Annual Review of Political Science*, 12: 225–41.

Hooghe, Liesbet and Marks, Gary (2016) *Community, Scale, and Regional Governance. A Postfunctionalist Theory of Governance, Volume II*. Oxford: Oxford University Press.

Hooghe, Liesbet, Marks, Gary, Schakel, Arjan H., Chapman Osterkatz, Sandra,

Niedzwiecki, Sara and Shair-Rosenfield, Sarah (2016) *Measuring Regional Authority. A Postfunctionalist Theory of Governance, Volume I.* Oxford: Oxford University Press.

Jennings, Ivor (1956) *The Approach to Self-Government.* Cambridge: Cambridge University

Keating, Michael (1988) *State and Regional Nationalism. Territorial Politics and the European State.* Brighton: Wheatsheaf.

Keating, Michael (1998) *The New Regionalism in Western Europe. Territorial Restructuring and Political Change.* Cheltenham: Edward Elgar.

Keating, Michael (2001) *Plurinational Democracy. Stateless Nations in a Post-Sovereignty Era.* Oxford: Oxford University Press.

Keating, Michael (2013) *Rescaling the European State. The Making of Territory and the Rise of the Meso.* Oxford: Oxford University Press.

Keating, Michael (2017) Contesting European Regions. *Regional Studies*, 51(1): 9–18.

Keating, Michael (2021) *State and Nation in the United Kingdom: The Fragmented Union.* Oxford: Oxford University Press.

Keating, Michael and Wilson, Alex (2014) Regions with Regionalism? The Rescaling of Interest Groups in Six European States. *European Journal of Political Research*, 53(4): 840–57.

Keating, Michael, Loughlin, John and Deschouwer, Kris (2003) *Culture, Institutions and Economic Development. A Study of Eight European Regions.* Cheltenham: Edward Elgar.

Kymlicka, Will (1995) *Multicultural Citizenship.* Oxford: Oxford University Press.

Kymlicka, Will (2007) *Multicultural Odysseys. Navigating the New International Politics of Diversity.* Oxford: Oxford University Press.

Lipset, Seymour Martin and Rokkan, Stein (1967) Cleavage Structures, Party Systems and Voter Alignments. In Lipset, Seymour Martin and Rokkan, Stein, *Party Systems and Voter Alignments*, New York: Free Press.

Loughlin, Martin (2003) Ten Tenets of Sovereignty. In Neil Walker (ed.) *Sovereignty in Transition.* Oxford: Hart.

MacCormick, Neil (1999) *Questioning Sovereignty. Law, State and Nation in the European Commonwealth.* Oxford: Oxford University Press.

McRoberts, Kenneth (2019) *Misconceiving Canada. The Struggle for National Unity.* Toronto: Oxford University Press.

Mann, Michael (1993) *The Sources of Social Power, volume II. The Rise of Classes and Nation-States, 1760-1914.* Cambridge: Cambridge University Press.

Marko, Joseph (2020) Law and Sociology. In Joseph Marko (ed.) *Human and Minority Rights Protection by Multiple Diversity Governance.* London: Routledge.

Nicolaïdes, Kalypso (2014) The Construction of European Democracy, <https://www.politics.ox.ac.uk/research-projects/the-construction-of-european-demoicracy.html> (last accessed 8 December 2022).

Nimni, Ephraim (2005) Introduction: The National Cultural Autonomy Model Revisited. In Nimni, Ephraim (ed.) *National Cultural Autonomy and its Contemporary Critics.* London: Routledge.

Ohmae, Kenichi (1995) *The End of the Nation State: The Rise of Regional Economies.* New York: The Free Press.

Piattoni, Simona (2010) *The Theory of Multi-Level Governance. Conceptual, Empirical, and Normative Challenges*. Oxford: Oxford University Press.
Piattoni, Simona and Polverari, Laura (2016) Introduction. In Piattoni, Simona and Polverari, Laura (eds) *Handbook on Cohesion Policy in the EU*. Cheltenham: Edward Elgar.
Renan, Ernest (1882) *Qu'est-ce qu'une nation ?* Conférence prononcée le 11 mars 1882 à la Sorbonne, <http://www.iheal.univ-paris3.fr/sites/www.iheal.univ-paris3.fr/files/Renan_-_Qu_est-ce_qu_une_Nation.pdf> (last accessed 25 November 2022).
Rokkan, Stein (1999) *State Formation, Nation-Building and Mass Politics in Europe. The Theory of Stein Rokkan*. Flora, Peter, Kuhnle, Stein and Urwin, Derek (eds). Oxford: Oxford University Press.
Sassen, Saskia (2000) *World Cities in a Global Economy*, 2nd edn. Thousand Oaks: Sage.
Scott, Allen (1998) *Regions and the World Economy. The Coming Shape of Global Production, Competition, and Political Order*. Oxford: Oxford University Press.
Smismans, Stijn (2008) New Modes of Governance and the Participatory Myth. *West European Politics*, 31(5): 874–95.
Tiebout, Charles (1956) A Pure Theory of Local Expenditures. *Journal of Political Economy*, 64: 416–24.
Walker, Neil (2019) Teleological and Reflexive Nationalism in the New Europe. In Jordana, Jacint, Keating, Michael, Marx, Alex and Wouters, Jan (eds) *Changing Borders in Europe. Exploring the Dynamics of Integration, Differentiation and Self-Determination in the European Union*. Abingdon: Routledge.

THREE

Dilemmas of Deliberative Democracy in the European Union: Why (Not) and How (Not)?[1]

Firat Cengiz

In this chapter, I discuss a relatively novel method of participatory democracy, namely deliberative democracy, and whether and how it could be implemented in the European Union (EU) to achieve a more inclusive and democratic process of policymaking. The reason for this is two-fold: first, deliberative democracy is an increasingly popular method for including citizens in the policymaking process. This popularity is reflected in the ever-increasing number of real-life examples of deliberative platforms as well as scientific deliberative experiments. The sheer popularity of deliberative democracy requires a mental and academic exercise on whether and how deliberative democracy could be implemented in the EU. Second, the representative democracy model on its own does not bode well to integrate citizens into policymaking, considering national representative democracies also suffer from chronic citizen disaffection (Doyle 2014; Armingeon and Guthmann 2014). As a result, replicating national representative institutions will not provide the fundamental shift in the EU–citizen relationship which is necessary to improve democracy in the EU.

As I discuss in this chapter, deliberative democracy is more likely to bring a shift in the EU–citizen relationship by providing citizens with a direct voice in decisions that fundamentally affect their lives and well-being. In the introductory chapter of this book, Bremberg and Norman discuss in detail the tensions and trade-offs between multiple democratic dilemmas the EU is facing and between different democratic models advocated to solve those dilemmas. This chapter contributes to this book's overall analysis of the

---

[1] I am grateful to the reviewers, editors and contributors of this book for their helpful comments on the previous versions of this chapter. All remaining errors are mine.

EU's democratic dilemmas by investigating the potential role of deliberative democracy in the EU's governance that is increasingly challenging the status of representative parliamentary democracy as the grand and dominant democratic theory.

In this chapter, I do not call for replacing the EU's established representative democratic institutions and structures with deliberative methods. In its original form, deliberative democracy was not proposed to replace but to strengthen representative democratic institutions (Dahl 1989: 340). Also, I do not perceive deliberative democracy as the ultimate panacea that is superior to representative democracy. On the contrary, I discuss the theoretical and practical dilemmas deliberative democracy faces both in general and in terms of its implementation in the EU. A key dilemma of deliberative democracy is that whilst being a potentially promising method of giving alienated citizens a voice in large, diverse and polarised societies, it is also more challenging to implement in societies with these qualities. As a result, deliberative democracy comes with several difficult questions particularly in the case of the EU, due to the size and diversity of the EU population and the complexities of EU decision-making processes, such as: can the diverse EU population realistically be included in deliberation based on the principle of equality in representation? What would be the implications of deliberation on the EU legislative regime in which three institutions representing member state, EU and citizen interests partake based on the principle of institutional balance (Art. 13(2) Treaty on European Union (TEU))? I discuss these questions in this chapter, although I do not offer exhaustive answers to them. The discussion of these questions ties in closely with Keating's extensive analysis of rescaling of democracy in this book. In his chapter, Keating argues that 'various arenas . . . need to be connected, or else power holders can merely delegate responsibility to new levels while constraining the real choices that can be made'. As I argue in this chapter, political institutions utilising deliberative platforms without offering citizens a real voice in political decisions is a real risk to deliberative democracy. As a result, very much in line with Keating's model of rescaling, it becomes inevitable to think about different levels of governance as overlapping and interdependent rather than separate and disconnected.

Deliberative democracy originates from Habermas's (2015a) work on communicative rationality. Since this original work, the extensive deliberative democracy scholarship has produced varieties of 'mini-public' models, such as citizens' assemblies, citizens' juries, and deliberative polls, that have been tested in different contexts. My position is neutral as to which one of these methods is superior and I do not suggest a specific model for the EU. Nevertheless, my position is grounded in the 'systemic approach' to deliberative democracy which I discuss later in this chapter. This comes with a criticism of the recent top-down pseudo-deliberation attempts in the EU, such as the 'citizens' dialogues' and 'citizens' consultations'.

The extensive deliberative democracy and democratic deficit scholarships have developed without a mutual communication and lesson drawing process. Therefore, the implementation of deliberative democracy in the EU is relatively uncharted territory. Previous research investigating deliberative democracy in the EU is extremely limited. Some of this research looks into the organisation of EU institutions that are not democratic in the popular sense, such as courts (Korkea-aho 2015) or the open method of coordination (de la Porte and Nanz 2004), whilst others advocate deliberative democracy without discussing how deliberative democracy could be implemented in the EU (see Smith 2013 as a rare exception). In this chapter, I face the challenge of making concrete suggestions for the implementation of deliberative democracy in the EU. However, these suggestions should be seen as building blocks for further extensive and transformative discussion rather than practised and proven methods ready to be implemented. As a result of this discussion, I put forward two key arguments in this chapter: first, despite the dilemmas emerging from the size and diversity of the EU population and the complexities of EU decision-making processes, it is possible to implement deliberative democracy in the EU. Second, deliberative democracy is likely to improve not only the democratic quality of EU decision-making processes but also the shared identity of EU citizenship.

The structure of this chapter is as follows: the next section discusses deliberative democracy and its potential to improve democracy in the EU. This is followed by a discussion of the limitations and drawbacks of deliberative democracy. The chapter then discusses attempts to implement deliberative democracy in the EU and their limitations. The penultimate section discusses how deliberative democracy could be implemented in the EU before the chapter closes with conclusions.

Deliberative Democracy: Giving Citizens a Voice?

Deliberative democracy originates from a communicative understanding of democracy in which citizens are considered capable of deciding on the political option that is in the best interest of society through open and free debate (Young 1996: 121). As one of the novel aspects, in deliberative democracy citizen preferences are considered endogenous to the political discussion process. In other words, unlike taking part in representative or direct democracy methods, such as voting in elections or referendums, citizens do not join the deliberative process with an already established opinion in the light of information and opinions made available to them outside of the deliberative process, most predominantly through national and international media and political campaigns. Citizens are expected to reconsider pre-established positions and reach a newly found common understanding as a result of hearing diverse and opposite 'reasoned arguments' as a part of the deliberative process (Chappell 2012: 52). This is what attributes the deliberative process and its political outcomes legitimacy (Curato et al. 2019). As it was shown, among others, by the Europolis experiment, citizens, indeed, are capable and likely to change pre-established opinions and formulate new ones by responding to public debate even on the most contentious and divisive subjects, such as environmental protection and immigration (Offe 2014; Fishkin 2014).

Notwithstanding the power of good argumentation and open discussion, why would deliberation be considered a legitimate method of decision-making in the eyes of citizens who do not personally partake in deliberation and result in a public willingness to comply with the result of deliberation? It is because citizens are more likely to trust decisions taken by their peers who, unlike professional politicians, are not expected to respond to the well-known trajectories and paternalism of professional politics, such as party agendas, disciplinary structures, re-election motives, regulatory capture, revolving doors or plain corruption (Fishkin 2014: 33; Crespy 2014: 83). As a result, fellow citizens would be considered more likely to make political choices, genuinely because they believe that that particular choice is in the best interest of society rather than responding to some other hidden political or economic motive.

Deliberation also has significant educative power, particularly for those citizens who partake in deliberation. This is because, unlike representative and direct democracy methods, in deliberation citizens do not cast a vote alongside millions of others with very little prospect of making a direct impact on the outcome (Fishkin 2014: 31). When citizens are given the opportunity and the responsibility to actively contribute to the political discourse, they have incentives to engage in a political education process on the subject concerned and form an informed and intelligent opinion.

Deliberation is also expected to strengthen mutual bonds and perceptions, particularly in societies that have been polarised by long-standing conflicts. Due to its positive contribution to the common identity-building process, deliberation has been used as a method of constitution-making and peacebuilding in societies divided by deeply entrenched conflicts, such as South Africa, Northern Ireland and more recently Iraq (Hart 2001; O'Flynn et al. 2019).

Deliberative democracy has become particularly popular since the 2008 economic and financial crisis. Deliberative democracy platforms have been created at national and local levels, particularly in polities that aim to re-establish their trust relationship with citizens, which include the Australian Citizens Parliament and the Belgian G1000 in addition to a plethora of scientific deliberative experiments (Fung 2003; Ryan and Smith 2014).[2] Most of these platforms follow the so-called 'mini-publics model', either in the form of deliberative polls or citizens' assemblies, which have proven to be the most popular among deliberative designs. These mini-publics originate from Robert Dahl's original idea of creating a 'mini-populous' that will bring together a sufficiently large number of citizens to ensure representation of different societal segments, yet small enough to ensure a high-quality, reasoned and open communication and discussion process in which all participants can contribute (Dahl 1989: 340).

Most recently, Ireland and Scotland have introduced almost identical citizens' assemblies composed of 100 citizens to debate and propose recommendations on a broad range of societal issues relevant to the future direction of these countries.[3] In other polities, mini-publics are permanently attached to political institutions. For instance, the Parliament of Ostbelgien in Belgium voted to establish a Citizens' Council to permanently complement the elected parliamentary chamber;[4] whereas in Vororlberg (Austria) and Gdansk (Poland) a certain number of citizens can petition the political institutions to convene a citizens' assembly (Chwalisz 2019).

Participation by citizens from different social locations, in terms of socio-economic class, race, gender, education level, minority status and so on is essential for the deliberative process and its outcomes to have sufficient legitimacy in the eyes of the entire society. Since citizens who do not partake in deliberation do not elect their citizen delegates to represent them in the deliberative process, they can only trust in the impartiality and robustness of deliberation if they believe that those deliberating on their behalf are ordinary citizens reflecting the qualities of the rest of the society and have not been chosen with a bias towards a particular group or view

---

[2] See also <http://www.participedia net> (last accessed 7 December 2022), a global database of novel, including deliberative, participatory designs.

[3] See <https://www.citizensassembly.ie/en/> (last accessed 7 December 2022) and <https://www.gov.scot/publications/research-report-citizens-assembly-scotland/> (last accessed 14 December 2022).

[4] See <https://www.foundationfuturegenerations.org/files/documents/news/20190226_dgpermanentcitizensassembly_pressrelease.pdf> (last accessed 7 December 2022).

(Chappell 2012: 69; Offe 2014: 440). To ensure this 'external inclusiveness', citizens are chosen using a method of random selection. Additionally, deliberative platforms should also aim to accomplish 'internal inclusiveness' by providing all citizens with an equal voice in the deliberative process and a high-quality deliberative discourse based on informed and respectful communication (Young 2000; Grönlund et al. 2014: 227). Nevertheless, despite novel methods and discourse quality measurements developed to ensure a genuinely democratic process, external and internal inclusivity are deliberative democracy platforms' most substantial limitations in terms of achieving the promises and potentials of deliberative democracy.

After a period of intense experimentation on a variety of subjects of socio-economic significance in different polities, now the deliberative democracy scholarship has taken a 'systemic turn'. In the systemic understanding, different parts of the political system, including representative institutions, the media, political parties, and all other outlets of political engagement and activism, are considered to form interdependent pieces of a single system rather than operating autonomously in separated realms (Mansbridge et al. 2012; Curato et al. 2019: 101). As a result, first, when it comes to the political practice of deliberative democracy, we cannot assume that a polity follows or accommodates deliberative democracy, simply because an ad hoc platform has been created to allow citizens to express their voices on an individual and isolated topic (Mansbridge et al. 2012: 5). But for deliberative democracy to be accommodated properly, all parts of the political sphere should be designed to follow the principles of high-quality deliberation. For instance, although they are traditionally considered representative rather than deliberative institutions, parliaments should also follow the principles of high-quality deliberation to reach legitimate and effective decisions reflecting the common good, which emerges from rational and mutually respectful discourse. Second, when it comes to the political science of deliberative democracy, it is not sufficient to engage in an isolated investigation, but to be able to fully understand whether and how deliberative democracy is practised in a polity, one needs to have a look at the full picture of how the political system functions including all of its parts and the interrelationships between those parts (Mansbridge et al. 2012: 26).

Needless to say, compared with the microscopic institutional approach, the macroscopic systemic approach makes more political sense whilst also setting extremely high standards and methodological complexities in terms of accomplishing deliberative democracy and scientifically investigating it. However, is the systemic approach as novel an understanding of deliberative democracy as it claims to be? After all, one of the original inspirations for deliberative democracy, Jürgen Habermas's communicative model, aspired at looking at and understanding the functioning of the 'public sphere' in its entirety, including all formal and informal institutions and outlets of political discourse (Habermas 2015b). Ultimately, it is well-known that political systems are a sum of interconnected informal and formal institutions which collectively influence outcomes, such as the complex and obvious relationship between media discourses and the actions of representative and direct democracy institutions. It is not surprising that Seyla Benhabib, writing in the early 1990s (the infancy of deliberative democracy), advocated a systemic approach without specifically naming it when she argued that deliberative democracy cannot be accomplished through ad hoc platforms, but that for it to happen the entire political system must consist of 'interlocking and overlapping networks and associations of deliberation [and] argumentation' (Benhabib 1996: 73–4).

Deliberative Democracy: But Citizens' Voices Might Be Limited!

Deliberative democracy sets itself the extremely ambitious goal of giving citizens a voice in political decisions, but its most significant limitation is the equality between the voices raised by citizens with different identities and socio-economic locations. This is the most fundamental dilemma of deliberative democracy, and it raises the question of whether deliberative democracy could accomplish its promised potential. Deliberative democracy's troubled relationship with equality emerges on two different, but equally important, levels: the meta-ethical level and the practical implementation level.

At the meta-ethical level, critical feminist scholars question the very foundation of deliberative democracy and the selection of qualities that deliberative democracy considers superior and attributing legitimacy to political discourse and outcomes (Young 1987; Gerber et al. 2019). Who and on what basis can decide that predominantly masculine qualities, such as impartiality, reasoned argumentation and rationality are more beneficial and necessary to reach a high-quality political discourse than predominantly feminine qualities such as open expression of emotions, affection, compassion or even anger (Mansbridge 1993, 2000)? From a feminist and egalitarian perspective, the selection of these normative qualities appears problematic, since those values indicate a particular way of argumentation and even persuasion that is reserved for those most privileged members of society, such as upper-class white men with high-quality private education. As a result, as another dilemma, deliberative democracy could potentially appeal to those elite European citizens who are already engaged with European politics, whilst disengaging alienated citizens whose contribution is needed to truly transform the EU–citizen relationship.

When it comes to the practical implementation level, deliberative democracy faces some significant challenges in terms of incorporating the voice of a diverse citizenship in the process. How can one reach out to those disenfranchised parts of society who are invisible in public records (such as Roma populations, other minorities, legal or illegal immigrants, the homeless and those living in extreme poverty) and make them appreciate deliberation as a valuable contribution to their not-so-positive experiences of citizenship? Critical studies investigating equality in deliberation find that it is extremely difficult for women who shoulder most of the unpaid care duties provided within the family and those precariously employed with unpredictable schedules to show up to deliberation (Kamarudin 2015; O'Hagan et al. 2019).

Even if those with little to no trust in political processes are convinced and able to enter the deliberative space, how can one make sure that their opinions are expressed and their voices are heard as loudly as those who have socio-economic privileges and the power of articulation on their side? Then perhaps deliberative democracy might be overestimating the contribution of voice and talk in the democratic process at the expense of silence and listening, which again feminist scholars see as a preference for masculine qualities over feminine qualities (Mansbridge 2000). Here deliberative democracy faces the age-old dilemma about the relationship between democracy and equality: is it possible to accomplish a truly democratic process that gives equal weight to all voices without creating a truly egalitarian society in the first place or is it necessary to create a truly democratic process that gives equal weight to all voices to be able to construct a truly egalitarian society? In any case, given the linguistic, cultural and socio-economic diversity of EU citizenship, it is not difficult to guess that it will be particularly challenging to ensure the internal inclusivity of deliberation in the context of the EU. Unsurprisingly, the Europolis experiment showed that middle-class educated citizens from Western Europe are more likely to influence the outcome of deliberation than their working-class counterparts from Eastern Europe (Offe 2014).

Additionally, deliberative democracy also faces some significant dilemmas of political design. First, deliberative democracy is envisioned to complement and not replace representative democratic institutions (Dahl 1989: 340). However, it is uncertain how deliberative platforms will make decisions and how these decisions will be incorporated by representative institutions into policymaking. Initially, a consensus was considered the gold standard (Habermas 2012) of deliberative decision-making, but it was later abandoned as an extremely ambitious standard. Instead, Gutmann and Thompson argue for a 'provisionally justified agreement' (1996: 93–4),

Dryzek and Niemeyer favour a 'meta consensus' on the contested values and disputed judgments (2010: 15), whereas Fishkin rejects group decisions altogether arguing that this would result in social pressure being put on individuals, and instead promotes deliberative polls (2009: 132–3). Although theoretically valuable, none of these abstract suggestions offers a sufficiently tangible form of decision-making that could inform real-life political and policy decisions of representative institutions. As discussed in the penultimate section of this chapter, anchoring deliberation into EU decision-making procedures raises even more fundamental dilemmas, not only because deliberative democracy is relatively novel in the EU but also because EU decision-making procedures are more complex than those of national representative democracies and involve negotiations between different institutions based on the principle of institutional balance.

Another potential and significant limitation of deliberative democracy is its reliance on expertise. In the context of deliberative experiments and platforms, citizens are expected to engage in a reasoned debate and exchange informed opinions about subjects that could be technical or completely new to citizens engaged in deliberation. To ensure that citizen opinions are informed and translatable into policy choices, deliberative platforms involve presentations of expert evidence informing citizens about different policy options and their relative costs and benefits. Foucault's powerful critique of the power of science illustrates that science and expertise are not neutral but have got significant political underpinnings (Foucault 1997, 1998). Not only could what does and does not count as science differ fundamentally from one era and context to the other, but also so-called scientific and expert opinions could have political undertones to implicitly coax citizens to favour one political choice over the others. Therefore, it is necessary to think carefully about the role of expertise in deliberation and its potential influence over citizens' opinions before deciding whether deliberative democracy offers a platform for citizens to voice their genuinely free opinions. This question becomes even more significant in the context of the EU, since those EU policies most influential on citizen welfare, such as the Economic and Monetary Union or Common Agricultural Policy, are extremely technical and therefore require an intense citizen engagement with expertise to decipher the basic underpinnings of those policies let alone to make decisions about them.

In addition and similar to direct democracy methods, such as referendums, deliberative democracy is potentially open to being captured by political institutions which could introduce deliberation in a specifically chosen subject to strengthen the legitimacy of their position. Political institutions could initiate pseudo deliberation experiments in soft issue areas with no obvious and immediate translation to real-life policy outcomes to manage relations with a politically disaffected public (Goodin and Dryzek 2006; Papadopoulos 2013: 147; Johnson 2015: 23). This seems to be the case for the recent 'Citizens' Consultations' and 'Citizens Dialogues' introduced to engage citizens with European politics at the EU and national levels. The same misgiving is also immediately visible in the recommendations proposed by Scotland's Citizens' Assembly, which appear beneficial to society overall (such as increasing income levels and affordable housing) but which, however, are also very vague and general and therefore not easily implementable by political institutions.[5]

Accordingly, critical feminist scholars argue that perhaps the problem of deliberative democracy is not so much one of design but the political nature of the issues that need to be debated and addressed for a truly egalitarian and democratic society to be established. It is unlikely for political institutions and interest groups, who are in the gatekeeper positions, to allow genuine civic engagement with agendas that will result in radical redistributions of power and resources (Cornwall and Goetz 2005).

Finally, another dilemma of deliberative democracy, particularly in the context of the EU, is how to create a holistic deliberative process that does not perceive policymaking as demarcated between rigid jurisdictional boundaries of sub-national, national and supranational levels. As argued in Keating's chapter in this book, this rigid perception of boundaries between policymaking at different levels has been one of the key weaknesses of the EU democracy theory. This rigidity falls short of igniting participatory enthusiasm in citizens who are directly affected by policy outcomes, notwithstanding which level of authority the policymaking power belongs to. This also potentially compromises the real-life impact of deliberation because the policymaking power to reflect on citizen voices could belong to a different level from the one that initiated the deliberative process.

Deliberative Democracy in the EU: Why?

The introduction to this volume discusses in detail the dilemmas of EU's democracy and some of the potential strategies that could be adopted to address those dilemmas. As is explained in the introduction, arguably the most dominant approach to democracy in the EU, namely the 'democratic deficit' approach, became increasingly prevalent in historical waves responding first to the EU's coming into existence as a result of the Maastricht

---

[5] See <https://www.gov.scot/publications/citizens-assembly-scotland-scottish-government-response-doing-politics-differently/> (last accessed 14 December 2022).

reforms with political (in addition to economic) pillars and more recently to the emergence of anti-democratic, populist right-wing political tendencies, particularly in Eastern Europe. The majority of the democratic deficit scholarship offers solutions inspired by the national representative democratic model, such as strengthening the relationship between citizens and the European Parliament, strengthening the role played by national parliaments in EU politics, or introducing directly elected positions in EU politics to create competitive politics at the EU level (see Hix 2008; Bellamy and Castiglione 2013; Nicolaïdis 2013; Nicolaïdis and Youngs 2014; see also Lacey in this volume).

Looking for the solution to the EU's democracy problem almost exclusively in directly elected representative institutions is not very convincing when those institutions also suffer from their very idiosyncratic problems of legitimacy, including continually decreasing election turnouts, political apathy particularly in younger and economically vulnerable parts of the populations, and increasing popularity of populist extreme right-wing political agendas (Armingeon and Guthmann 2014). As a result, it could be argued that similar to the supranational representative institutions, national representative institutions also suffer from a legitimation crisis and they also need to rethink their relationship with citizens. Hence, the need to look for alternative outlets of citizen participation outside representative democracy.

A key reason for the lack of interest in innovative participatory democracy methods in EU scholarship is the presumed absence of citizenship that shares a sufficiently strong mutual trust and loyalty bound to collectively engage in a democratic process (Nicolaïdis 2013; see also Seubert in this volume). The sense of community and physical and social closeness to the issues discussed is one of the key aspects which makes a deliberative platform successful in terms of attracting sufficient citizen interest and commitment. It is not surprising that citizens would feel more strongly about the regeneration of an old dump site in their neighbourhood than how the EU distributes its regional development funds, as the implications on citizens' economic, social and physical well-being are significantly more direct in the first example than the second. Nevertheless, we need to acknowledge that the relationship between EU citizenship and democracy constitutes another fundamental dilemma. Although it is assumed that the absence of a common identity contributes to citizens' lack of interest in EU politics, limited opportunities for collective engagement with EU-level issues could potentially be one of the contributing factors to the relatively weak common identity between EU citizens in the first place. Accordingly, rethinking the EU's relationship with citizens in the light of the principles and ambitions of deliberative democracy and opening up platforms and spaces in which citizens can collectively discuss EU-level issues with an impact on their well-being could contribute to the emergence of a common political sphere and strengthen the sense of shared identity among citizens.

Recent examples involving the European Citizens' Initiative (although not a deliberative democracy method) show that democratic innovations could lead to increased civic and political engagement with EU-level policies and issues and that scepticism towards democratic innovations based on the diversity of EU citizenship is not entirely justified. Although the European Commission has rejected the vast majority of legislative proposals submitted through the European Citizens' Initiative, the mechanism itself provided an outlet for citizens to more critically and deeply engage with EU-level politics and issues, as reflected, among others, in the EU-wide political campaigns involving the Transatlantic Trade and Investment Partnership[6] and the right to water,[7] which started as a European Citizens' Initiative. As a result, if successfully implemented, deliberative democracy could contribute to the democratisation of the EU in two ways: by providing an alternative outlet for citizen participation and by contributing to the common identity of European citizenship.

Deliberative Democracy in the EU: How Not?

EU institutions and political figures are not oblivious to the EU's chronic unpopularity with citizens. Since the 2001 White Paper on Governance, there have been several reforms and reform proposals to strengthen the relationship with citizens and to change the EU's public image. Given its increasing popularity across the globe at local and national levels, deliberative democracy has not been unnoticed by EU institutions and politicians. Nevertheless, both historic and recent attempts for deliberation in the EU suffer from two fundamental problems: first, they are based on the misunderstanding that the key problem in EU democracy is not insufficient citizen participation but insufficient citizen education about how the EU works. Second, these attempts were not based on a systemic understanding of deliberation. As a result, rather than critically rethinking the role of deliberation and citizen participation in the EU political system as a whole, these attempts produced ad hoc subject-specific platforms with no effect on policy outcomes.

Early examples of deliberation include several projects initiated by different EU institutions to engage in a dialogue with citizens on different subjects. However, these were not genuinely deliberative projects, as they

---

[6] See <https://actions.sumofus.org/a/stop-ttip> (last accessed 7 December 2022).
[7] See <https://www.right2water.eu> (last accessed 7 December 2022).

rarely allowed citizens to communicate directly with each other (Yang 2013; Smith 2013: 202). The most significant early example of deliberation was the Convention on the Future of Europe which was convened to accomplish the ambitious objective of drafting a constitution for the EU set by the 2001 Laeken Declaration. Nevertheless, the Convention did not satisfy the fundamental principles of deliberative democracy either, as it brought together 'stakeholders', mainly national and EU politicians; in other words, the European elite, rather than citizens (Karolewski 2011). Perhaps this provides one of the explanations for the unpopularity of the result (the Constitutional Treaty) which citizens rejected in the Dutch and French referendums.

As a result of yet another White Paper on the Future of Europe (European Commission 2017), and connected to the processes of elections and political leadership changes at both the EU and national levels, a series of new initiatives have recently been launched to regenerate the EU's relationship with citizens. European Commission President Ursula von der Leyen's agenda for 'a new push for European democracy'[8] gave birth to the so-called 'citizens' dialogues', which are question and answer (Q&A) sessions between citizens and national and local politicians (European Commission 2019). As part of this process, a 'Citizens' Panel on the Future of Europe' was convened which drafted an online survey on the future of Europe to be communicated to EU citizens.[9] On the other hand, French President Macron's 2017 Pynx speech[10] initiated a six-month process of 'citizens' consultations', in which several EU-related issues were opened for discussion at the national level, albeit with significant differences across the member states in the subject matters, the numbers of consultations initiated and the procedures followed (Białożyt and Le Quiniou 2019).

The EU's interest in rekindling its relationship with citizens seems promising at first. Also, as another positive element, unlike previous attempts, recent initiatives involve simultaneous dialogues with citizens taking place at both supranational and national levels. Nevertheless, citizens' consultations and dialogues still seem to suffer from the EU's chronic misunderstanding of the key problem in its relationship with citizens. Similar to previous experiments with deliberative democracy, the

---

[8] See <https://ec.europa.eu/info/strategy/priorities-2019-2024/new-push-european-democracy_en> (last accessed 7 December 2022).

[9] See <https://futureu.europa.eu/en/assemblies/citizens-panels?locale=en> (last accessed 14 December 2022).

[10] See <https://www.theguardian.com/world/2017/sep/07/emmanuel-macron-calls-for-solidarity-as-he-vows-to-lead-eu-rebuild> (last accessed 14 December 2022).

recent initiatives seem to be designed to improve communication with citizens rather than increasing citizens' participation in EU politics and policies. This reflects the perception that citizens struggle to disentangle the complex policymaking processes followed and policies produced in Brussels; thus, they punish the unknown at every opportunity (see Yang 2013: 19; Doyle 2014: 114). As a result, to improve the effectiveness and efficacy of EU-level policymaking and to avoid the repetition of past crises, such as rejections of major Treaty amendments, citizens should be educated about the EU. For instance, one of the key conclusions of the citizens' consultations is the need to improve particularly young citizens' understanding of the EU by redesigning national curriculums (Białożyt and Le Quiniou 2019: 327).

Also, citizens' dialogues and citizens' consultations do not reflect a systemic rethinking of the EU–citizen relationship and systemic integration of deliberation into the EU political system. Neither of these initiatives is officially tied to policymaking processes and it is unclear whether and how they will affect real-life policy outcomes. Additionally, the 'Citizens' Panel on the Future of Europe', rather than involving citizens in the discussion of tangible and ongoing issues central to EU's governance and decisive in its future (such as economic governance or migration), opened the discussion with the abstract subject of the EU's future, despite the myriad of previous initiatives on this subject with no visible outcome or influence on EU policies.

In the light of the feminist critique of deliberative democracy, it could be argued that unless actors and institutions with political power are willing to relinquish some of their power to citizens in areas that are linked to EU governance and citizens' well-being, we should abandon all hope for democracy in the EU. Similarly, the ad hoc, piecemeal and disconnected deliberative platforms initiated at the national and supranational levels do not satisfy the conditions of a systemic approach to deliberative democracy. For citizens, the most direct indicator of the success of a political system is their individual experiences of citizenship, which in the context of EU governance are influenced by aggregated and territorially overlapping political decisions taken at local, regional, national and supranational levels (see also Keating in this volume). Hence, the EU's never-ending frustration with citizens' misunderstanding of its organisation. In this sense, the simultaneous initiation of national and supranational deliberative spaces appears as a move in the right direction, whereas the disconnection between the supranational and national spaces and the absence of tangible impact on policymaking appear as missed opportunities.

As argued by Keating in this volume, territorial and disaggregated policymaking could be strategically utilised by opportunistic political institutions in multilevel polities. Political institutions could scale the responsibility of taking decisions upwards or downwards to reduce citizens' influence on policy outcomes. This risk is particularly acute in the context of deliberative democracy, since, as discussed in this section, evidence from previous experiences shows the potential for political institutions to strategically utilise deliberative democracy to legitimise their actions without a genuine motive to reflect citizens' voices in the policy outcomes. Therefore, in the context of multilevel polities, it is particularly vital to embrace a systemic understanding of deliberation simultaneously influencing policy outcomes at multiple levels to ensure that deliberation leads to democratic, not pseudo-democratic, outcomes.

Deliberative Democracy in the EU: How?

In the final section of this chapter, I discuss whether deliberative democracy could be implemented in the EU and the dilemmas that need to be addressed for this to happen. Deliberative democracy is not only complicated to implement in the EU for obvious reasons, such as the size and diversity of EU citizenship and its disaffection with EU politics, but also when thinking about deliberative democracy in the EU in practical terms, one has to draw on a blank canvas, because deliberative democracy scholarship is almost completely silent when it comes to the implementation of deliberative democracy in multilevel polities, such as the EU. Arguably, the key reason for this is the limited communication between deliberative democracy and EU democracy scholarships, which have prevented the emergence of mutual learning and development of models incorporating expertise from both fields.

As I mentioned in the previous section, a truly systemic approach to deliberative democracy in the EU would involve a reconsideration and even a reconfiguration of all political and policy spheres, formal and informal, supranational, national, regional and local, in the light of deliberative principles. Perhaps one of the fundamental mistakes in the EU democracy scholarship has been the perception of political spheres as segregated between regional, national and supranational levels based on who has the authority of policymaking in a certain area rather than envisioning deliberative spaces organised based on subject areas central to citizens' well-being and influenced by collective but at times uncoordinated actions of political institutions of different levels. The organisation of such deliberative spaces is not necessarily a task for the centralised EU level, but local, regional and national political organisations could also collaborate to create deliberative spaces on issues that are of common concern to citizens provided that they are willing to give citizens a voice in the subject matter and to incorporate deliberative outcomes into policy decisions.

Needless to say, a holistic reconsideration of the EU political sphere in its entirety falls beyond the scope of this chapter. Instead, I will confine myself to having a systemic look at the key EU decision-making processes, namely the ordinary Treaty amendment procedure, the ordinary legislative procedure and the adoption process of long-term EU strategies, and I will discuss how citizen deliberation could be permanently and institutionally embedded into these processes.

Deliberation involving EU citizens can potentially be complex and costly given the size and cultural and linguistic diversity of EU citizenship. There is extensive literature on different methods for reducing the costs of deliberation, such as limiting the number of issues deliberated or using deliberation on an ad hoc basis, deliberation through elected representatives or using online technologies for communication between citizens (Dryzek and Niemeyer 2010: 25). I am not going to replicate the discussions about the costs and benefits of these different approaches and how they limit the democratic power of deliberation. Limiting issue areas to be deliberated or using deliberation on an ad hoc basis opens the door for political institutions to manipulate the deliberative process and to initiate deliberation only on minor issues or when they need to legitimise their positions. Deliberation between elected representatives replicates the already existing elite deliberation processes (such as deliberation in the European Parliament, in the case of the EU). Finally, online deliberation is an imperfect substitute to direct communication between citizens for many reasons and could result in inequalities in citizens' contribution to deliberation based on the digital divide (Stranberg and Grönlund 2014). In any case, the experiences of citizens' consultations and dialogues illustrate that linguistic and cultural diversity does not render deliberation prohibitively costly in the EU (European Commission 2019).

In the light of Article 48 TEU, Treaty amendments are initiated by the European Council upon a request from the European Commission, European Parliament or a government of a member state. The substance of Treaty amendment proposals is discussed in a Convention composed of representatives of national parliaments, the European Parliament, the Commission and the heads of state or government of the member states. The Convention makes decisions based on consensus. In order words, the Treaty amendment process involves elite deliberations and consensus between the highest political institutions of European governance, similar to constitutional amendment procedures of many polities. Direct election relationship between citizens and national and EU parliaments and direct or indirect election relationships between citizens and government and state executives provide the main source of legitimacy of the Treaty amendment process, which takes place distantly from citizens who do not enjoy any direct or indirect contribution to the process. On the other hand, the ordinary legislative procedure is initiated with a legislative proposal by the European Commission, which is adopted upon agreement between the Council and the European Parliament as a result of phases of readings and possibly a conciliation procedure (Art. 294 Treaty on the Functioning of the European Union (TFEU)). Similar to the Treaty amendment procedure, citizens do not participate in the legislative procedure indirectly or directly. The direct election relationship between citizens and the European Parliament and the indirect election relationships between citizens and the Commission and national government representatives in the Council attribute legitimacy to the process. In general, the EU political system operates based on the logic of 'institutional balance' which ensures that the decisions reflect a compromise reached as a result of negotiations between member state, EU and citizen interests represented respectively by the European Council or the Council of the European Union, European Commission and European Parliament (Art.13(2) TEU). This makes the EU political system and the incorporation of citizen deliberation more complicated than in national representative democracies.

How can the Treaty amendment and ordinary legislative procedures be reformed to include an element of deliberative democracy? Citizens could be involved in the process of deciding how the current procedures could be reformed to include deliberation. In his original formulation, Dahl suggested that two deliberative platforms can be created to debate first the subjects of constitutional or legal reforms (agenda-setting deliberation) and second the substance of the reform proposals. Similarly, in the context of the EU, a 'meta-deliberation' process could be initiated to involve citizens in the debate of how the Treaty should be reformed to include a deliberative element in the Treaty amendment and legislative processes.

The European Citizens' Initiative presents an opportunity for citizens to propose potential EU legislation, although it is ultimately subject to the European Commission's discretion and other high procedural thresholds (see Art. 11 TEU), and as a result has not been utilised successfully on many occasions (Karatzia 2017). Nevertheless, the framework of the Citizens' Initiative constitutes a promising starting point for further reform to include a deliberative element in the Treaty amendment and legislation processes. First of all, it could be discussed how the current remit of the Citizens' Initiative could be extended also to include Treaty amendment proposals. Second, similar to the citizens' councils and assemblies established respectively in Austria and Poland, citizens could be given the power to convene a deliberative process to discuss either constitutional or legislative issues utilising the Citizens' Initiative procedure. As an alternative, to increase the democratic credentials of citizens' initiatives, a deliberative element, such as a citizens' assembly, could be incorporated into citizens' initiatives and the Commission's discretion on whether to put the suggested legislative proposal into action could be lifted for citizens' proposals that emerge from a deliberative process.

When it comes to the substantive debate of the Treaty reforms and legislative proposals, citizen deliberation could take place either in one of the EU institutions empowered to take part in the process (such as the Convention in the context of Treaty amendments and the European Parliament in the context of the legislative process) or simultaneously but separate from formal institutions. There are different costs and benefits for either option. If deliberation takes place within formal institutions, citizens' proposals have a better chance of getting accepted. However, citizens are more likely to engage in informed and free debate resulting in original proposals if deliberation takes place outside the paternalism of political institutions (Geissel and Gherghina 2016). Therefore, if the former option is chosen then measures and procedures should be adopted to ensure citizens' equal participation in the debate with politicians who are experienced in political discourse. If the latter option is chosen, then measures and procedures should be established to make sure that political institutions duly reflect on and discuss citizen proposals. For instance, it could be made obligatory for political institutions to discuss citizens' proposals in a way that is fully transparent to citizens, report on the results of the discussion, and put forward substantive justifications if citizens' proposals are rejected.

Long-term EU strategies, although not having any binding power and being set forth mostly in soft law measures, can still make a significant impact on citizens' economic and social well-being. This, for instance, was the case for Lisbon and later Europe 2020 Agendas which steered the EU economic policies openly towards a neoliberal paradigm in the light of economic growth and competitiveness objectives. Such EU strategies are decided and enacted in an ad hoc basis when the previous strategies are out of date or there is a new political challenge that needs to be addressed. Similarly, deliberative processes and platforms could be convened on an ad hoc basis to involve citizens in the discussion of new strategies.

Needless to say, citizens participating in deliberation must represent EU citizenship as accurately as possible in terms of nationality, socio-economic background, racial and cultural characteristics, minority status and so on. This can be satisfied with stratified random selection and the addition of missing citizen demographics, subject to the limitations of internal and external inclusivity discussed in detail in this chapter. In the context of EU strategies, if the issue in question is likely to affect the status and well-being of certain clusters of citizens more directly (such as strategies on equality) then those clusters of citizens should be given particular priority in the selection process of citizens. It should not be a significant problem to decide on the number of citizens partaking in deliberation per member state, as the number of Members of the European Parliament (MEPs) for each member state offers a solution to this question that has worked effectively other than the minor issue of the slight over-representation of smaller member states. As long as the deliberative platform has internal and external inclusivity and there is political willingness to translate citizen opinions to tangible outcomes, the specific design of the deliberative platform, for example whether it should be a citizens' assembly or a deliberative poll, is less imperative, as there is no evidence about the superiority of one form of deliberation over another.

What would be the potential implications of citizen deliberation on the principle of institutional balance underlying the EU political system? It could be argued that embedding deliberation into EU decision-making procedures could upset this principle by tilting the balance towards the over-representation of citizen interests at the expense of other interests. This is unlikely to happen because at present the EU political regime suffers from an under-representation of citizen interests. Considering the limitations of representation of citizen interests through the European Parliament documented extensively in the democratic deficit literature and partially discussed in this article, providing citizen interests with another entry point to the EU political system is unlikely to jeopardise the principle of institutional balance. It could also be argued that embedding deliberation into the EU political system could potentially further clog the EU decision-making procedures which already suffer from efficiency problems due to the presence of several institutions representing different interests. It cannot be denied that institutionalised citizen deliberation could potentially further decrease the speed of EU decision-making, particularly in issues that are subject to stark divisions between EU citizens and institutions. Nevertheless, this does not automatically translate into inefficiency in EU decision-making. On the contrary, clear citizens' preference could attribute legitimacy to certain policy choices over others, and as a result, could prevent or reduce costly and time-consuming negotiations between the three EU institutions.

Needless to say, the institutional reforms proposed here (other than the ones regarding EU strategies) will require amendments to the founding Treaties, which might be considered politically and economically costly. Aversion to Treaty amendments in the EU after the failed constitution experiment is well known. However, Commission President van der Leyen promised a 'new push for democracy' as part of her selection agenda, including a potential Treaty reform (von der Leyen 2019). If there is a time to institutionalise deliberative democracy in the EU through Treaty reform, it is now.

Conclusions

The EU is increasingly perceived as a polity of perpetual crises. Its unsatisfactory democratic credentials (the 'democratic deficit') have been the subject of endless debates, particularly since the Maastricht reforms. Is it possible to further democratise the EU or do we have to accept that this is as democratic as the EU can get? Its unique institutional structure coupled with its economic policy objectives could mean that the EU will always have a distant relationship with citizens and any discussion of democratisation in the EU will have only purely academic value (see also McNamara in this volume).

However, if there is any hope for further democratisation in the EU, then increasingly popular deliberative democracy provides a promising outlet to draw lessons from. As discussed extensively in this chapter, deliberative democracy is not a panacea for creating perfect relationships with citizens. Nevertheless, deliberative democracy represents a novel alternative to tried and failed methods to strengthen representative democratic institutions, subject to its very own idiosyncratic dilemmas.

The existing and limited scholarship on deliberative democracy in the EU has refrained from suggesting concrete reform proposals. There have been historic (such as the Convention on the Future of Europe) and recent (such as citizens' consultations and dialogues) attempts to implement deliberation in the EU, but none of these attempts followed a systemic approach and produced tangible policy outcomes. Thus, it is not surprising that they did not result in any significant improvement in the EU's democracy and its relationship with citizens. Against this background, this chapter aimed to discuss deliberative democracy with its potentials and limitations and to propose concrete reforms for the implementation of deliberative democracy in the EU. The proposals of this chapter are not cast in stone; they represent an attempt to open a potentially very productive conversation.

References

Armingeon, Klaus and Guthmann, Kai (2014) Democracy in Crisis? The Declining Support for National Democracy in European Countries, 2007-2011. *European Journal of Political Research*, 53: 423–42.

Bellamy, Richard and Castiglione, Dario (2013) Three Models of Democracy, Political Community and Representation on the EU. *Journal of European Public Policy*, 20(2): 206–23.

Benhabib, Seyla (1996) Toward a Deliberative Model of Democratic Legitimacy. In Benhabib, S. (ed.) *Democracy and Difference*. Chichester: Princeton University Press, pp. 67–94.

Białożyt, Wojciech and Le Quiniou, Romain (2019) Europe's Deliberative Instruments: Has the EU Delivered? In Blockmans, Steven and Russack, Sophia (eds) *Deliberative Democracy in the EU*. Brussels: CEPS.

Chappell, Zsuzsanna (2012) *Deliberative Democracy: A Critical Introduction*. New York: Palgrave.

Chwalisz, Claudia (2019) A New Wave of Deliberative Democracy, Carnegie Europe, 26 November, <https://carnegieeurope.eu/2019/11/26/new-wave-of-deliberative-democracy-pub-80422> (last accessed 25 November 2022).

Cornwall, Andrea and Goetz, Anne Marie (2005) Democratising Democracy: Feminist Perspectives. *Democratization*, 12(5): 783–800.

Crespy, Amandine (2014) Deliberative Democracy and the Legitimacy of the European Union: A Reappraisal of Conflict. *Political Studies*, 62(1): 81–98.

Curato, Nicole, Hammond, Marit and Min, John B. (2019) *Power in Deliberative Democracy*. New York: Palgrave.

Dahl, Robert A. (1989) *Democracy and Its Critics*. New Haven: Yale University Press.

De la Porte, Caroline and Nanz, Patricia (2004) OMC – A Deliberative Democratic Mode of Governance? The Case of Employment and Pensions. *Journal of European Public Policy*, 11(4): 267–88.

Doyle, Natalie J. (2014) Governance and Democratic Legitimacy: The European Union's Crisis of De-Politicisation. In Isakhan, Benjamin and Slaughter, Steven (eds) *Democracy and Crisis*. New York: Palgrave, pp. 108–24.

Dryzek, John and Niemeyer, Simon (2010) Deliberative Turns. In Dryzek, J., *Foundations and Frontiers of Deliberative Governance*. New York: Oxford University Press.

European Commission (2017) White Paper on the Future of Europe. Brussels.

European Commission (2019) Citizens' Dialogues and Citizens' Consultations – Key Conclusions. Brussels.

Fishkin, James S. (2009) *When the People Speak: Deliberative Democracy and Public Consultation*. Oxford: Oxford University Press.

Fishkin, James S. (2014) Deliberative Democracy in Context: Reflections on Theory and Practice. In Grönlund, K., Bächtiger, A. and Setälä, M. (eds) *Deliberative Mini-Publics*. Colchester: ECPR Press, pp. 27–39.

Foucault, Michel (1997) Sex, Power, and the Politics of Identity. In *Ethics: Subjectivity and Truth*. London: Penguin.

Foucault, Michel (1998) *The Will to Knowledge*. London: Penguin

Fung, Archon (2003) Survey Article: Recipes for Public Spheres: Eight Institutional Design Choices and Their Consequences. *Journal of Political Philosophy*, II(3): 338–67.

Geissel, Brigitte and Gherghina, Sergiu (2016) Constitutional Deliberative Democracy and Democratic Innovations. In Reuchamps, M. and Suiter, J. (eds) *Constitutional Deliberative Democracy in Europe*. Colchester: ECPR.

Gerber, Marlène, Schaub, Hans-Peter and Mueller, Sean (2019) O sister, where art thou? Theory and Evidence on Female Participation at Citizen Assemblies. *European Journal of Politics and Gender*, 2(2): 173-95.
Goodin, Robert E. and Dryzek, John S. (2006) Deliberative Impacts: The Macro-Political Uptake of Mini-Publics. *Politics & Society*, 34(2): 219-44.
Grönlund, Kimmo, Bächtiger, André and Setälä, Maija (2014) Towards a New Era of Deliberative Mini-Publics. In Grönlund, K., Bächtiger, A. and Setälä, M. (eds) *Deliberative Mini-Publics*. Colchester: ECPR Press.
Gutmann, A. and Thompson, D. (1996) *Democracy and Disagreement*. Cambridge: Harvard University Press.
Habermas, Jürgen (2012) *Between Facts and Norms*. Cambridge: Polity.
Habermas, Jürgen (2015a) *The Lure of Technocracy*. Cambridge: Polity.
Habermas, Jürgen [1962] (2015b) *The Structural Transformation of the Public Sphere*. London: Polity.
Hart, Vivien (2001) Constitution-Making and the Transformation of Conflict. *Peace and Change*, 26(2): 153-76.
Hix, Simon (2008) *What's Wrong with the European Union and How to Fix It?* Cambridge: Polity.
Johnson, Genevieve F. (2015) *Democratic Illusion*. Toronto: University of Toronto Press.
Kamarudin, Shariza (2015) Gender Responsive and Participatory Budgeting in Penang: The People-Oriented Model. In Ng. C. (ed.) *Gender Responsive and Participatory Budgeting*. London: Springer.
Karatzia, Anastasia (2017) The European Citizens' Initiative and the EU Institutional Balance: On Realism and the Possibilities of Affecting EU Law-Making. *Common Market Law Review*, 54(1): 177-208.
Karolewski, Ireneusz P. (2011) Pathologies of Deliberation in the EU. *European Law Journal*, 17(1): 66-79.
Korkea-aho, Emilia (2015) *Adjudicating Governance*. New York: Routledge.
Mansbridge, Jane (1993) Feminism and Democratic Community. *Nomos*, 35: 339-95.
Mansbridge, Jane (2000) Feminism and Democracy. *The American Prospect*, 5 December 2000, <https://prospect.org/civil-rights/feminism-democracy/> (last accessed 25 November 2022).
Mansbridge, Jane, Bohman, James, Chambers, Simone, Christiano, Thomas, Fung, Archon, Parkinson, John, Thompson, Dennis F. and Warren, Mark E. (2012) A Systemic Approach to Deliberative Democracy. In Parkinson, John and Mansbridge, Jane (eds) *Deliberative Systems*. London: Cambridge University Press.
Nicolaïdis, Kalypso (2013) European Demoicracy and Its Crisis. *Journal of Common Market Studies*, 51(2): 351-69.
Nicolaïdis, Kalypso and Youngs, Richard (2014) Europe's Democracy Trilemma. *International Affairs*, 90(6): 1403-19.
Offe, Claus (2014) The Europolis Experiment and Its Lessons for Deliberation on Europe. *European Union Politics*, 15(3): 430-41.
O'Flynn, Ian, Sood, Gaurav, Mistaffa, Jalal and Saeed, Nawhi (2019) What Future for Kirkuk? Evidence from a Deliberative Intervention. *Democratization*, 26(7): 1299-1317.

O'Hagan, Angela, et al. (2019) Evaluation of Participatory Budgeting Activity in Scotland: 2016-2018, <https://www.gov.scot/publications/evaluation-participatory-budgeting-activity-scotland-2016-2018-2/> (last accessed 25 November 2022).

Papadopoulos, Yannis (2013) *Democracy in Crisis*. New York: Palgrave.

Ryan, Matthew and Smith, Graham (2014) Defining Mini-Publics. In Grönlund, K., Bächtiger, A. and Setälä, M. (eds) *Deliberative Mini-Publics*. Colchester: ECPR Press.

Smith, Graham (2013) Designing Democratic Innovations at the European Level: Lessons from the Experiments. In Kies, R. and Nanz, P. (eds) *Is Europe Listening to Us?: Successes and Failures of EU Citizen Consultations*. Farnham: Ashgate.

Strandberg, Kim and Grönlund, Kimmo (2014) Online Deliberation: Theory and Practice in Virtual Mini-Publics. In Grönlund, K. Bächtiger, A. and Setälä, M. (eds) *Deliberative Mini-Publics*. Colchester: ECPR.

Von der Leyen, Ursula (2019) Opening Statement in the European Parliament, Brussels, <https://ec.europa.eu/commission/presscorner/detail/en/SPEECH_19_4230> (last accessed 25 November 2022).

Yang, Mundo (2013) Europe's New Communication Policy and the Introduction of Transnational Deliberative Citizens' Involvement Projects. In Kies, R. and Nanz, P. (eds) *Is Europe Listening to Us?: Successes and Failures of EU Citizen Consultations*. Farnham: Ashgate.

Young, Iris M. (1987) Impartiality and the Civic Public: Some Implications of Feminist Critiques of Moral and Political Theory. In Benhabib, S. and Cornell, N. (eds) *Feminism as a Critique*. New York: Oxford University Press.

Young, Iris M. (1996) Communication and the Other: Beyond Deliberative Democracy. In Benhabib, S. (ed.) *Democracy and Difference*. Chichester: Princeton University Press, pp. 120–35.

Young, Iris M. (2000) *Inclusion and Democracy*. New York: Oxford University Press.

FOUR

Dilemmas of EU Citizenship: The Persistent Divide between Economic and Political Integration

Sandra Seubert

The continuous economic integration of the European common market has arguably paved the way for establishing a bundle of transnational rights which in the course of further European integration was suposed to become a comprehensive citizenship status. The introduction of 'Union Citizenship' in the Treaty of Maastricht (1992) was an explicit attempt to transcend the economic logic: integrating the existing worker's rights of free movement and equal treatment into a transnational citizenship status raised the expectation of empowering political subjects and leaving a primarily market-oriented dynamic of European integration behind. But so far, the political meaning of this transnational status has remained deficient: European Union (EU) citizens are still mainly addressed as workers or consumers but rarely as conscious political agents, who deliberate and decide issues of common concern as equals in a pan-European space.

Despite the ever-increasing influence of European politics on the everyday life of citizens political agency is still predominantly linked and channelled through the national context.[1] Normatively, citizenship combines membership

---

[1] Whether this has changed in the course of recent events is debatable: the EU's multiple crises have raised attention to European issues considerably (Grande and Kriesi 2016), there has been an increasing (although still low) voter turnout in the last European elections (<https://www.europarl.europa.eu/news/de/press-room/20191029IPR65301/final-turnout-data-for-2019-european-elections-announced> (last accessed 8 December 2022)) and also pro-European activism is arguably on the rise (Seubert 2021). Recently the 'Conference on the Future of Europe', an ambitious European experiment of transnational citizen deliberation, running from May 2021 until May 2022, took up ideas for reform (<https://futureu.europa.eu> (last accessed 8 December 2022)). Given the pandemic and the EU's

in a bounded community with the political status of an equal. In the national context this status is supposed to be secured by the constitutionalisation of fundamental rights which empower the subjects to actually make use of legal entitlements, previously the privilege of a particular social estate or class. The political meaning of modern citizenship has evolved in the course of democratic revolutions and struggles that have taken place since European Enlightenment. Its normative promise – freedom and equality under self-enacted laws – nevertheless covers a persistent dilemma: formal political equality coexists with a continuing inequality of social status, that is reproduced under capitalist conditions and reappears in the European context with a vengeance. Given the EU's persistent 'joint-decision trap' the functioning of the internal market is shielded from democratic decision-making rather than the other way round (Scharpf 2009). The tension between political equality and inequality of social status was supposed to be evened out by national welfare state regimes (Offe 2013; Bude and Staab 2016). But while welfare state regimes remained mainly nationally organised they have come under pressure in the course of deepening global interdependencies and processes of denationalisation and Europeanisation.[2]

The introduction of EU citizenship can certainly be interpreted as an expression as well as a reaction to these kinds of developments. So far, major debates about citizenship in Europe have revolved around (and criticised) EU citizenship as originating in market integration, presupposing that it is nothing more than a complementary add-on, leaving national citizenship more or less unchanged and unquestioned (Bauböck 2019). But not least tendencies of democratic backsliding in several EU member states raise the question of whether and how European citizenship rights ought to be substantiated and defended at all levels. This relates to the larger challenge of reinterpreting the normative promise of democratic citizenship beyond the national–supranational binary in a compound, multilevel system like the EU.[3] The

geopolitical challenges related to the Russian aggression, attention for this event remained limited and results vague (for an overview and first assessment, see Alemanno 2022).

[2] What is more, the nation as the major social reference group for claims to equality and inclusion is itself put into question. Theories of post-national membership interpret this process in detail and highlight how different dimensions of citizenship, such as privileges of political membership, entitlements to rights and collective identity, have become disaggregated in the course of global economic developments and they discuss the establishment of an international human rights regime after the Second World War (Soysal 1994; Benhabib 2006, 2016).

[3] While for some applying the inherited understanding of citizenship is just a 'category mistake', others argue for a reinterpretation and point to the constructive power

chapter addresses this challenge by reconsidering EU citizenship's dilemma as situated between economic and political integration and aims to reassess its democratic aspirations and constraints in a multilevel constellation. It starts from the assumption that EU citizenships' conceptual core is ambivalent: free movement of persons is part of the 'Four Freedoms' of the market. At the same time the principle of non-discrimination recalls a citizenship paradigm of equal treatment. This leads to rivalling legitimatory demands. So far, the constitution of EU citizenship is divided along conflicting economic and political logics. As argued, EU citizenship contributes to an expansion of certain citizenship rights but at the same time risks the dissolution of others. Since in the current EU system the economic and the social are constitutionally decoupled, EU citizenship reintroduces a link between economic activity and full entitlement to rights, which national social citizenship was supposed to overcome. The fact that the existing arrangements allow for considerably unequal levels of empowerment and protection on a pan-European scale provokes the question of whether the EU is really on the way to develop a democratic citizenship regime that is worth the name. The challenge of rethinking the tension between political equality and social status in light of the specific context of the EU's economic and political order is addressed in Section 3. It is concluded that the particular citizenship constellation in the EU demands strengthening the connection between EU citizenship and fundamental rights. Although differentiation might be needed to leave room for a variety of social, economic and cultural arrangements, it is only acceptable to the extent that this does not endanger EU citizens' basic status as political equals. What is more, the rhetoric of protecting diversity must not be abused to mask and perpetuate relations of domination, that is, inequalities, but rather take 'democratic minimum' standards into account that give EU citizenship the substance that is needed for making it meaningful for people's lives and thus possible to identify each other as committed to a common venture.

Beyond the Market Paradigm?

When the project of European integration was already deemed to be suffering from a deep sense of malaise and public disaffection in the late 1980s, the establishment of EU citizenship in the Treaty of Maastricht (1992) carried hopes for strengthening the EU's legitimacy and addressing what was

---

of legal concepts which, by being sensitive to social change, can slowly but steadily shape expectations and thereby have a transformative impact on citizen's understanding of the political world in which they live (for the former position, see e.g. Majone 2005; for the latter see e.g. Kostakopoulou 2008; Besson and Utzinger 2008).

increasingly perceived as a democratic deficit. The more the process of European integration had proceeded substantially, the more deficient the EU's legitimacy drawn from its international organisation of political authority had become. While political advocates framed the introduction as a paradigm shift, critics saw it as nothing more than 'old wine in new bottles'. Economic integration, based on the 'four freedoms' and culminating in economic and monetary union (EMU), had paved the way for the new citizenship status: worker mobility had been the bedrock upon which the entire construction of European Rights had been built (see Maas 2007). But while free movement of persons was certainly desirable to ensure the common market, it was not at all necessary to frame the related claims as individual rights, and even more as citizenship.[4] Bringing the existing rights together in a comprehensive status indeed contained a political message: it raised the expectation of moving beyond a state-centred logic of European integration, and establishing a direct link between EU institutions and EU citizens.

While political supporters argued that the idea of the European Union requires an integrative space, in which European citizens play a central and fundamental role, sceptics warned that this introduction was 'little more than a cynical exercise in public relations' (Weiler 1998: 10). In their view the language of citizenship contained a promise that the EU was far from being able to fulfil. The actual rights related to the new status remained rather thin and there was no radical 'new beginning', expressed, as one might expect, through the common will of the peoples of Europe to join together and form a polity.[5]

Conceptually EU citizenship's cornerstones are the right to mobility and the right to non-discrimination.[6] The relation of these cornerstones is more conflictual than it might seem at first sight. Freedom of movement for persons has developed as one of the 'four freedoms' – freedom of goods,

---

[4] Other regional integration efforts (such as the North American Free Trade Agreement (NAFTA), Mercosur) have provided individuals with some rights but none have developed into citizenship (cf. Shaw 2007; Maas 2017: 646).

[5] Political support for the new citizenship status (which in fact was the result of a compromise) came from a left-liberal power constellation assembled around the aim of challenging the internal market dispositive. It included initiatives from the European Parliament and also from the European Trade Union's Association, civil society organisations and pan-European intellectuals (for a reconstruction of this process, see Maas 2007; Buckel 2013: 90–7).

[6] Cf. Art. 21 Treaty on the Functioning of the European Union (TFEU) which guarantees the right 'to move and reside freely within the Territory of the member states'. The 'non-discrimination principle' demands that 'any discrimination on grounds of nationality shall be prohibited' (Art. 18 TFEU).

services, capital and labour – that form the basis of EU law (Barnard 2010; Kadelbach 2011). Having a right to free movement opens the door for border crossing, but it does not grant an unconditional right to residency. Insofar as free movement is not only to do with entering but also residing in a country, legal residency is dependent on being economically self-supporting.[7] Hence, the right to move appears primarily as a right to be economically active, to seek employment or run a business, across the Union. This has given rise to the criticism that EU citizenship is nothing more than a 'market citizenship' (Everson 1995; Shuibhne 2010).

Non-discrimination, on the other hand, expresses a right to equal treatment: no EU citizen in any EU member state shall be put in a position more disadvantaged than that of a national citizen or a third country national. In principle, the right to equal treatment expresses a move beyond the economic rationale: persons can expect to be treated on an equal footing and be integrated in the host society.[8] But the political logic of equal treatment and the economic logic of free movement are not as easy to mediate as functionalist theories of a 'spill-over' might suggest and rather get caught up in serious tensions.[9] Applying the rationale behind the 'four freedoms' all the way

---

[7] Council Directive 2004/38/EC of 29 April 2004. Legal residence is restricted for those who are likely to become 'a burden on the host country's social assistance system' or a threat to public security and public health (EC, Memo/1/1041, <https://eur-lex.europa.eu/legal-content/EN/TXT/?uri=CELEX%3A32004L0038> (last accessed 14 December 2022).

[8] The European Court of Justice (ECJ) has contributed to gradually expanding the rights relating to EU citizenship to non-economically active persons (students, pensioners, job seekers). While some interpreted this as an attempt to re-embed the European market, although with limited success, others criticise the Court's activism as a democratically problematic constraint on policymaking (for the former position, see Buckel (2013: 93); for the latter Schmidt (2018: 12)). Recently, the ECJ has been engaged in a partial roll-back from previous (more expansive) interpretations of EU citizenship rights (see Shuibhne 2015 who criticises that in recent case law the 'hegemonic attribution of supremacy to secondary law vis à vis the Union's legal order' strengthens the discretion of national law, in particular with regard to social rights). As an example, see the ECJ ruling in *Dano v Jobcenter Leipzig* (2014) C-333/13.

[9] As for instance Wolfgang Streeck has prominently argued in the context of the financial crisis, it is unlikely that an 'ever closer union' will ever follow the currency union; on the contrary, stabilising the European currency has brought up the nations against each other as never before in the postwar era (Streeck 2013). Crisis management has brought inherent contradictions to the fore and has worked towards a technocratic, authoritarian implementation of a 'capitalist monoculture' (Offe 2015; White 2013). For a democratic reform proposal, see Hennette et al. (2017).

down, would either have meant creating a European common marketplace and letting people circulate freely like goods without restrictions, or it would have suggested creating a common social space, next to the market, in which the citizenship logic with its principle of (political and social) equality could have been fully displayed (Weiler 1998; in a similar vein, see Eleftheriadis 2014: 779). Neither has been the case. Despite the apparent analogy of the 'four freedoms' it has been perfectly well understood from the beginning that the free movement of persons is a completely different issue from the free movement of goods. As Dagmar Schiek points out, non-discrimination of persons in the host state contrasts with the country-of-origin principle applied to the free movement of products (following 'Cassis de Dijon', 1979, Case 120/78), especially because as persons are not considered as a commodity traded across borders, they enjoy the right to equal treatment in their host state (Schiek 2017: 355–6). Non-discrimination can thus be interpreted as an important element of decommodification. People cannot simply be regarded as 'factors of production', to be shifted and allocated at will. What is more, their movement has a collective component: freedom of movement for persons, when leading to residence, affects the composition of the social entity that is the reference group of citizenship – the 'people'.

With the non-discrimination principle the European citizenship regime has so far followed an idea of horizontal integration: opening national polities and their citizenship regimes to one another. EU citizenship primarily entitles a person to be treated as a national citizen in the respective state, that is, like an Italian in Italy, like a French(wo)man in France and so on. Being an EU citizen is thus deeply mediated through a national framing (Azoulai 2017: 179). Ideally, the 'non-discrimination principle' presupposes a reciprocal give and take: 'I admit you into my place and treat you as a fellow citizen, if you pledge to do the same if I come to your place and ask to be treated as a fellow citizen' (Ferrera 2016: 800). However, in the current institutional set-up member states remain primarily responsible for realising non-discrimination, that is, substantially underpinning the rights of EU citizens (Seubert 2019). In an asymmetrical constellation as the current one, member states are relatively unequal in social, cultural and economic resources and divide into sending and receiving countries. What can be observed under these conditions is that the non-discrimination principle tends to be hollowed out when receiving countries are not willing to bear the 'burdens of hospitality' (Ferrera 2016). Currently this 'hollowing-out' works, for instance, through restrictive interpretations of legal residency requirements.[10] It also works through withholding

---

[10] All EU member states have some kind of 'habitual residence test' but what constitutes the benchmark of habitual residence varies between states. Since it is not defined under EU law, guidance is vague. See 'Report on the rights and obligations of

equal treatment by extensively allowing the posting of workers. People moving as posted workers cannot claim equal treatment individually by relying on their Treaty rights, since posting is framed as an expression of their employer's freedom to provide services.[11] To the extent that these practices are tolerated, the EU insufficiently protects and enforces the equal treatment guarantee for its citizens. The problem with 'market citizenship' is that those who are most in need of protection from commodification are unlikely to benefit at all from EU citizenship rights.[12]

This mismatch has motivated calls to move beyond the economic rationale of the 'four freedoms'. Taking freedom of movement as the sole reference point for the idea of Union citizenship seems deeply misleading. It conceals the fact that the coexistence of democratic citizenship and competitive market economy rather creates dilemmas than a state of 'natural' harmony.[13] In its current shape EU citizenship is accused of promoting

---

citizens and non-citizens in selected countries', bEUcitizen Project Deliverable 10.1., 39–43, <https://doi.org/10.5281/zenodo.11346> (last accessed 8 December 2022).

[11] See for the respective case law: Case C-438/05 *International Transport Workers Federation, Finish Seamen's Union v Viking Line* (2007) ECR I-10779; Case C-341/05 *Laval un Partneri Ltd v Svenska Byggnadsarbetareförbundet* (2007) ECR I-11767.

[12] Currently this is particularly true for mobile employees, seasonal and posted workers, from Eastern Europe (as an attempt to address the issue see e.g. *European Trade Union Confederation Comments on the Commission Guidelines for Seasonal Workers*, 8.9.2020, <https://www.etuc.org/en/documents> (last accessed 8 December 2022); also the fair mobility initiative of the *Deutsche Gewerkschaftsbund* (DGB), <http://www.faire-mobilitaet.de> (last accessed 8 December 2022)). It is also true for workers in the so called 'new economy' who are trapped in semi-formality as underemployed or with casual contracts (cf. Abraham et al. 2010).

[13] Presupposing decommodification as a hallmark of democratic citizenship, the idea of 'market citizenship' is probably an oxymoron. For a critical discussion, see Kochenov (2017: 49–50); Menéndez and Olson (2020: 61–3). In Thomas Marshall's seminal study this conflict is described as a tension between 'status' and 'contract': after a differential status (associated with class) was replaced by a uniform status of citizenship (which provided the foundation of equality), rights of citizenship were defended against bargaining in the economic sphere (by collective actors, e.g. trade unionism which pushed for the transition of collective civil rights into basic (social) rights. 'To have to bargain for a living wage in a society which accepts the living wage as a social right is as absurd as to have to haggle for a vote in a society which accepts the vote as a political right' (Marshall 1992: 40). Marshall's distinction between status and contract and his insistence on two conflicting logics doesn't imply that he disputes the interdependency of markets and polities. To the contrary. Indeed, markets cannot function properly without political framing (see McNamara in this volume).

a 'patchwork of personhoods' (O'Brien, 2013: 1643).[14] Critiques therefore call for broader construction of personhood in EU law and suggest that EU citizenship should develop towards a further integrated unitary status. This raises questions about EU citizenship's substance which have frequently been avoided.

The Promise of Democratic Citizenship and Its Limits in the EU

The modern concept of citizenship combines membership in a political community with the political status as equals. In the influential tradition of Thomas Marshall's (1992) study on citizenship and social class, citizenship is conceived as a full membership status which entitles its holders to a bundle of rights and respective duties. Along the Marshallian Triassic, citizenship rights are commonly subclassified as civil, political and social rights. These rights are different in character: whereas civil rights tend to be negative and mainly demand omissions, social rights demand positive action, active engagement and commitment which presupposes some kind of 'social contract' (Lessenich and Mau 2005). The social dimension is vastly contested in debates about EU citizenship since the presuppositions for thick solidarity arrangements are supposed to be missing (Sangiovanni 2013). This argument neglects, though, that in the past social rights have been effectively used in nation-building processes to build up solidarity in the first place – the causality may well work the other way around (Seeleib-Kaiser 2018). Social rights are a necessary complement of political rights: by enabling and empowering citizens to actually make use of their formal political equality social rights substantially underpins a full membership status. In turn, from the perspective of democratic citizenship, political rights have an exceptional quality. They establish the legal status of

---

[14] See O'Brien (2013: 1643); Kochenov (2017: 41). In order to be entitled to equal treatment the ECJ has created a 'real link' criterion which, at first sight, seems less economic, thus pointing towards a broader direction (Case C-542/09 *Commission v Netherlands*, 4.6.2012). But, as O'Brian remarks, this requirement is still interpreted in a very limited sense: it is mainly the fact of participating in the employment market which is supposed to establish a sufficient link of integration. There is thus a systemic misrecognition of socially necessary work beyond wage work, in particular care work and community work, which leads (at best) to derivative protection due to dependency on a (wage) worker. For a critique of the gender-bias of EU citizenship see for example Naldini and Knijn (2018). For a productive adjustment of the real link-criterion, see de Witte (2015).

the citizen in a reflexive way: as entitlement to participating in a process of law-making political rights are the presupposition for the further democratic interpretation of all other rights (see Habermas 1992; Besson and Utzinger 2008). Citizens shall not only have access to rights provided and determined by others but equal access to a process of law-making in which the content of these rights is publicly debated and decided upon. From this perspective political rights should be considered the normative core of democratic citizenship.

As outlined above, according to the principle of non-discrimination EU citizenship entitles its holder to be treated as a national citizen in the respective state. By relating to national citizens, the right to equal treatment constitutes a relative status of equality for EU citizens: relative to the level of protection in the respective member state. With regard to substance this status is ambivalent: it guarantees equal treatment in the national domain but allows for unequal levels of protection on a European scale.[15] Arguments in defence of the logic of horizontal integration frequently stress that this arrangement does not stretch commitments of solidarity too far. Since the main content is not a complete scheme of political status and social protection, EU citizenship remains substantially thin, but this is interpreted as a strength rather than a weakness: EU citizenship is interpreted as a 'procedural citizenship' that entitles its holder to nothing more (but also nothing less) than access to the variety of 'communitarian' solidarity arrangements existent in the different member states (de Witte 2015: 130–9; Bellamy 2019).

The weakness comes to the fore, though, when we shift our attention to the normative core of democratic citizenship: political rights. In the European citizenship constellation political rights for EU citizens are made dependent on residency without demanding naturalisation. This is, so far, a remarkable normative transformation. But the shift to a residence-based principle of access to political rights is not applied 'all the way down': EU citizenship entitles voting rights for communal and European, but not national elections.[16] It is obvious that under these conditions EU citizenship is not a full status of political empowerment: for those who move it remains an entitlement to protection defined by others, that is, the national citizens. Without national voting rights the moving EU citizen has only very limited possibilities of co-authoring precisely those laws that substantially underpin their status according to the non-discrimination principle. The

---

[15] As can currently be observed this concerns social rights but also affects civil and political rights (Granger 2018: 182–7).
[16] Access to political rights on the national level presupposes naturalisation, that is, the acquisition of national citizenship (for a critical discussion see Bauböck 2019).

fact that they keep their national voting rights in the country of origin is a rather weak compensation, in particular for long-term residents, and perpetuates the (self-)perception as foreigner rather than fellow citizen.

In principle EU citizenship is supposed to constitute a direct – vertical – link to the EU's institutions. But the logic of horizontal integration and its national framing of access to full social and political rights severely hinders a distinctive identification with a European citizenship status, being anchored in a pan-European political space and related to a European society of shared values and practices. In particular when it comes to changing the 'rules of the game', that is, the Treaties as the EU's formal 'constitution', it is clear that EU citizens are not in the driver's seat. So far EU law lacks a proper balance between the economic and the social, but any attempt to change this faces considerable barriers. In the current institutional system which gives dominant power to the Council, that is, national governments with an incentive to play off allegedly national interests against each other, a transnational coding of social and political conflicts remains difficult. Even European Parliament election procedures favour national cleavages. The European Parliament (EP) is a supranational parliament but it is elected through twenty-seven different national voting procedures. These procedures are dependent on national election laws and differ immensely (Shaw 2015). As a consequence, it hard to get traction for European issues in the largely separate national debates and the emergence of a political identity as European fellow citizens is severely hindered. This affects the effectiveness of EU citizens' political rights as equals.[17]

Moving beyond the Divide: Towards Democratic Minimum Standards

If and how a 'citizen paradigm' can and should be applied to the EU is a deeply contested question, and is related to far-reaching debates about the EU's character as a supranational polity.[18] Historically, at the time of

---

[17] Cf. Seubert et al. (2018). For the question of whether the EU's multiple crises have provoked a Europeanisation of (national) public discourse, see Grande and Kriesi (2016).

[18] Currently different 'grand theories', such as EU demoicracy (in intergovernmental or transnational variants) or European federalism are competing to tackle this challenge (see e.g. Nicolaidis 2012; Cheneval and Schimmelfennig 2013; Fossum and Jachtenfuchs 2017). Compared to the traditional state model, the EU has weaker coercive means, weaker socialising ability, an inconsistent system of territorial control, no sovereign tax base and no competence in fiscal matters (Neyer 2012: 20–2; Eriksen 2014: 74–6). For the distinction and defence of a 'citizen paradigm' versus a 'market paradigm' see Kochenov (2013).

founding, nation-states were deeply discredited and their destructive potential still a vivid memory. European integration was considered a means of national (self)containment, of taming the nation-state and making it 'safe for democracy' (Eriksen 2014: 45). 'The traumatic experiences of the interwar period and of the Second World War had rendered painfully clear the extent to which the political fortunes of European states were dependent on a stable continental, if not international political order' (Menéndez and Olsen 2020: 34). The internal market was considered a means to this end, but not an end in itself. Seen in this light, the project of European integration was never only an economic but from the beginning also a normative project with a greater goal in mind. It aimed at fundamental innovation in the realm of political relations: a federation of states, overcoming their historical hostilities by voluntarily increasing their economic and social interdependencies, opening up their borders and reaching out to connect democracy and human rights on a new level of political organisation.

By detaching entitlement to rights from privileges of national membership and collective identity EU citizenship exemplifies the disaggregation of different dimensions of citizenship which have previously been closely related. This might indicate a decline of the traditional, unitary conception of citizenship, but it might also give rise to new modalities of political membership. Nevertheless, in its current state the European citizenship regime raises concerns that it will undercut former levels of democratic empowerment and protection. Protagonists of intergovernmental variants of demoicracy argue that a multilevel governance system like the EU should not be measured along the same standards as a unitary nation-state (see e.g. Bellamy 2019).[19] This suggests that a European citizenship status cannot be modelled after the traditional nation-state example at all. But one might doubt that the national, unitary model can easily be applied to a supranational entity like the EU, and nevertheless reach out to determine basic democratic standards that a transnational citizenship status must meet in order not to undermine the basic ideas of political and social equality – standards that distinguish a transnational citizenship regime from a regional rights regime in general.

From a historical perspective, a unitary citizenship status became the dominant model of membership, although created, more often than not, through a process of nationalisation which was repressive, if not violent in character (Kymlicka 2009: 61–6). The doctrine of nationalism undergirded state efforts to create and reinforce a homogenous national citizenry, bringing

---

[19] In contrast, integrationist accounts take the democratic and social state, as it has developed in the postwar era, as a benchmark and complain that EU citizenship is still torn between two possible articulations: 'proto-citizenship' and supranationality (Menéndez and Olsen 2019: 69–74).

together and finally substituting more diverse loyalties of corporations, associations and communities. This was, no doubt, an ambivalent project, but it contributed at the same time to establishing the normative ideal of political and social equality which has become the hallmark of modern democratic citizenship (Habermas 1992: 634–5; Fahrmeir 2007). The nationalisation of citizenship operated as a catalyst for processes of democratisation, overcoming old corporate structures and creating a new sense of togetherness as 'peoplehood' (Smith 2015).

The unitary form of citizenship is still predominantly taken to be the norm. But in multilevel, federal constellations like the EU a multilevel form of citizenship seems more appropriate. 'Multilevel citizenship' is characterised as a compound citizenship where citizens are members of different levels of political organisation, which coexist on a given territory and have, to some extent, autonomy.[20] In this constellation, rights might indeed vary across the constituent units, in relation to social, economic and cultural diversity (Maas 2017: 648; Fossum and Jachtenfuchs 2017; van den Brink 2019). It is thus an important normative task to distinguish acceptable from unacceptable rights diversity. If differentiated forms of citizenship are considered more appropriate for multilevel polities like the EU, the question is about the threshold which helps to determine whether differentiated forms of citizenship are still democratic in any qualified sense. This is a particular challenge under conditions of heterogeneity and power asymmetry (which has increased even more since EU enlargement). The EU in particular proclaims being 'united in diversity' – a self-set standard which in the wake of multiple crises has raised considerable doubts (Bauböck 2017). In particular the economic and financial crises have revealed deep divisions between advocates of austerity politics and debt-relief, and the smouldering rule of law crisis exposes a severe misrecognition of the EU's fundamental values. In this situation 'differentiated integration' (if not disintegration) seems to be a more likely scenario than deeper integration, and an even more differentiated form of European citizenship appears as the necessary consequence.[21]

---

[20] Maas characterises multilevel citizenship as a type of citizenship which encompasses federal citizenship (within states) and supranational citizenship (beyond states) (Maas 2017: 657). What distinguished a citizenship regime from a human rights regime are some means in involving individual citizens in decision-making, that is, own legislation and eventually also a sense of peoplehood (ibid: 646).

[21] Differentiated integration is for instance proposed as one of five scenarios in the *White paper on the Future of Europe* (issued by the European Commission in March 2017): Scenario 3 'Those who want more do more' (<https://digital-strategy.ec.europa.eu/en/news/white-paper-future-europe-avenues-unity-eu-27> (last accessed 8 December 2022); see also Blockmans 2014).

But any plea for differentiation raises the question of the common ground, the shared basis, on which all member states and citizens commonly stand. For European citizenship, and for any transnational form of citizenship more generally, this provokes the question of how much (substantial) differentiation a citizenship regime can tolerate without abandoning the normative basis of equality enshrined in an idea of 'constitutional citizenship' that member states are supposed to share (Shaw 2020).

In the national context 'citizenship as equality' has arguably become the dominant representation of what citizenship means today – but this norm has also been challenged, as philosophical and political debates about 'justice and the politics of difference' demonstrate (Young 1990). Even though related to a different context, insights from these discussions are also relevant in the European realm where the institution of a supranational citizenship is still under construction and the standards of equality largely contested. A major point in philosophical debates about balancing equality and diversity is to distinguish between two categories of differences: on the one hand variations of social practices and institutions that are expressions of the diversity of human forms of life, and, on the other hand, differences that are an effect of power asymmetries and oppression – such as effected by class, race and gender (Fraser 1997: 203–4; Young 2002). With regard to the egalitarian ideals of democracy, the first category of differences can be affirmed for the sake of pluralism, while the second category should be eliminated for the sake of justice.

Can this distinction between two categories of differences – differences that are related to pluralism and differences that are the result of injustices – also be applied to a politics of diversity in the EU? In a multilevel constellation with huge heterogeneity, drawing this line is certainly much more difficult and in its concrete consequences a matter of political debate. So far the EU is hardly appropriately addressed as a context of justice. Under conditions of considerable wealth disparities and in the absence of sufficient EU-wide solidarity arrangements, the opportunities to profit from market integration are unequally distributed. This allows the relatively well-off countries to take advantage of economic exchange and the right to free movement without symmetrically bearing the costs.[22] Since in the EU

---

[22] Interestingly political debates on 'welfare tourism' and 'abuse' of free movement rights are dominated by the perspective of receiving countries and tend to leave the social costs of free movement for sending countries aside. This leads, for example, to the proposal that countries with high inflow of EU migrants ought to be compensated for their additional costs (Sangiovanni 2013: 240). The social costs of moving for sending countries – labour drainage, 'care-chains' and 'EU-orphans' – are hardly counted (for the precarious situation of migrant care workers see e.g. Luppi et al. 2018).

economic and social spheres are decoupled, 'protection of diversity' (e.g. how 'we' organise 'our' welfare state) can well mean conservation of power asymmetries and maintaining or increasing inequality.[23] On the other hand, the project of 'making equal citizens' is surrounded by continuous contestation (Maas 2017: 664). It is discredited as the 'Eurocrat's dream' (Chalmers et al. 2017) – a top-down approach to which citizens rightfully react with suspicion when they feel they are rhetorically addressed without ever being involved in any serious way. The critique misses the point, though, under conditions in which the rhetoric of diversity is mainly in the mouths of the more powerful actors who profit from the status quo, that is, from maintaining a national framing of justice. Diversity might be protected wherever it does not endanger equality. However, collective action and 'harmonisation' are required when basic freedoms and equality of European citizens are at stake.

Take a recent example: the demand for differentiation with reference to the concept of 'constitutional identity'. This concept has gained increased popularity as a juridical and discursive means for claiming a right to deviate from the common ground of European law. Developed as a doctrine to shield areas of the national legal systems from the influence of European law, the question is whether it has the potential to protect or rather to weaken if not undermine the process of European integration. The concept of 'constitutional identity' made room for Great Britain (and Poland) to opt-out of the EU Charter of Fundamental Rights on the basis of arguments of constitutional pluralism.[24] Yet, a conflict over the binding character of a Charter of Fundamental Rights is certainly not a minor issue – it goes to the core of the EU's 'constitutional identity' itself. With reference to a similar reasoning, in France the republican principle of 'laïcité' is considered part of its 'constitutional identity' although a strict application is arguably in conflict with the basic religious freedoms of its Muslim population.[25] Reference to 'constitutional

---

[23] A constellation characterised by an imbalance of power, giving rise to critiques of the EU as a neo-imperial actor (Zielonka 2015).

[24] The Charter of Fundamental Rights was a result of the Convention procedure of 2002/03 and was originally meant to become part of a constitution. After this attempt had failed the Charter nevertheless came into effect through the Lisbon Treaty Treaty, Art. 6(1) Treaty on European Union (TEU), thereby becoming a binding source of primary law.

[25] Cf. Laborde (2008). A recent escalation of the 'affair du foulard' was the debate on whether mothers wearing headscarves should be allowed to accompany their children on school trips (<https://www.lemonde.fr/les-decodeurs/article/2019/09/25/pourquoi-les-meres-voilees-ont-bien-le-droit-de-participer-aux-sorties-scolaires_6012998_4355770.html> (last accessed 8 December 2022)).

identity' also plays an important role in landmark EU rulings of the German Constitutional Court (BVerfG) in its decade-old scuffle about competing competencies with the ECJ. In the German context 'constitutional identity' is supposed to be applied as a purely legal concept (the BVerfG understands itself as a *'Grundrechtsgericht'*), but a certain extent of indeterminacy and arbitrariness is unavoidable, as critics warn, which makes the concept inherently problematic.[26] No doubt, the protection of diversity is an important issue in a Union with different legal traditions and socio-economic paths of development, cultural traditions and historical experiences. But these examples give rise to the concern that what might in fact be protected with reference to 'constitutional identity' as protection of diversity are more powerful members over weaker ones and societal majorities over minority voices. This raises doubt that the concept of 'constitutional identity' can plausibly function as a normative guideline to determine the space for legitimate diversity within a general idea of equal European citizenship.

Another candidate for this task might be the concept of 'instrumental differentiation'. In a context of huge heterogeneity, it aims at restricting diversity to those issues that do not undermine citizen's equality in any serious way and are rather pragmatic in character (Bellamy 2019: 188–93). This could probably work if we were able to presuppose a simple consensus on what aspects of the integration process count as 'instrumental' and which ones touch normative essentials. While setting the height of one's own railway platforms might be an example for 'instrumental differentiation', as Richard Bellamy suggests, not participating in the euro is certainly not (Bellamy 2019: 189).[27] Taking part in the common currency comes along with benefits but also duties which are linked to the core of the EU's economic constitution. It is rightfully criticised that the stability-criteria in the Treaties have a quasi-constitutional status and are thus shielded from political contestation (Grimm 2016). But this should rather be an argument

---

[26] Fabbrini and Sajó (2019: 467–9). Since the recent escalation caused by the ruling on the Public Sector Purchase Program (PSPP) of the European Central Bank (ECB) in May 2020, the BVerfG finds itself in the delicate situation of needing to make clear why its proclaimed prerogative of checking European primary law differs from claims to do the same, for example, in Hungary or Poland (Goldmann 2020: 49–53).

[27] Bellamy distinguishes between instrumental, constitutional and legislative differentiation which he considers a means of managing diversity. Referring to de facto opt-outs in the Treaties his analytical distinctions seem rather arbitrary though: as an example of 'constitutional differentiation' he names the 'Danish Protocol' prohibiting the purchase of second homes by non-Danes next to the non-participation in the European Policy on Defense and Security (ibid: 191).

for addressing the political vacuum than downplaying their importance as a technicality. What could be understood from the start (but was not articulated aloud) is that a common currency without a common financial and economic policy is bound to fail. Thus, a common currency is a step towards more political integration in the future. Those who didn't want to participate in this endeavour might have understood this quite well. Not participating was apparently indeed taken as a minor issue, a possibly temporary deviation or a tolerated peculiarity of a few individual actors, when in fact the introduction of a common currency was a material 'constitutional moment'. It is a major example of 'integration by stealth', a process developing behind the back of the citizens, creating systemic interdependencies but without being publicly debated and argued for.[28]

A prominent caricature portrays the EU as a potential 'super-state', promoting standardisation, ambitious to regulate every single detail of everyday life. The truth in this picture is the pervasive systemic dynamic related to economic and monetary integration, backed up by substantial Treaty provisions (i.e. the stability criteria). This narrative tends to ignore, though, that the EU, when it comes to the democratic core of its constitution, is rather weak. It cannot act in policy areas where it is not given the power to act by the member states, and this paralysis not only produces considerable problems of collective action in various policy fields but also serious injustices. In those dimensions that are central for democratic citizenship the EU rather has too few competencies than too many. If one does not want to dismiss the talk of 'Union Citizenship' as pure decoration and legitimation politics and prefers to take the normative promise of democratic citizenship seriously, defining (and protecting!) some kind of 'democratic minimum' for EU citizens is crucial. Following James Bohman, 'democratic minimum' refers to the capacity of political agents to initiate deliberation which ought to be entrenched in various basic rights. It presupposes the 'normative powers' to publicly challenge the rules of cooperation and thus captures the radical implication of (only temporarily domesticable) constituent power. In principle normative powers transcend delimitations of already constituted demoi (Bohman 2007: 93–7).

---

[28] Of course, there might be good reasons to be sceptical about the whole project of introducing a common currency among states that differ immensely in their socio-economic development. But leaving this aside, being a member and not taking part is not a technicality but still a way of free riding: profiting from trade facilitations by avoiding exchange rates with a lot of partners who themselves have given up their currency while keeping one's own. Had everybody insisted on keeping their own, an economic area with easy trade conditions due to a single currency simply wouldn't exist.

The 'democratic minimum' thus incorporates the reflexive loop mentioned above regarding political rights: empowerment to participate in a process of law-making as a precondition to substantiate all other rights. At the same time, this loop abstracts from (and questions any) concrete institutionalisation. This constitutes another dilemma: for democracy to be sustained the 'democratic minimum' is required, but sustaining democracy is itself dependent on some *'minimum institutional requirement'*, including those basic rights that guarantee the 'democratic minimum' in the first place (Eriksen and Fossum 2018; italics in original).

In the heterogeneous EU context, strengthening the connection between EU citizenship and fundamental rights (as laid down in the Charter of Fundamental Rights of the European Union) would be a first step to support this minimum institutional requirement. Since, as argued above, free movement alone is not sufficient to constitute citizenship and horizontal non-discrimination guarantees only a relative status of equality, establishing a robust vertical link between EU citizens and EU institutions is crucial. Otherwise, the current set-up can rightly be criticised for reintroducing a connection between citizenship and economic status that the democratic welfare state of the postwar era was supposed to even out. It will continually be criticised for constituting an ideological frame, which sits uneasily with the normative promise of democratic citizenship inherited from the national context, including a redistributive dimension as the basis of substantial citizenship rights (Kochenov 2013, 2017: 28).

Conclusion

The introduction of a European citizenship status was supposed to strengthen the EU's legitimacy and address its democratic deficit. While its purpose has always been to some extent contested, the further development of EU citizenship got stuck in dilemmas of rivalling legitimatory demands. Uneasily positioned between the economic and political logic of free movement and non-discrimination, EU citizenship's democratic determination is today more uncertain than ever and in need of substantial backup.

The advancement of market integration induced and at the same time restricted the evolution of a European citizen status. Intimately linked to mobility it contributed to opening up national boundaries and, via the non-discrimination principle, facilitated access to rights on the basis of residency rather than nationality. But the genesis in market integration caused frictions that have not appropriately been addressed until today. In order to substantiate a European citizen status, the EU needs to complement its fragmented constitution and be strengthened in matters of fundamental rights protection. This has to go hand in hand with political empowerment on the basis of a 'democratic minimum', fostering social cohesion on the national and supranational level.[29] The EU's political makeup continues to be a site of contestation with centripetal and centrifugal forces tearing in different directions. In this situation deepening and enlarging citizenship rights might not work well together. But while balancing equality and diversity is important in a multilevel polity, setting a core of normative standards at EU level is crucial to ensure the normative purpose of the Union in a comprehensive sense. The protection of diversity must not undermine the 'democratic minimum' of European citizenship. The EU has already laid down normative essentials which new members have to accept – the problem is that it does not guarantee them once the step inside is taken.[30] Following the idea of a reflexive loop implied in the 'democratic minimum', standards shall be open to debate, subject to a process of public deliberation which addresses European citizens as political agents, as co-legislators of commonly binding norms.

In light of scenarios of differentiated integration, the future of EU citizenship seems to face a choice between a weak, integrated status for all or a stronger differentiated status for some. Both alternatives have their particular risks, also depending on whether they are temporary or permanent derogations. Substantiated citizenship rights among a 'core' that moves towards deeper cooperation in economic and social policies could, if a positive example, increase the motivation for those outside to join, thus saving the idea of a democratic transnational citizenship status from being hollowed out. Instead of entering into always refined reflections about exceptions, differentiations and opt-outs, European citizens need to engage

---

[29] As long as, for example, taxation remains a national prerogative and minimum EU taxation rules are missing, states will play off 'national interests' against each other and use tax dumping to attract businesses. Under these conditions a common European tax policy which tracks EU citizen's interests equally is impossible. For an instructive discussion of models of social protection for a multilevel polity such as the EU, see Claassen et al. (2019).

[30] Apart from the overarching Art. 2 TEU which encompasses the Copenhagen Criteria, this is mainly the Charter of Fundamental Rights – to be complemented by a Democracy Charter (see Nemitz and Ehm 2019). For tackling the rule of law crisis see the EP's demand for an EU mechanism on democracy, the rule of law and fundamental rights. This should be an annual independent review which assesses, on an equal footing, the compliance of all member states with the values stipulated in Art. 2 TEU (<https://www.europarl.europa.eu/legislative-train/theme-area-of-justice-and-fundamental-rights/file-eu-mechanism-on-democracy-the-rule-of-law-and-fundamental-rights> (last accessed date 8 December 2022)).

in a catching-up debate about their common interests and commitments, in particular across the political and social conflicts that their fragmented economic constitution produces.

References

Abraham, K., Spletzer, J. and Harper, M. (2010) *Labor in the New Economy*. Chicago: University of Chicago Press.

Alemanno, Alberto (2022) Unboxing the Conference on the Future of Europe and its Democratic Raison d'être. *European Law Journal*, 26: 484–508.

Azoulai, Loic (2017) Transfiguring European Citizenship: From Member State Territory to Union Territory. In Kochenov, D. (ed.) *EU Citizenship and Federalism*. Cambridge and New York: Cambridge University Press, pp. 178–203.

Barnard, Catherine (2010) *The Substantial Law of the EU: The Four Freedoms*, 3rd edn. Oxford and New York: Oxford University Press.

Bauböck, Rainer (2017) Still United in Diversity? The State of the Union Conference, 2017, Address, <https://hdl.handle.net/1814/67448> (last accessed 2 December 2022).

Bauböck, Rainer (ed.) (2019) *Debating EU Citizenship*. Springer Open.

Bellamy, Richard (2019) *A Republican Europe of States*. Cambridge and New York: Cambridge University Press.

Benhabib, Seyla (2006) *Another Cosmopolitanism*. Oxford and New York: Oxford University Press.

Benhabib, Seyla (2016) Dämmerung der Souveränität oder das Aufstreben kosmopolitischer Normen? Eine Neubetrachtung von Staatsbürgerschaft in Zeiten des Umbruchs. In *Kosmopolitismus ohne Illusionen*. Berlin: Suhrkamp, pp. 160–90.

Besson, Samantha and Utzinger, André (2008) Towards European Citizenship. *Journal of Social Philosophy*, 39(2): 185–208.

Blockmans, Steven (2014) *Differentiated Integration in the EU. From the Inside Looking Out*. Brussels: Center for European Policy Studies (CEPS).

Bohman, James (2007) *Democracy across Borders: From Demos to Demoi*. Cambridge, MA and London: MIT Press.

Buckel, Sonja (2013) *'Welcome to Europe': Die Grenzen des europäischen Migrationsrechts*. Bielefeld: transcript.

Bude, Heinz and Staab, Philipp (2016) *Kapitalismus und Ungleichheit*. Frankfurt a.M. and New York: Campus.

Chalmers, D., Jachtenfuchs, M. and Joerges, C. (2017) *The End of the Eurocrats' Dream. Adjusting to European Diversity*. Cambridge: Cambridge University Press.

Cheneval, Francis and Schimmelfennig, Frank (2013) The Case for Demoicracy in the European Union. *Journal of Common Market Studies*, 51(2): 334–50.

Claassen, R., Gerbrandy, A., Princen, S. and Segers, M. (2019) Four Models of Protecting Citizenship and Social Rights in Europe: Conclusion to the Special Issue 'Rethinking the European Social Market Economy'. *Journal of Common Market Studies*, 57(1): 159–74.

De Witte, Floris (2015) *Justice in the EU. The Emergence of Transnational Solidarity.* Oxford: Oxford University Press.

Eleftheriadis, Pavlos (2014) The Content of EU Citizenship. *German Law Journal,* 15(5): 777–96.

Eriksen, Erik O. (2014) *The Normativity of the European Union.* Basingstoke: Palgrave.

Eriksen, Erik O. and Fossum, Jan-Erik (2018) Deliberation Constrained: An Increasingly Segmented European Union. In Bächtinger, A., Dryzek, J., Mansbridge, J. and Warren, M. (eds) *The Oxford Handbook of Deliberative Democracy.* Oxford: Oxford University Press.

Everson, M. (1995) The Legacy of the Market Citizen. In Shaw, J. and More, G. (eds) *New Legal Dynamics of European Union.* Oxford: Clarendon Press, pp. 73–89.

Fabbrini, F. and Sajó, A. (2019) The Dangers of Constitutional Identity. *European Law Journal,* 25: 457–73.

Fahrmeir, Andreas (2007) *Citizenship: The Rise and Fall of a Modern Concept.* New Haven and London: Yale University Press.

Ferrera, Maurizio (2016) The Contentious Politics of Hospitality. Intra-EU Mobility and Social Rights. *European Law Journal,* 22(6); 791–805.

Fossum, J. E. and Jachtenfuchs, M. (2017) Federal Challenges and Challenges to Federalism. Insights from the EU and Federal States. *Journal of European Public Policy,* 24(4): 467–85.

Fraser, Nancy (1997) *Justice Interruptus.* New York: Routledge.

Goldmann, Matthias (2020) As Darkness Deepens: The Right to be Forgotten in the Context of Authoritarian Constitutionalism. *German Law Journal,* 21: 45–54.

Grande, E. and Kriesi. H.-P. (2016) Introduction: European Integration and the Challenge of Politicisation. In Huetter, S., Grande, E. and Kriesi, H.-P. (eds) *Politicising Europe. Integration and Mass Politics.* Cambridge: Cambridge University Press, pp. 3–31.

Granger, Marie-Pierre (2018) The Protection of Civil Rights and Liberties and the Transformation of Union Citizenship. In Seubert, S. et al. (eds) *Moving Beyond Barriers.* Cheltenham and Northampton, MA: Edward Elgar.

Grimm, Dieter (2016) Die demokratischen Kosten der Konstitutionalisierung. Der Fall Europa. In *Europa ja - aber welches?* München: C. H. Beck.

Habermas, Jürgen (1992) *Faktizität und Geltung.* Frankfurt a.M.: Suhrkamp.

Hennette, S., Piketty, T., Sacriste, G. and Vauchez, A. (2017) *Für ein anderes Europa. Vertrag zur Demokratisierung der Eurozone.* München: C. H. Beck.

Kadelbach, Stefan (2011) Union Citizenship. In Bogdandy, Armin and Bast, Jürgen (eds) *Principles of European Union Law.* Oxford: Hart Publishing, pp. 443–78.

Kochenov, Dimitry (2013) The Citizenship Paradigm. University of Groningen Faculty of Law Research Paper Series No. 08/2013, <http://ssrn.com/abstract=2274404> (last accessed 2 December 2022).

Kochenov, Dimitry (2017) On Tiles and Pillars: EU Citizenship as a Federal Denominator. In Kochenov, D. (ed.) *EU Citizenship and Federalism. The Role of Rights.* Cambridge: Cambridge University Press, pp. 3–82.

Kostakopoulou, Dora (2008) The Evolution of European Union Citizenship. *European Political Science,* 7(3): 285–95.

Kymlicka, Will (2009) *Multicultural Odysseys*. Oxford: Oxford University Press.
Laborde, Cécile (2008) *Critical Republicanism: The Hijab Controversy and Political Philosophy*. Oxford: Oxford University Press.
Lessenich, Stephan and Mau, Steffen (2005) Reziprozität und Wohlfahrtsstaat. In Adloff, Frank and Mau, Steffen (eds) *Vom Geben und Nehmen. Zur Soziologie der Reziprozität*. Frankfurt a.M. and New York: Campus.
Luppi, M., Oomkens, R. and Gal, J. (2018) Precarious Migrant Care Workers in Italy, Israel and the UK. In Knijn, T. and Naldini, M. (eds) *Gender and Generational Division in EU Citizenship*. Cheltenham and Northampton, MA: Edward Elgar, pp. 140–60.
Maas, Willem (2007) *Creating European Citizens*. Lanham and Plymouth: Rowman & Littlefield.
Maas, Willem (2017) Multilevel Citizenship. In Shachar, A. et al. (eds) *The Oxford Handbook of Citizenship*. Oxford: Oxford University Press, pp. 643–68.
Majone, Giandomenico (2005) *Dilemmas of European Integration: The Ambiguities and Pitfalls of Integration by Stealth*. Oxford: Oxford University Press.
Marshall, Thomas H. (1992) *Citizenship and Social Class*. London: Pluto Press.
Menéndez, Agustín José and Olsen, Espen D. H. (2020) *Challenging European Citizenship. Ideas an Realities in Contrast*. Cham: Palgrave Macmillan.
Naldini, Manuela and Knijn, Trudie (2018) *Gender and Generational Division in EU Citizenship*. Cheltenham and Northampton, MA: Edward Elgar.
Nemitz, P. and Ehm, F. (2019) Strengthening EU Democracy and its Resilience against Autocracy: Daring more Democracy and a European Democracy Charter. Research Paper in Law, College of Europe, Brügge.
Neyer, Jürgen (2012) *The Justification of Europe*. Oxford: Oxford University Press.
Nicolaidis, Kalypso (2012) The Idea of European Demoicracy. In Dickson, Julie and Eleftheriadis, Pavlos (eds) *Philosophical Foundations of European Union Law*. Oxford: Oxford University Press, pp. 247–74.
O'Brien, Charlotte (2013) I Trade, Therefore I Am: Legal Personhood in the European Union. *Common Market Law Review*, 50: 1643–84.
Offe, Claus (2013) Participatory Inequality in the Austerity State: A Supply Side Approach. In Streeck, Wolfgang and Schäfer, Armin (eds) *Politics in the Age of Austerity*. Cambridge: Polity, pp. 196–218.
Offe, Claus (2015) *Europe Entrapped*. Cambridge and Malden: Polity Press.
Sangiovanni, Andrea (2013) Solidarity in the European Union. *Oxford Journal of Legal Studies*, 33(2): 213–41.
Scharpf, Fritz W. (2009) Legitimacy in the Multilevel European Polity. *European Political Science Review*, 1(2): 173–204.
Schiek, Dagmar (2017) Perspectives on Social Citizenship in the EU. In Kochenov, D. (ed.) *EU Citizenship and Federalism. The Role of Rights*. Cambridge: Cambridge University Press, pp. 341–70.
Schmidt, Susanne K. (2018) *The European Court of Justice and the Policy Process*. Oxford: Oxford University Press.
Seeleib-Kaiser, Martin. (2018) Citizenship, Europe and Social Rights. In Seubert, S. et al. (eds) *Moving Beyond Barriers. Prospects for EU Citizenship*. Cheltenham and Northampton, MA: Edward Elgar, pp. 158–77.

Seubert, Sandra (2019) Shifting Boundaries of Membership: The Politicisation of Free Movement as a Challenge for EU citizenship. *European Law Journal*, 14 December, DOI: 10.1111/eulj.12346, 1–13.

Seubert, Sandra (2021) Reframing Political Space. Pro-European Mobilisation and the Enactment of European Citizenship. *Citizenship Studies*, 25(1): 72–89.

Seubert, Sandra, Eberl, Oliver and Gaus, Daniel (2018) Political Inequality and Democratic Empowerment in the European Union: The Role of the European Parliament. In Levi-Faur, David and van Waarden, Frans (eds) *Democratic Empowerment in the European Union*. Cheltenham: Edward Elgar Publishing Limited, pp. 40–62.

Shaw, Jo (2007) *The Transformation of Citizenship in the European Union: Electoral Rights and the Restructuring of Political Space*. Cambridge: Cambridge University Press.

Shaw, Jo (2015) European Added Value of a Reform of the EU Electoral Law. Making EU Elections More European and Improving EU Democratic Legitimacy and Governance. Research paper for the Directorate General for Parliamentary Research Services, European Parliament, pp. 2–116.

Shaw, Jo (2020) *The People in Question. Citizens and Constitutions in Uncertain Times*. Bristol: Bristol University Press.

Shuibhne, Niam Nic (2010) The Resilience of EU Market Citizenship. *Common Market Law Review*, 47(6): 1597–1628.

Shuibhne, Niam Nic (2015) Limits Rising, Duties Ascending: The Changing Legal Shape of Union Citizenship. *Common Market Review*, 52(4): 889–937.

Smith, Rogers M. (2015) *Political Peoplehood*. Chicago and London: University of Chicago Press.

Soysal, Yasemin (1994) *Limits of Citizenship: Migrants and Postnational Membership in Europe*. Chicago: University of Chicago Press.

Streeck, Wolfgang (2013) *Gekaufte Zeit*. Berlin: Suhrkamp.

Van den Brink, Martijn (2019) The Promises and Drawbacks of European Union Citizenship for a Polycentric Union. In van Zeben, Josephine and Bobic, Ana (eds) *Polycentricity in the European Union*. Cambridge: Cambridge University Press, pp. 163–85.

Weiler, Joseph (1998) To Be a European Citizen: Eros and Civilization. Working Paper Series in European Studies, University of Wisconsin-Madison.

White, Jonathan (2013) Emergency Europe. *Political Studies*, 13 September, DOI: 10.1111/1467-9248.12072.

Young, Iris M. (1990) *Justice and the Politics of Difference*. Princeton: Princeton University Press.

Young, Iris M. (2002) *Inclusion and Democracy*. Oxford: Oxford University Press.

Zielonka, Jan (2015) The Uses and Misuses of the Imperial Paradigm in the Study of European Integration. In Behr, Hartmut and Stivachtis, Yannis A. (eds) *Revisiting the European Union as Empire*. London and New York: Routledge, pp. 45–58.

FIVE

European Capitalism without European Democracy? Democratic Dilemmas and Markets in the European Union[1]

Kathleen R. McNamara

Capitalism has long been understood to generate thorny dilemmas for democracy. Unbridled market dynamics can lead to social and economic inequalities that are in tension with democracy's ideals of equality and equal treatment for all. The historical democratic governance of markets, however, has not necessarily eased those effects, and a true version of democratic capitalism has proven elusive in national settings. Today's European Union (EU) is particularly challenged in addressing the dilemmas produced by the clash between the logic of markets and the values of democracy. While the EU is a deeply integrated single economic space where markets span national borders, the practices and processes of democracy continue to be rooted largely in the nation-state. I argue in this chapter that 'European capitalism without European democracy' is a key source of democratic dilemmas in the European order, one that has contributed to the broader challenges of the rise of anti-system and populist parties across Europe.

In assessing these dilemmas, while most EU scholarship has focused on how economic policies are themselves part of the EU's well-known democratic legitimacy deficit, I take a different approach. Instead of seeing the EU as a unique case, I situate the EU's dilemmas within the broader historical trajectory of modern nation-states, specifically, the tensions between free-market capitalism and the workings of democracy that are endemic to all national political orders. Drawing on an extensive literature in comparative

---

[1] I thank the editors and participants in this volume for their helpful comments, and acknowledge the outstanding research assistance of Makala Forster in preparing this essay.

politics, I evaluate some of the key responses that democratic nation-states have taken to meet the challenges of capitalism, namely, regulation and redistribution. I then consider what these national lessons might suggest for the EU today, highlighting the lack of redistribution in the EU context. In particular, I argue that scholars, citizens and political leaders must more directly confront the lack of electoral mechanisms of representational democracy if they wish to strengthen democratic capitalism in the EU through redistribution. Assessing the tensions and trade-offs around markets and democracy is critical to finding a sustainable path forward for the EU and its citizens.

My assessment also highlights the need to rethink the widely held conventional wisdom that market logics and political logics unfold in separate spheres, and instead, to grapple with the reality that market logics intertwine with political logics in reciprocally causal ways. While representational democracy has the potential to blunt social and economic inequality, it can also deepen it, if those politics empower only the wealthy and result in capture of governance. On the other hand, political interventions should not be seen as anathema to robust capitalism as they may actually make markets work more efficiently. These lessons about how markets are structured by, and structure, politics must be built into any conclusions about how to use a strengthened European democracy to manage European capitalism today.

The rest of the chapter proceeds as follows. I first discuss conventional approaches to the question of markets and democracy in the EU, and outline their limits. I then delve into an alternative view of how the logics of markets and democracy interact, outlining some of the key tensions that arise. The next section delineates how two key mechanisms, regulation and redistribution, have functioned at the national level to mediate the tensions between capitalism and democracy, and evaluates the degree to which they can do so at the European level. The final section highlights the necessary role of electoral politics and representation in democratising European markets through the critical missing policy area of EU redistribution, ultimately producing a more stable European polity. My preliminary assessment suggests that rather than a necessary unravelling of the European project, in the post-pandemic era, the drivers are in place to move in the direction of more robust European-level political participation and electoral competition, and thus more sustainable resolutions to the tension between European capitalism and European democracy.

Markets and Democracy in the EU

Conventional discussions about markets and democracy in the European Union have tended to overlook the role of electoral politics and representation.

Instead, they have made a deficit of democratic legitimacy, not democracy itself, the focal point of analysis and policy recommendations. While the question of legitimacy is critical, this framing has allowed us to sidestep some of the deeper tensions and trade-offs at work, particularly around the role of electoral contestation, while bracketing the immense literature on this question in national settings that might prove helpful in assessing the health of the EU's political order.

A robust discussion around the 'democratic deficit' of the EU took place following the deepening of the Maastricht Treaty in the 1990s, as the editors discuss in their introductory chapter, yet scholars examining the single market, the euro, or other economic policy and market developments tended to focus more narrowly on the concept of legitimate authority, an emphasis that has continued in the wake of the eurozone crisis (Scharpf 1999; Schmidt 2020). This was driven in part by an understanding of the EU as a governing, not representative, authority, more similar to an international organisation than a nation-state (McNamara 2018). Two arguments, in both the literature and in popular discussions, were used to refute the idea that there were serious democratic shortcomings for the EU in the area of political economy.

The first argument was that consensual decision-making around widely shared values, and uncontested policies driven by technocratic expertise, provides adequate legitimacy for the EU (Majone 1998; Moravcsik 2002), a contention roundly disputed by many (Bickerton 2011; Follesdal and Hix 2006; Mair 2006). Legitimacy is a claim to a broadly accepted principle or value that shores up the right of that political authority to rule (Weber 2009). Moreover, a legitimate political authority is one that is recognised as having the consent of its citizens for its governance. A path to legitimacy therefore might be to argue that the EU represents appropriate delegation to a technocratic set of experts who are carrying out policies that do not involve politically contestable values or choices (Moravcsik 1998). Such type of delegation has been framed as unproblematic in the example of independent central banks, that are claimed to be outside the bounds of distributional politics, although that assumption has been contested (McNamara 2002). The rejection of the EU as its own form of representational political order allows one to deftly sidestep the question of potential democratic deficits. For much of the EU's existence, it also dramatically lessened attention to the role of trade-offs and contestation in the governance of European markets, in comparison to democratic processes in the national settings (McNamara 2019b).

A second argument refuting such democratic shortcomings around the deep market integration of the EU contends that, as with international organisations, member state citizens can directly petition their national leaders about EU governance, obviating the need for direct representation or EU level contestation (Majone 1998; Moravcsik 2002). Indeed, a set of conventional arguments about the EU's legitimacy rests in what we could call 'democratic subsidiarity'. For most of the EU's existence, the link between markets and democracy has run primarily through the nation-state, sidestepping the EU entirely. This implicit version of subsidiarity, whereby the nation-state is assumed to be responsible for accountability for offsetting the costs and risks that come with unbridled markets, has been the dominant method of dealing with the tensions of democratic capitalism in the EU. An open and highly integrated single European market that allows for national sovereignty over welfare state policies and other market-correcting policies has been the historical bargain that underpinned the development of the European project and provided a particular type of argument for resolving the dilemma of European capitalism without European democracy.

These arguments, about technocracy and sovereignty, fall short in the reality of the EU today. The intrusiveness of the EU's governance over those who live within its borders is such that the EU should be considered a political order, not simply a site of delegated technocratic legitimacy or international organisation underpinned by sovereign states with their own internal democratic representation. The increasing politicisation of the EU over the past few decades is evidence of the need for the EU to go beyond its foundational legitimation processes (de Wilde et al. 2016; Hooghe and Marks 2009; Kriesi 2016).

Instead, as this volume asserts, the EU should be conceptualised as its own political order: an innovative and consequential form of political organisation that exercises significant political authority over the citizens of its member states (Hix 2018; McNamara 2015). The EU decisively shapes everyday life in Europe, in areas ranging from monetary policy to economic regulation, to agriculture, to environmental and social policies, to anti-discrimination policies. Not only has authority over internal matters been transferred, but the EU has also been given authority to act externally on behalf of its members – acting as a unified foreign policy actor in a number of areas including international trade negotiations (Hill et al. 2017; Smith 2017). On the macroeconomic side, the creation of the single currency and transfer of monetary policy authority to the European Central Bank for the nineteen countries that adopted the euro raised the stakes on the democratic shortcomings of the EU. The legitimation of the EU's monetary policy governance, and after the eurozone crisis, fiscal governance has been deeply challenged, negating the notion that citizens are best protected from the tumult of markets when central banks are independent from politics, obviating the need for direct national governmental control over decision-making (McNamara 2002; Tucker 2019).

Yet even with the multiple and ongoing intersecting migration, eurozone and Brexit crises that have buffeted the EU in recent years, the primary reaction of European leaders has not been to unravel the Union, but rather to deepen and extend European authority across various policy arenas. In tandem, and not unexpectedly, there has been a dramatic increase in the levels of 'contestation and politicisation regarding the shape and form of the European political order' (Bremberg and Norman in this volume). Thus, grappling with the democratic processes and practices in the EU remains a vital task, one increasing in importance as EU governance, and particularly for our purposes, market deepening, continues to grow.

Markets and Politics through a Comparative Historical Lens

A simple definition of democracy is a good starting point to navigate the dilemmas inherent in the ways in which markets and democracy interact in the EU today. Noting that there are many types and institutional configurations of democracy across time and place, Schmitter and Karl offer a helpful general approach to democracy: 'Modern political democracy is a system of governance in which rulers are held accountable for their actions in the public realm by citizens, acting indirectly through the competition and cooperation of their elected representatives' (Schmitter and Karl 1991: 4). This system of governance expresses itself in specific sets of ideas and practices around democracy, even as it is also found in formal institutions. Those include political representation, accountability and participation by citizens, and likewise dovetails with constitutionalism, rule of law and a sense of sovereign control in the international realm, all elements of European democracy taken up by other chapters in this volume.

In the case of the EU, these conceptions and practices of democracy constitute multiple and overlapping claims, reflecting the varieties of democracy across the EU member states themselves. But the juxtaposition of democracy and capitalism creates a host of particular challenges beyond the tensions inherent in democracy itself. In the case of the interaction between markets and democracy, the historical experiences of European states provide a very helpful lens with which to evaluate the EU's record. These national experiences suggest the value of representation in electoral democracy as the mechanism for easing the key tensions of European capitalism without European democracy. Indeed, today's EU member states have all, to one degree or another, used the mechanisms of elections and political parties internally to domestically mediate the non-democratic nature of markets and the destabilising impacts they have on citizens. It is therefore electoral democracy and representation that is the focus of this chapter's assessment of how to manage the tensions and trade-offs within the practices of the EU's mix of markets and democracy.

Accepting the premise that market integration in the EU must be evaluated through a more demanding democratic lens, one rooted in the idea of the EU as a political order in its own right, rather than relying on technocratic legitimation or sovereign delegation only, leads us to an evaluation of how national polities have dealt with the interaction of the two logics of modern capitalism and modern democracy.

Markets and Politics

Much of our common understanding of the relationship between markets and democracy is premised on the notion that they are two separate spheres, inherently in conflict with each other. Democracy is premised on the idea of equal treatment, in this view, whereas capitalism inevitably works to concentrate wealth in ways that skew away from this ideal. However, rather than seeing the two logics as necessarily conflictual or naturally separate from each other, appreciating how market logics intertwine with political logics in reciprocally causal ways provides a more realistic and fruitful approach to balancing out the dilemmas of democratic capitalism. Doing so allows us to see that the inequalities and social stratification that we assume are automatically generated from capitalism might instead need to be located as much in the workings of democracy as the markets themselves – as well as understanding that political interventions may, under the right conditions, make markets work better rather than impeding them. In this view, the political contestation that arises from a healthy democracy itself may be key in creating functional markets, rather than damaging them, echoing this volume's editors' emphasis on contestation as an intrinsic part of European democracy. Thus, the model of the EU as an elite governance system, rather than one based on democratic representation and contestation, is called into question, despite the conventional understandings of the value of democratic subsidiarity or delegated decision-making outlined above. A brief overview of the literature on democracy and capitalism in comparative political economy makes this clear.

The starting point for rejecting the false dichotomy between political and market logics is the observation that political institutions, in all their legal, administrative, symbolic, electoral and coercive capacities, provide the critical infrastructure to make capitalism work – providing information, insurance against risk and the enforcement of contracts, to name but a few elements of that infrastructure. It is no accident that capitalism and democracy have historically coincided, joined in a symbiotic if conflictual relationship (Berman 2006; Polanyi 1944). From the work of new institutional economists such as Douglas North and others who focused on the need for institutions (both political and within markets themselves), to the large literature on Varieties of Capitalism that demonstrates the ways in which states crucially support and shape market activity, a large theoretical and empirical literature makes clear how markets require politics, rather than being separate (Hall 2001; North 1991).

Directly to this point, Neil Fligstein has argued that

> the entry of countries into capitalism pushes states to develop rules about property rights (who owns what), governance structures (that determine and organize fair competition), rules of exchange and conceptions of control (status hierarchies that work to stabilize markets by privileging dominant players). (Fligstein 2002: 36)

These rules provide crucial frameworks that set actors' expectations and shared understandings, allowing for collective action, while establishing categories and classifications that do the work of making sense of these markets and what actors' roles are within them. The work that is done by this political architecture is absolutely essential for complex markets to even come into being. Politics is also a crucial underpinning for the transformation of markets, as with the move to the knowledge economy over the past three decades, a transition that was built on a set of government policies that created the capacity for firms to move into new technologies, create new types of innovative (if often risky) financial instruments and shed traditional labour relations in the process of creating the gig economy (Iversen and Soskice 2019). Thus, instead of the conventional assumption that markets and politics are two separate logics, if one views markets as they really are, embedded within the larger social and political structures of their particular time and place, we can start to see the tensions around democracy in the EU in a very new light.

A model of markets and politics as intertwined also allows us to more easily see how capitalism mediated through democratic politics can readily produce situations where powerful corporate interests use democratic processes to stabilise markets for their own gain. Rather than market actors embracing Schumpeter's trope of 'creative destruction', firms often seek to dampen competition and stabilise markets to lock in their advantages around their own market dominance (Fligstein 2002; Wu 2018). This might be through capture of regulatory processes to favour the existing firms, or predatory market practices by the corporations themselves that create barriers to entry, as has been widely reported in the tech industry's billion-dollar dominance of very few companies like Microsoft, Facebook, Apple, Amazon and Google. In addition, as market actors become wealthier, they will also seek to guard and extend that wealth through regressive tax systems that privilege both their corporate entities and their personal income and wealth. This points to the need for democracy to truly represent the needs of all its citizens in both redistributive policies and policies that make markets more truly competitive rather than structured to favour powerful actors. In this telling of the trade-offs and tensions around democracy and capitalism, we might have things backwards if we assume it is capitalism that is the problem – both democracy and capitalism need to be understood as potentially producing inequality or social stratification, 'depending on the purposeful policy decisions made by democratic governments' (Berman 2019).

If we accept my argument about the reality of intertwining of market and political logics and the potential for democracy to lock in economic equality, what specific policies might make EU markets 'democratic' in a way that produces better outcomes for the majority of citizens, while protecting the most vulnerable? At the national level, there are two main categories of activities that shape whether a particular system of governance around a capitalist system is democratic in this way: regulation and redistribution. These activities can be thought of as types of democratic practices on their own, if they are done in a way that addresses the needs of the citizenry broadly understood, rather than targeted to a small group of powerful actors or interests. I now turn to considering each, before evaluating them specifically in terms of how strengthening electoral mechanisms and democratic representation at the EU level might help to confront the tensions arising from European markets without European democracy.

Regulation and the Rise of the Modern State

Regulation is the first key category of political and legal infrastructures necessary for markets to function effectively. The slow spread of market exchange, trade and capitalism and their linkages to political development and state formation have historically been built directly on centralisation and development of regulation (Poggi 1978; Spruyt 1994). As economic activity becomes more integrated and complex, societal actors make claims on the state to stabilise and regulate markets against the volatility inherent in market growth. Rules are drawn up, often by national level courts, to enable markets to function. While accomplished through political mechanisms, the drawing up of regulatory infrastructure is not only reliant on democratic processes, as discussed below.

The history of comparative political development is instructive as to how markets and politics interact to produce such governance. The roots of the modern nation-state are found in Western Europe as early as the late Middle Ages, as trade and monetisation of the economy began to push forward the rise of cities and towns and of a nascent commercial class with a new stake in the logics of rule and organisation (Spruyt 1994). While the self-governing systems of the early merchant fairs arose as a way for economic actors to trade, it was not enough (Greif 2006; Milgrom et al. 1990). Public, not private, authority could more fully address the needs of these new social groups for more routinised, regularised systems of rule: everything from the standardisation of weights and measures to promote more fair and efficient trade, to the development of monetary systems to allow for complex markets to arise around trading systems for goods and agricultural products, to the standardisation of time as clock towers in town squares regulated the new working day needed (Ruggie 1993). In the US case, the historical deepening of policy capacity in Washington was the result of the increasing demands for stable rules on the part of an increasingly complex capitalist economy in the nineteenth century and onwards (Skowronek 1982). The creation of a market system, accompanied by the establishment of legal institutions and an administrative bureaucracy, has historically ended up centralising authority over time, as a newly deepened polity is constructed alongside the newly enlarged market.

Regulation has arisen in a variety of governance settings historically, however, and is not tied only to democracy. Over time, as Spruyt and others detail, monarchs were the actors to establish regulations around trade (the King's foot as a standardised measurement, for example) and early Italian city-states or the Hanseatic League or the Holy Roman Empire were the political orders that generated the terms under which markets could expand and grow more complex within and across political boundaries (Spruyt 1994). But the modern nation-state has used regulation as a key tool to address citizen concerns about unbridled markets, as expressed through democratic representation and electoral party politics. Returning to Schmitter and Karl's definition of democracy, as rulers are 'held accountable for their actions in the public realm by citizens, acting indirectly through the competition and cooperation of their elected representatives', the regulation of market activity is a key element in that activity. How might we then evaluate the EU's own regulatory activities in terms of their functions in providing democratic capitalism?

The EU as a Regulatory State?

Regulation is the central arena for democratic governance of the EU's market, but it is not unproblematic as a beacon of democratic processes (Caporaso 1996). The single market formed the centrepiece of the early European project with the Treaty of Rome's emphasis on the four freedoms (freedom of movement, goods, services and capital) (Egan 2001). It has grown up alongside a robust set of rules around its workings, anchored in the ever increasing power and scope of the Court of Justice of the European Union (formally the European Court of Justice) (Kelemen 2011). These EU regulations both act as a way to tame the market towards the needs of European citizens, and thus represent a sort of output legitimacy even if they do not have clear channels of representation and democratic process to do so.

R. Daniel Kelemen has termed the EU 'the most influential regulator in the world', given its shaping of the rules on

> everything from food safety, to the roaming tariffs for mobile phones, to the content of prospectuses for traded securities, to the carbon emissions from passenger planes, to capital requirements for banks, to the recyclability of consumer electronics, to the cookies on websites, to the tuition charged to European students who study in other EU countries, to working hours, to rules on workplace discrimination, to the pension eligibility of migrant workers, to mergers of companies and divorces of married couples. (Kelemen 2016: 73)

There is no doubt about the extensiveness of the EU's regulatory apparatus, but it falls short of a democratising of the European single market project akin to what we see in national settings.

The early establishment of a common market in Europe under the 1958 Treaty of Rome created an institutional framework for a 'common market free from distortions to competition' (Art. 3), meaning tariffs and quotas, and thus is generally understood as a fairly understated version of liberalisation. The Single European Act (SEA) of 1985, however, was a much more profound set of disruptions of national control and an opening to the European-wide flow of goods, services, people and capital. The role of the European Commission's directives in implementing the SEA's treaty goals and that of the free movement of capital, individuals and services, and that of the Court of Justice of the European Union (CJEU) in ensuring that the single market laws are interpreted and applied across the member states has bolstered the EU's regulatory state status. However, these processes, rooted as they are in the Commission and the Court, not the European Parliament, mean that the processes at work do not reflect the type of representational, electoral democratic politics that produce regulatory regimes in national democracies.

Second, recall my argument above that democracy can be a source of increasing or decreasing inequality and general social welfare depending on whose interests are being met. The question is whether EU regulations have largely been in the service of European citizens or whether they represent a case of industry capture, reflecting the preferences of the most powerful economic actors and the industry itself. In the post-SEA era, there is evidence on both sides of this question. An early evaluation provides evidence demonstrating the EU's bolstering of labour rights through the CJEU's rulings upholding labour mobility (Caporaso and Tarrow 2009). Others similarly point to the court's emphasis on extending gender rights and other protections on social identity as examples of the more progressive nature of its regulatory schemes (Pollack and Hafner-Burton 2000). However, multiple critics of the scope and intensiveness of the single market project have instead argued it is a fully neoliberal effort marked by corporate capture, where the rules favour the narrow interests of the monied class (Buch-Hansen and Wigger 2010; Gill 2003, 2017). A more balanced assessment is likely to conclude that while the EU has had elements of its framework that privilege the upper classes and corporate interests, it also has moved forward on many elements of worker protection in line with what we would imagine a democratic practice should look like in this realm (Nedergaard 2020). But importantly, while the outputs of EU regulation may be protection of social and economic inequality and resist industry capture, the formulation of these regulatory structures does not occur through electoral and representational democracy, but rather through the Commission and the courts.

National Redistribution and a Social Safety Net

Policies and programmes of redistribution are the second category of national solutions that have arisen to confront the challenges of democratic capitalism. Redistribution is generated from the need to offset, compensate and reduce the risks arising from the working of capitalist markets. It is at the heart of the solutions to the types of democratic dilemmas and trade-offs presented by the intertwining of capitalism and democracy. A huge literature in comparative political economy has described and analysed the growth of the welfare state in Europe and the advanced economies, which began in the second half of the nineteenth century, took hold in the postwar era and faced increasing stress by the end of the twentieth century into the present day (Pierson 1994). A brief overview of these processes of comparative political development provides a useful template for understanding the EU's situation today.

While many early industrialising polities instituted various types of 'poor laws' to alleviate the stark poverty of the lower classes, and experimented with labour laws, social insurance and health funding, it was Bismarck who first introduced a more comprehensive, large-scale set of social insurance policies in the 1880s (Polanyi 1944). The cataclysmic social and economic devastation of the world wars and great depression meant that as democracy expanded, the demands for redistributive policies that would provide a social safety net for citizens became impossible to deny. The welfare state grew apace, albeit in various forms as the different political and economic systems of postwar Europe grappled with the needs of their citizens (Esping-Andersen 1990).

The development of modern-day electoral politics around redistribution occurred along traditional left–right lines of contestation. During the postwar period political parties organised themselves in terms of support for more or less redistribution, and a bigger or smaller welfare state and role for the state in the economy. Esping-Anderson captured well the historically unique class coalitional politics that produced variations in the development of the three 'worlds of welfare capitalism' in the European nation-states that acted to mediate markets through democratic processes. The class compromise that allowed for a relatively stable equilibrium to develop around enough redistribution to keep the lower classes from seeking to overthrow the capitalist system, but without jeopardising profit for capital, is viewed as fundamental to the ways that markets and democracy developed to coexist in the West (Przeworski and Wallerstein 1982).

A now well-established literature demonstrates the ways in which these redistributive policies and programmes of modern states are not in opposition to, but rather essential for, the working of modern markets. The Varieties of Capitalism literature lays out in empirical detail the ways in which national capitalisms have varied depending on how democratic demands have played out – with national economic performance never beholden to a non-interventionist, separation of markets from political governance and redistribution. Empirically demonstrating the ways in which markets need politics to function, as argued in the first section above, scholars like Stephen Vogel have argued that 'marketcraft' is an essential function of states that can provide benefits to the pursuit of effective and efficient markets (Vogel 2018). Katharina Pistor has documented how financial assets themselves only exist because of law and the state, not outside them. Financial trusts, corporate asset pools and the Investor State Dispute Settlement mechanism all come into being through projects of 'legal encoding' (Pistor 2019). So once again, the notion of a bright red line between the logics of markets and the logics of democracy is put to doubt – with implications for how we might think about resolving the tensions in the EU's democratic foundations today.

In sum, democracy in the context of modern nation-states provides a robust if contested mechanism for squaring the circle of the tensions produced by capitalist markets. As Jonathan Hopkin writes, 'Democracy has the potential to curb capitalism's inherent tendency to generate inequality. This very inequality can undermine the ability of democratic institutions to ensure that the economy works for the majority' (Hopkin 2020a). But that potential is not always realised – in fact, in the last thirty years, national democracy has produced a widening of inequality, not its decrease. While electoral politics as the mechanism of democracy should result in a shaping of the market into one that works for the majority of people, rather than a small investor class, democracy has not always delivered on that promise. Examining the various ways in which national electoral politics has and has not translated into democratic legitimation of markets is a helpful exercise when considering the limits and the opportunities afforded by the EU's emergent political order.

The EU as a Redistributive State?

In considering democratic practices that temper the potentially unequal impact of markets, the redistributive policies of the modern welfare state are critically important to the postwar era, as described above. Yet, the EU has had only very modest redistributive activities and no real welfare state at the European level. The underlying, necessary foundation for the modern national welfare state is the power to tax, borrow and spend, a capacity that the EU has been almost entirely lacking. Instead, the EU relies almost entirely on national budgetary contributions and has an overall budget that is only about two per cent of the total tax revenue of the twenty-seven EU members (Genschel and Jachtenfuchs 2011; Kelemen 2013: 219–20).

Unlike the regulatory parallels drawn above between nation-states and the EU, the differences between the EU and national polities are therefore stark. Extensive redistribution of the sort that is key to democratic capitalism in Europe is simply absent in the EU, although as will be discussed below, there are some steps being taken to develop the EU's 'own resources' for redistribution in the Next Generation Initiative. The EU does have some direct redistribution in the form of structural funds, which have historically been a key source of economic aid and development in certain needy regions of Europe (Hodson 2012). Also, the Common Agricultural Policy is a major redistributive intervention in the economy, albeit for farmers only, a dramatically smaller part of the European population than at the start of the EU (Snyder 2012).

The EU has also played a redistributive role, but one that is arguably regressive rather than progressive, with the creation of the eurozone and the austerity policies that followed from the global and eurozone financial crisis. Rather than redistributing to the more needy states, the eurozone crisis ended up economically shifting funds to the wealthier states of the EU. While some might justify this outcome using the 'saints and sinners' narrative about free-spending debtor nations versus the sober orthodoxy of the Northern creditor states, this simplified dichotomy obscures the ways in which private lenders have made large profits off the states required to dramatically cut back on their government spending and public services (Matthijs and McNamara 2015).

Because these avenues for redistribution in the EU are implicit and oblique, they do not effectively address the democratic dilemmas of market integration in the EU. The hidden, technocratic nature of the current policies does not provide a path for democratic demands to effectively reshape economic outcomes in the ways that the welfare state's redistributive mechanisms do at national level. These EU policies thus do not create the necessarily politically contested and overt trade-offs that we see in the cases of national welfare state redistribution. Counterintuitively, the hidden nature of the EU's redistribution means that democratic contestation cannot serve as a mechanism to make social stability and sustainable policies more likely in the way it would in healthy national democratic settings with electoral mechanisms for robust representation.

However, the pandemic has prompted an important set of policy responses that might indicate a new way forward for true redistributive policies in the EU. With the Next Generation EU initiative (NGEU), the EU has proposed an unprecedented approach to the challenges of governing the EU's economy, one with a series of very ambitious goals that remain to be realised, but do seem to be a bridge to a more Europeanised version of democratic capitalism. First is the recovery package comprised of €750 billion, with €390 of the money distributed as grants (Gambaro and Massara 2020). The funding is to be allocated to programmes that are EU priorities, such as the 'European Green Deal', which funds sustainable infrastructure and jobs in clean energy. The goal is to strengthen the EU single market by funding infrastructure, social programmes and providing assistance to businesses most impacted by the crisis. The negotiations over this programme were openly debated and subject to wide media coverage and national engagement, providing the sort of democratic contestation I argue is necessary for a sustainable democratic capitalism in the EU.

NGEU is unprecedented for several important reasons. First, because the EU 'may incur debt at an unprecedented scale' and second, because of the distribution of grant monies without strings attached (*The Economist* 2020).

Also, in the last economic crisis a decade ago, the EU and Northern countries took a position against redistribution across the EU, arguing that it was not the role of wealthier nations to take on the debts of poorer nations. The NGEU deal is designed to benefit the countries suffering the most (which include the Southern countries), dramatically different from how the EU and Northern countries responded to the debt crisis a decade ago. However, underlying tensions between countries persist. For example, the Dutch prime minister created an oversight body that could potentially cause issues if the tool is not used in good faith; 'any government can object to another's spending plans, delaying and complicating disbursements' (*The Economist* 2020). Even more important, although there is language about 'rule of law' in the policy, redistribution is to be provided to Hungary and Poland, states currently violating the EU's bedrock principles of liberal democracy (Kelemen 2020). This speaks to the trade-offs that come with democratic contestation and debate over the difficult issue of how to collectively cushion the impacts of open markets across the EU member states.

A key part of the innovation of the NGEU approach is the elevation of the idea of the EU's 'own resources' as the foundation for these redistributive activities. Previously, as discussed above, the EU's revenue was relatively limited, and included custom duties, a percentage of value-added tax collected by EU countries, and gross national income-based revenue from EU countries (66 per cent of revenue in 2018). The EU 'Own Resources' is a new source of revenue for the EU budget, in order to cover the costs related to the recovery plan. On 16 September 2020, the voice of direct democracy in the EU, the Members of the European Parliament, voted to make it possible for the EU to raise this money legally, linking it also to the lower-level democratic participation of the member states:

> The Council adopts the decision by unanimity after having consulted the European Parliament. Before entering into force, foreseen for January 2021 together with the new MFF [Multiannual Financial Framework], the ORD [Own Resources Decision] needs to be ratified by the parliaments of all member states. (European Parliament 2020)

The source of revenue could include a range of taxes, such as a tax on unrecycled plastic and on goods imported into the EU from countries with lower climate-change rules. Also under consideration is taxing digital giants and extending an EU carbon dioxide emissions trading scheme into the maritime and aviation sectors.

The Next Generation EU initiative is a therefore a potentially powerful and innovative way forward for the EU's challenges, as it creates a buffer for markets in a way that aligns with twenty-first century democratic demands, and moves the EU closer to having a truly redistributive capacity. But even if this creates new powers for the EU, they will remain in a broader EU institutional framework for governance where policies of regulation and redistribution still do not have the electoral link to citizens needed for democratic practice in the classic sense. I turn to this final issue below.

The Missing Democratic Practices in the EU

If we think of the EU as a system of modern capitalism in a democratic setting, even the brief comparison to the experiences and policies of traditional nation-states offered above points to the stresses and tensions in the contemporary European political order. An analysis of the tensions between markets and democracy in the EU requires changing our assumptions about market logics themselves – that instead of markets versus states, we should see markets as reliant on political authority for the generation of rules, the redistribution of economic benefits and the creation of social solidarity that is needed to underpin their effective functioning. At the same time, we need to be cognisant of the potential for democracy to generate policies that produce unequal effects across society, rather than seeing democracy as the answer and inequality generated by market dynamics alone. When applying these lessons to the EU, what stands out is how the attenuated nature of democratic representation and citizenship in the EU exacerbates the potential for tensions between markets and politics and the democratic dilemmas that arise.

These tensions can be squarely located in the incomplete nature of one specific and crucial element in the EU case: electoral politics. While the EU has many of the key parts of the political infrastructure for markets – most centrally in the form of the Court of Justice of the European Union providing the broader institutional structures and expectations necessary for the functioning of the single European market – it is keenly lacking in the electoral mechanisms that underpin markets and democracy in nation-states. The sustainability of both democracy and capitalism has historically been situated on the response of electoral parties to voters demands for cushioning of the impact of markets through the building of a welfare state and social safety net alongside deepening markets. Healthy, functioning democracy can potentially solve, or at least mediate, the tensions of markets, through electoral mechanisms – avoiding the rampant inequality in life experience that unbridled capitalism may generate.[2]

---

[2] For a thorough analysis of the complexities and tensions of this type of representative politics in the EU, see Christopher Lord's analysis of the construction of indirect legitimacy in this volume.

I began this chapter by noting the essential challenge the EU faces as a political order: the disjuncture between transnational markets and national electoral systems. The tensions of European capitalism without European democracy have contributed to the rise of anti-system or populist politics over the past decade, exacerbated by the economic hardships and austerity policies around the eurozone crisis (Hopkin 2020b; Schmidt 2020). The limited nature of democratic capitalism in the EU, from a relatively strong regulatory apparatus to the very weak redistributive institutions, combine with technocratic governance to further democratic tensions and feed into the inability of mainstream traditional centrist parties to keep their voting base happy, leading to the growth of anti-system, populist and anti-EU parties.

What might the potential options for the EU be around these challenges of democratic practices going forward? Today's global political economy has heightened the tensions, raised the stakes and revealed the nature of the transformations in political life that globalisation has wrought (McNamara and Newman 2020). The global pandemic is increased the already high levels of inequality and social stratification, while climate change and environmental sustainability are creating existential challenges. The digital revolution has brought new ways of interacting over Zoom during the pandemic for some, while increasing surveillance capacities and electoral interference. The pandemic has also exposed the transformations in political authority, and the multiple layers of powerful actors, that transcend simple models of nation-states in control of their citizens' destinies. The EU's shifting sites of authority seem to be the new normal, as regions, localities, nation-states, groups of states and the EU itself all interacted to address the pandemic.

The most straightforward way to deal with the challenges of European capitalism without European democracy is to simply renationalise markets. That way, European capitalism would become national capitalism, with markets matching their democratic foundations in each country. Of course, this is in a sense the putative point of Brexit: to regain sovereignty over all of the regulatory and other activities of the EU by leaving the Union. However, as the points made above about the global pandemic's challenge to national control indicate, renationalising is not a practical option for both material and political reasons. Indeed, EU publics at this point do not seem to favour any sort of exit from the EU; the unwinding of the European project would be, as has been seen with the UK, an excruciatingly painful exercise that is very, very unlikely. A scaled-back and more possible version of this would be a turn towards a differentiated EU, allowing for much more variation in policies (Lavenex and Krizic 2019; Leuffen et al. 2012). Here, domestic democratic demands could theoretically more directly determine the extent and nature of market integration and governance (de Vries 2018).

However, we should also consider whether the conditions may be in place for a deepening of Europe as a polity, rather than its loosening. An elaborate system of European regulation already exists, and the Pandora's box of a fiscal role for the EU has been opened with the pandemic financing package of the NGEU. But what is needed is a new commitment to building pan-European political parties and mechanisms of contestation and representation, and to ensure that these upgraded democratic politics do not widen inequality but rather work to lessen it. Simon Hix has laid out the specifics of how the EU might build in such electoral accountability (Hix 2008). The past ten years of EU politics can be understood as a trajectory of events that demonstrate a new political willingness and coalitional conditions that make such accountability more likely. The European Parliament's 2019 elections were remarkable for the level of overt contestation and turnout, taking place in an unprecedently high-profile way across the EU member states (McNamara 2019a); the 2019 *Spitzenkandidaten* debate focused attention on the need to link the choice of the Commission president to formal electoral politics (Fotopoulos 2019), and more broadly, the mass politics around Brexit has created a new awareness of the critical issues that membership in the EU engages for its citizens. Finally, and ironically, it has tended to be the far right, Eurosceptic parties that have recently organised at the European-level most successfully (McDonnell and Werner 2019), but an example of the pathway to a more robust representational democracy at the EU level has been forged in their actions. The trade-off of the tranquillity of consensus-based, technocratically insulated policy creation for the loud and often unpleasant pull and haul of democratic politics is one that the EU has already been forced to confront. Although these are but small steps forward, the ground appears to be shifting such that renationalisation may be less likely than continued forward movement to politicise the EU around a more overt set of electoral politics.

Conclusion

The EU is unique in its particular combination of capitalism without democracy, but both the tensions and potential solutions for that conundrum are echoed in the history of democratic capitalism in the nation-state. I have outlined some of the ways in which the EU may be able to replicate the methods by which polities have historically constructed bridges between markets and politics, using regulation and redistribution. But truly moving the EU towards a full expression of these institutions of democratic capitalism will take a revolutionary shift.

Most important is to match European capitalism with European democracy by Europeanising electoral politics such that there is true democracy of the sort defined by Schmitter and Karl at the start of this chapter: 'Modern political democracy is a system of governance in which rulers are held accountable for their actions in the public realm by citizens, acting indirectly through the competition and cooperation of their elected representatives' (Schmitter and Karl 1991: 4). The other contributions in this volume detail the various changes and transformations necessary to create political representation, accountability and participation at the European level – which can seem an almost unimaginable task. Although ambitious, history does show us that new emergent polities have, over time, built institutions of democracy to extend over a larger demos, redrawing the political identities of their citizens. The US case offers some suggestive examples of the ways in which politics can be transformed from their roots in subunit institutions, parties, identities and practices to a broader unified level over time, and how that might be possible in the EU case (McNamara and Musgrave 2020). Situating the EU case within the broader history of comparative political development so as to provide analytic leverage on the tensions and challenges is a necessary first step.

The EU is very much a work in progress, one that has gone much further in its building of a transnational polity and a governance form beyond the state than any other entity. Despite having some of the key mechanisms, such as regulation, that might allow for the peaceful coexistence of democracy and capitalism, the relative lack of redistributive powers in the EU is a crippling obstacle that must be overcome, in tandem with a true Europeanising of electoral politics. There is much work of political imagination, political leadership and political deal-making that needs to happen for the EU to be truly democratic in its governance over markets. While the fallout from the last decade of eurozone, migrant and, most recently, COVID-19 crises have unexpectedly moved European closer to that goal, much remains to be done. Facing up to the dilemmas inherent in the interaction of democratic politics and capitalist markets is a first step.

References

Berman, Sheri (2006) *The Primacy of Politics: Social Democracy and the Making of Europe's Twentieth Century*, 1st edn. New York: Cambridge University Press.

Berman, Sheri (2019) Capitalism and Democracy: What If We Have It Backwards? *Social Europe* (blog), <https://www.socialeurope.eu/capitalism-and-democracy> (last accessed 2 December 2022).

Bickerton, Chris J. (2011) Europe's Neo-Madisonians: Rethinking the Legitimacy of Limited Power in a Multi-Level Polity. *Political Studies*, 59(3): 659–73. https://doi.org/10.1111/j.1467-9248.2010.00872.x.

Buch-Hansen, Hubert and Wigger, Angela (2010) Revisiting 50 Years of Market-Making: The Neoliberal Transformation of European Competition Policy. *Review of International Political Economy*, 17(1): 20–44.

Caporaso, James A. (1996) The European Union and Forms of State: Westphalian, Regulatory or Post-Modern? *JCMS: Journal of Common Market Studies*, 34(1): 29–52. https://doi.org/10.1111/j.1468-5965.1996.tb00559.x.

Caporaso, James A. and Tarrow, Sidney (2009) Polanyi in Brussels: Supranational Institutions and the Transnational Embedding of Markets. *International Organization*, 63(4): 593–620. https://doi.org/10.1017/S0020818309990099.

De Vries, Catherine E. (2018) *Euroscepticism and the Future of European Integration*. Oxford: Oxford University Press.

Egan, Michelle P. (2001) *Constructing a European Market: Standards, Regulation, and Governance*, 1st edn. Oxford and New York: Oxford University Press.

Esping-Andersen, Gosta (1990) *The Three Worlds of Welfare Capitalism*. Princeton: Princeton University Press.

European Parliament (2020) Vote on Own Resources: MEPs Clear Way for COVID-19 Recovery Plan', News, European Parliament, 16 September, <https://www.europarl.europa.eu/news/en/press-room/20200910IPR86815/vote-on-own-resources-meps-clear-way-for-covid-19-recovery-plan> (last accessed 2 December 2022).

Fligstein, Neil (2002) *The Architecture of Markets: An Economic Sociology of Twenty-First-Century Capitalist Societies*. Princeton: Princeton University Press.

Follesdal, Andreas and Hix, Simon (2006) Why There Is a Democratic Deficit in the EU: A Response to Majone and Moravcsik. *JCMS: Journal of Common Market Studies*, 44(3): 533–62. https://doi.org/10.1111/j.1468-5965.2006.00650.x.

Fotopoulos, Stergios (2019) What Sort of Changes Did the Spitzenkandidat Process Bring to the Quality of the EU's Democracy? *European View*, 18(2): 194–202. https://doi.org/10.1177/1781685819879862.

Gambaro, Edoardo and Massara, Giulia (2020) Next Generation EU: The Commission's Proposal for the European Recovery, Greenberg Traurig LLP, 10 June, <https://www.gtlaw.com/en/insights/2020/6/next-generation-eu-the-commissions-proposal-for-the-european-recovery> (last accessed 2 December 2022).

Genschel, Philipp and Jachtenfuchs, Markus (2011) How the European Union Constrains the State: Multilevel Governance of Taxation. *European Journal of Political Research*, 50(3): 293–314. https://doi.org/10.1111/j.1475-6765.2010.01939.x.

Gill, Stephen (2003) A Neo-Gramscian Approach to European Integration. In Cafruny, Alan W. and Ryner, Magnus (eds) *A Ruined Fortress?: Neoliberal Hegemony and Transformation in Europe*. Lanham: Rowman & Littlefield, pp. 47–70.

Gill, Stephen (2017) Transnational Class Formations, European Crisis and the Silent Revolution. *Critical Sociology*, 43(4–5): 635–51. https://doi.org/10.1177/0896920516656920.

Greif, Avner (2006) *Institutions and the Path to the Modern Economy: Lessons from Medieval Trade*. Cambridge: Cambridge University Press.

Hall, Peter A (ed.) (2001) *Varieties of Capitalism: The Institutional Foundations of Comparative Advantage*, illustrated edn. Oxford and New York: Oxford University Press.

Hill, Christopher, Smith, Michael and Vanhoonacker, Sophie (2017) *International Relations and the European Union*, 3rd edn. New European Union Series. Oxford and New York: Oxford University Press.

Hix, Simon (2008) *What's Wrong with the European Union and How to Fix It*. Cambridge: Polity Press.

Hix, Simon (2018) Decentralised Federalism: A New Model for the EU. In Martill, Benjamin and Staiger, Uta (eds) *Brexit and Beyond: Rethinking the Futures of Europe*. London: UCL Press, pp. 72–80.

Hodson, Dermot (2012) Regional and Structural Funds. In Jones, Erik, Menon, Anand and Weatherill, Stephen (eds) *The Oxford Handbook of the European Union*. Oxford: Oxford University Press

Hooghe, Liesbet and Marks, Gary (2009) A Postfunctionalist Theory of European Integration: From Permissive Consensus to Constraining Dissensus. *British Journal of Political Science*, 39(1): 1–23. https://doi.org/10.1017/S0007123408000409.

Hopkin, Jonathan (2020a) Postwar Prosperity Depended on a Truce between Capitalism and Democracy, Aeon, <https://aeon.co/essays/postwar-prosperity-depended-on-a-truce-between-capitalism-and-democracy> (last accessed 2 December 2022).

Hopkin, Jonathan (2020b) *Anti-System Politics: The Crisis of Market Liberalism in Rich Democracies*. Oxford and New York: Oxford University Press.

Iversen, Torben and Soskice, David (2019) *Democracy and Prosperity: Reinventing Capitalism Through a Turbulent Century*. Princeton: Princeton University Press.

Kelemen, R. Daniel (2011) *Eurolegalism: The Transformation of Law and Regulation in the European Union*. Cambridge, MA: Harvard University Press.

Kelemen, R. Daniel (2013) Building the New European State? In Genschel, Philipp and Jachtenfuchs, Markus (eds) *Beyond the Regulatory Polity*. Oxford: Oxford University Press.

Kelemen, R. Daniel (2016) Regulation in the European Union. In Bignami, Francesca and Zaring, David (eds) *Comparative Law and Regulation: Understanding the Global Regulatory Process*. Cheltenham: Edward Elgar Publishing, pp. 73–91.

Kelemen, R. Daniel (2020) Europe's Faustian Union, *Foreign Policy* (blog), <https://foreignpolicy.com/2020/07/30/europes-faustian-union/> (last accessed 2 December 2022).

Kriesi, Hanspeter (2016) The Politicization of European Integration. *JCMS: Journal of Common Market Studies*, 54: 32–47. https://doi.org/10.1111/jcms.12406.

Lavenex, Sandra and Krizic, Ivo (2019) Conceptualising Differentiated Integration: Governance, Effectiveness and Legitimacy, *EU IDEA*, <https://archive-ouverte.unige.ch/unige:129347> (last accessed 6 December 2022).

Leuffen, Dirk, Rittberger, Berthold and Schimmelfennig, Frank (2012) *Differentiated Integration: Explaining Variation in the European Union*. Basingstoke: Palgrave MacMillan.

McDonnell, Duncan and Werner, Annika (2019) *International Populism: The Radical Right in the European Parliament*. London: C. Hurst & Co Publishers Ltd.

McNamara, Kathleen R. (2002) Rational Fictions: Central Bank Independence and the Social Logic of Delegation. *West European Politics*, 25(1): 47–76. https://doi.org/10.1080/713601585.

McNamara, Kathleen R. (2015) *The Politics of Everyday Europe: Constructing Authority in the European Union*. Oxford: Oxford University Press.

McNamara, Kathleen R. (2018) Authority under Construction: The European Union in Comparative Political Perspective. *JCMS: Journal of Common Market Studies*, 56(7): 1510–25. https://doi.org/10.1111/jcms.12784.

McNamara, Kathleen R. (2019a) The New European Parliament Will Balance Dramatically Different Ideologies and Interests. *Washington Post*, <https://www.washingtonpost.com/politics/2019/05/29/new-european-parliament-will-balance-dramatically-different-ideologies-interests/> (last accessed 2 December 2022).

McNamara, Kathleen R. (2019b) When the Banal Becomes Political: The European Union in the Age of Populism. *Polity*, 51 (October).

McNamara, Kathleen R. and Musgrave, Paul (2020) Democracy and Collective Identity in the EU and the USA. *JCMS: Journal of Common Market Studies*, 58(1): 172–88. https://doi.org/10.1111/jcms.12978.

McNamara, Kathleen R. and Newman, Abraham L. (2020) The Big Reveal: COVID-19 and Globalization's Great Transformations. *International Organization*, 1–19. https://doi.org/10.1017/S0020818320000387.

Mair, Peter (2006) *Ruling the Void: The Hollowing of Western Democracy*, 1st edn. London and New York: Verso.

Majone, Giandomenico (1998) Europe's 'Democratic Deficit': The Question of Standards. *European Law Journal*, 4(1): 5–28. https://doi.org/10.1111/1468-0386.00040.

Matthijs, Matthias and McNamara, Kathleen R. (2015) 'The Euro Crisis' Theory Effect: Northern Saints, Southern Sinners, and the Demise of the Eurobond. *Journal of European Integration*, 37(2): 229–45. https://doi.org/10.1080/07036337.2014.990137.

Milgrom, Paul R., North, Douglass C. and Weingast, Barry E. (1990) The Role of Institutions in the Revival of Trade: The Law Merchant, Private Judges, and the Champagne Fairs. *Economics and Politics*, 1(2): 1–23.

Moravcsik, Andrew (1998) *The Choice for Europe: Social Purpose and State Power from Messina to Maastricht*, 1st edn. Ithaca: Cornell University Press.

Moravcsik, Andrew (2002) In Defence of the Democratic Deficit: Reassessing Legitimacy in the European Union. *Journal of Common Market Studies*, 40(4): 603–24.

Nedergaard, Peter (2020) The Ordoliberalisation of the European Union? *Journal of European Integration*, 42(2): 213–30. https://doi.org/10.1080/07036337.2019.1658751.

North, Douglass C. (1991) *Institutions, Institutional Change and Economic Performance*. 2nd edn. Cambridge and New York: Cambridge University Press.

Pierson, Paul (1994) *Dismantling the Welfare State?: Reagan, Thatcher and the Politics of Retrenchment*. Cambridge: Cambridge University Press.

Pistor, Katharina (2019) *The Code of Capital: How the Law Creates Wealth and Inequality*. Princeton: Princeton University Press.

Poggi, Gianfranco (1978) *The Development of the Modern State: A Sociological Introduction*, 1st edn. Palo Alto: Stanford University Press.

Polanyi, Karl (1944) *The Great Transformation: The Political and Economic Origins of Our Time*, 2nd edn. New York: Beacon Press.
Pollack, Mark A. and Hafner-Burton, Emilie (2000) Mainstreaming Gender in the European Union. *Journal of European Public Policy*, 7(3): 432-56. https://doi.org/10.1080/13501760050086116.
Przeworski, Adam and Wallerstein, Michael (1982) The Structure of Class Conflict in Democratic Capitalist Societies. *American Political Science Review*, 76(2): 215-38. https://doi.org/10.1017/S0003055400186952.
Ruggie, John Gerard (1993) Territoriality and Beyond: Problematizing Modernity in International Relations. *International Organization*, 47(1): 139-74.
Scharpf, Fritz (1999) *Governing in Europe: Effective and Democratic?* Oxford: Oxford University Press.
Schmidt, Vivien Ann (2020) *Europe's Crisis of Legitimacy: Governing by Rules and Ruling by Numbers in the Eurozone*, 1st edn. Oxford: Oxford University Press.
Schmitter, Phillipe C. and Karl, Terry Lynn (1991) What Democracy Is . . . and Is Not. *Journal of Democracy*, 2(3): 3-16.
Skowronek, Stephen (1982) *Building a New American State: The Expansion of National Administrative Capacities, 1877-1920*. Cambridge: Cambridge University Press.
Smith, Michael E. (2017) *Europe's Common Security and Defence Policy: Capacity-Building, Experiential Learning, and Institutional Change*. Cambridge: Cambridge University Press.
Snyder, Francis (2012) CAP. In Jones, Erik, Menon, Anand and Weatherill, Stephen (eds) *The Oxford Handbook of the European Union*. Oxford: Oxford University Press
Spruyt, Hendrik (1994) *The Sovereign State and Its Competitors: An Analysis of Systems Change*. Princeton Studies in International History and Politics. Princeton: Princeton University Press.
The Economist (2020) The EU's Leaders Have Agreed on a €750bn Covid-19 Recovery Package, *The Economist*, 21 July, <https://www.economist.com/europe/2020/07/21/the-eus-leaders-have-agreed-on-a-eu750bn-covid-19-recovery-package> (last accessed 2 December 2022).
Tucker, Paul (2019) *Unelected Power: The Quest for Legitimacy in Central Banking and the Regulatory State*. Princeton: Princeton University Press.
Vogel, Steven K. (2018) *Marketcraft: How Governments Make Markets Work*. Oxford and New York: Oxford University Press.
Weber, Max (2009) *The Theory of Social and Economic Organization*. New York: Simon and Schuster.
Wilde, Pieter de, Leupold, Anna and Schmidtke, Henning (2016) Introduction: The Differentiated Politicisation of European Governance. *West European Politics*, 39(1): 3-22. https://doi.org/10.1080/01402382.2015.1081505.
Wu, Tim (2018) *The Curse of Bigness: Antitrust in the New Gilded Age*. New York: Columbia Global Reports.

SIX

Beyond Democratic Minimalism: How Democratic Contestation Can Support European Integration

Joseph Lacey

All political communities have an interest in adopting a regime that will ensure the preservation of the community and solve the social and economic problems it faces. Democracy, understood as a scheme of collective self-government, has been defended as a regime-type that is well-suited to these tasks. Part of the way in which it does this is by providing fair conditions for policy contestation and public debate, so that different values and interests held across the society can feed into decision-making. Although often a bumpy road, this process is at least expected to produce the 'community-integration' good of peaceful and civil conflict resolution, as well as some of the 'epistemic' goods required for well-informed and well-justified policy outcomes.

Not all political communities, however, are created alike. In some cases, certain aspects of the democratic process may be counter-productive when it comes to producing the goods of community integration and policy effectiveness. This is especially true in what have been referred to as 'deeply divided societies' (Taylor 1993). Although most democratic societies are diverse, deep diversity refers to societies where different ways of belonging mark out some of the central political fault lines. These lines of division tend to include nationality, language, religion and even ethnicity. Deeply diverse societies are often seen as facing a democratic dilemma when it comes to institutional design: a) adopt a standard model of contestatory democracy and put the goods of community integration and problem-solving effectiveness at greater risk; or b) attenuate some of the more contestatory attributes commonly associated with democratic systems to better preserve these goods. At least part of the reason for the perceived tension at the heart of this dilemma is the tendency for political contestation to run hot in deeply diverse societies as different social segments pursue strategies of maximum extraction for the benefit of their segments at the expense of more optimal outcomes for the whole (Miller 1995: 91–7; Moore et al. 2014: 159). This not only creates obstacles to problem-solving, it also makes it more difficult for citizens from different segments to identify with one another or their common political institutions as constituting an appropriately integrated body politic. As a result, disintegrative demands – from decentralisation or federalisation to complete secession – tend to become forceful in deeply divided societies.

Commonly, the democratic dilemma facing deeply divided societies is addressed by opting for the latter trade-off: taking the heat out of political contestation through institutional design as a means of improving problem-solving and reducing disintegrative pressures. Consociational models of democracy, practiced today in the purest form in Belgium and Northern Ireland, are among the stand-out examples of this trade-off. On this model, political contestation is reduced through an electoral system that produces power-sharing among the politically divided segments of the society. Furthermore, there are mechanisms in place to ensure that the most contentious issues between the segments are depoliticised and resolved through grand bargaining *in camera* at the elite level (Lijphart 1977).

Some have described the EU as a consociation in its own right (Papadopoulos and Magnette 2010). Precisely because it is a deeply divided society, along national lines at the very least, from the beginning the EU has developed a unique power-sharing system of governance that has been largely depoliticised and elite-driven in accord with consensual decision-making rules and norms. Compared to the familiar national consociational cases, however, the deadening of political contestation has historically taken on an extreme form in the EU. This has been for a variety of reasons that are related to the 'rescaling' of democracy in the EU context (see Keating in this volume), including the lack of a common European public sphere for political debate (Lacey 2016), the historically low-salience and technical nature of many EU competences (Moravcsik 2008) and the difficulty that national parliaments and citizens have in monitoring executive behaviour at the European level (Hurrelmann and Debardeleben 2009).

In the EU case (Mair 2007), and in the case of national consociations (Stojanović 2019), scholars have raised concerns about the viability of political communities that institute democratic processes without sufficient opportunities for public contestation. On this perspective, the long-term solution to the democratic dilemma facing deeply divided societies is not to trade-off democratic contestation to secure problem-solving effectiveness and community integration. There are two reasons for this. First, sacrificing too much democratic contestation involves its own risks for the very goods that this measure is supposed to protect. By failing to sufficiently incentivise public contestation and the associated citizen engagement entailed by this, the political system bases itself on a fragile legitimacy that alienates citizens from their political institutions. This, in turn, provides fertile ground for anti-system politics to emerge which, by their nature, seek to demonstrate the flaws of the existing system by actively undermining the goods of community integration and problem-solving effectiveness. Second, in deeply divided societies, it appears that democratic contestation may be only contingently in tension with these goods. Under appropriate institutional designs, it is argued, democratic contestation can make the kind of contributions to problem-solving effectiveness and community integration in deeply divided societies that it can make in those societies that do not suffer such deep divisions (Reilly 2012; Lacey 2017a; Stojanovic 2020; McNamara and Musgrave 2020). On this contestatory perspective concerning the democratic dilemma faced by deeply divided societies then, consociation-style depoliticisation is at best a temporary stopgap that can under certain circumstances give a political community time to develop the maturity and resilience for a more contestatory democratic politics.

This chapter seeks to build on the case for enhancing democratic opportunities for contestation in the EU by arguing that the costs of trading-off democratic contestation to serve community integration and problem-solving effectiveness may be even greater than they first appear. The standard critique of this trade-off is concerned about the rise of opposition to the system because of a lack of opportunities for contestation within the system (Mair 2007). My contribution is to draw attention to the impacts of depoliticisation on the ability of the system to defend itself against critique, especially from anti-system politics. In brief, I maintain that in the absence of democratic contestation about the EU, citizens are more likely to maintain ambivalent attitudes towards this political system. Under such depoliticised conditions, pro-European political actors will lack the incentive to develop strong communicative practices that forge more definite and informed public support for the EU. At an opportune moment, such as a period of crisis that implicates the EU, citizens' ambivalent attitudes can be easily exploited by political entrepreneurs who colourfully and vigorously make the case against (some aspect of) European integration. On these occasions, it is suggested that pro-European political actors will lack the communicative resources necessary to forcefully confront this critique and may be even electorally incentivised to accommodate it in some way.

A common approach to questions of democracy in the EU that I and many others have adopted in previous work, and which has its own merits, is to start with a grand normative theory or vision of the EU and then to work out what kind of democratic institutions would be compatible with that theory (Cheneval and Schimmelfennig 2013; Lacey 2017a; Bellamy 2019). However, in line with the benefits of the dilemma-driven approach outlined by Niklas Bremberg and Ludvig Norman in this volume, this chapter suspends such normative presuppositions. Rather than asking what kind of contestatory or non-contestatory institutions follow from a particular conception of the EU – whether liberal nationalist or federalist or demoicratic – this chapter analyses the normative tensions faced by the EU in attempting to maintain its stability while securing the democratic goods of community integration and problem-solving effectiveness. Whether or not this analysis and its institutional implications resonate with one or other grander normative theory of the EU is a separate matter that will not be addressed in this contribution.

The chapter proceeds as follows. In the next section, I outline the competing minimalist and participatory positions within traditional democratic theory on the purpose of contestation, explaining how they relate to the more specific debate on democratic contestation in the EU. Following this, I explore the nature of democratic contestation in the EU, which has been driven by Eurosceptical political entrepreneurs. In successive sections, I look at three primary venues or democratic opportunity structures where the EU has been politicised: national parliaments, the European Parliament (EP) and referendums on European issues. Each case clearly demonstrates the risk of democratic contestation for European integration, thus confirming that the tension animating the democratic dilemma faced by deeply diverse societies like the EU is a real one. However, each case also demonstrates the risks associated with too few opportunities for democratic contestation. While no specific democratising reforms are favoured in this chapter, the final section concludes that there appear to be special advantages to a) connecting the outcome of EP elections to executive office via the Commission; and b) developing a scheme of citizen-called European-wide referendums on legislative issues within the EU's competences. Most notably, these democratic reforms are expected to make commissioners and European political groups publicly visible. This is significant since they are typically more motivated to consistently communicate a pro-European message than national representatives.

The Purpose of Democratic Contestation

Contestation is a core value of any democratic theory, though the nature and extent of contestation that is favoured by any theory is dependent on how the purpose of contestation is understood. Perhaps the starkest contrast on this point are the minimalist and participatory theories of democracy. Both theories agree that democratic contestation contributes to community integration and problem-solving effectiveness, but in very different ways. According to the first articulator of the minimalist theory of democracy, Joseph Schumpeter (2003), democratic contestation should be limited to free and fair competitive elections between political leaders. A minimal degree of community integration will be secured by virtue of the fact that free and fair competitive elections allow for the peaceful transition of power, at least to the extent that electoral losers feel that they have a chance at winning in the future. Problem-solving effectiveness, however, is ensured to the extent that political leaders are exclusively tasked with delivering outcomes for the community. For Schumpeter (2003: 259–61), and other competitive democrats (Aachen and Bartels 2016), citizens are most competent over areas where they have responsibility. On issues in their workplaces and even their local communities, Schumpeter claimed that citizens were more than capable of rationally forming 'definite individual volitions' concerning what should be done. In national (and certainly international) politics, by contrast, Schumpeter insisted that citizens generally do not form such definite volitions. As a result, when asked for their views on political issues for which they have no direct responsibility, he maintained that citizens are not fully rational and can therefore be easily manipulated, leading to worse outcomes if leaders are incentivised to take heed of these views. For Schumpeter, insofar as possible, citizens' involvement in the democratic process is best limited to choosing personalities whom they trust in leadership positions.

Participatory democrats (Pateman 1970, 2012; Barber 1984) do not doubt the community-integrating function of elections, nor do they necessarily doubt the importance of leadership for effective problem-solving. However, they believe that both goods can be better secured through a fuller engagement of citizens in the democratic process. On the one hand, by entering an inclusive public debate resulting in collective decisions, participatory democrats believe that democratic contestation helps to build community ties with fellow citizens by bringing them into direct contact with one another, allowing for mutual understanding despite disagreement. On the other hand, by connecting the political process with the concerns of citizens on an ongoing basis, participatory democrats believe that problem-solving effectiveness will be improved as political leaders become better informed about citizen experiences and perspectives and what might be the limits of public acceptability for certain policies.

Unlike the minimalist theory of democracy, participatory democrats do not take citizens' irrationality in political matters as a given. Participatory democrats recognise the incentive structure between having responsibility in some sphere of life and forming definite volitions when it comes to deciding upon issues in such spheres. Their proposal, however, is to give citizens responsibility for decision-making through democratic opportunity structures, so that they are incentivised to form definite volitions on at least the most important issues. Participatory democrats are more optimistic than Schumpeter about the possibility of elections to incentivise citizens to form considered views on important issues, while they urge the need to offer further opportunities for participation (such as referendums) that could also incentivise the formation of definite volitions. In doing so, participatory democrats believe, citizens become more politically sophisticated over time, thus improving their capacity to make rational contributions to political debate.

Democratic Contestation and European Integration

The debate between minimalist and participatory democrats becomes sharper in deeply diverse political communities, like the EU. As we have seen, such communities appear to face a democratic dilemma, whereby forms of democratic contestation that are commonly considered to be intrinsic to the idea of democracy have the potential to have especially negative consequences for the goods of community integration and problem-solving effectiveness. To the extent that all member states have directly elected governments, the possibility of democratic contestation is necessarily built into the EU's architecture. This is not in dispute. What is a matter of debate is the extent to which contestation should be facilitated and incentivised through democratic institutional design. Concerns have reigned over the establishment of the EP as an electoral body and various institutional tweaks proposed to politicise it still further (Bartolini 2006). Meanwhile, the politicising effects of national referendums on European integration (Moravcsik 2008) and proposals for European-wide referendums have been commonly viewed as problematic (Bellamy et al. 2019: 297–9).

At the founding of the European Communities, the democratic dilemma facing it as a deeply divided polity had been decided in a very clear way. Community integration and problem-solving effectiveness were to be prioritised above democratic contestation. Institutional architects of the Communities, such as Claude Monnet (Featherstone 1994) and influential theorists of international integration (Mitrany 1966) were convinced that opportunities for public contestation over Europe would undermine community integration and problem-solving effectiveness. This position was driven in no small part by concerns that politicisation of European integration would entrench public positions that were nationally self-interested and thereby limit the autonomy of political representatives at European level, as well as related Schumpetarian concerns about citizens' capacities to properly understand high politics and technical policy areas. As a result, the EU has been developed along the lines of what Turkuler Isiksel (2017) calls a 'functional constitution', which articulates a legal architecture and institutional format that is driven by the goals of solving particular sets of problems (with the single market as the focus in the EU case). For the likes of Monnet and Mitrany, without being subject to democratic contestation, European institutions have the potential to produce some of the community integration effects that could stand in for those that Schumpeter and participatory democrats respectively associate with democratic contestation. European integration, it was believed, would win citizens common allegiance by both securing the good of peaceful conflict resolution on the international stage, and through the unique functional capacity of its institutions to deliver good and otherwise unattainable policy outputs.

Although the EU has become more politicised, in both domestic electoral systems and through the EP at the European level in particular, contemporary accounts emphasise that the functionalist approach to the EU's democratic dilemma continues to dominate. This can be seen, for example, in the empowerment of the EU's technocratic institutions (including the European Central Bank and Commission) and its intergovernmental institutions dedicated to elite bargaining *in camera* (including the European Council and the Eurogroup), during and following periods of crisis (White 2019). These empowerments largely came at the expense of the EP and national parliaments, themselves hotbeds of political contestation during the euro crisis and 2015 refugee crisis especially. Significantly, the functionalist approach can be seen also within the EP itself as it eschews democratising reforms in favour of those that would limit the impact of the emergent far-right on its operations (Norman 2021).

This chapter will not aim to be comprehensive in considering all of the historic and contemporary justifications for the EU's predominant functional approach towards the democratic dilemma of deep diversity. Instead, it will focus on Stefano Bartolini's (2006) especially powerful and influential formulation of the rationale for a democratic minimalism in the EU, which is well-attuned to contemporary realities. What generates political heat about the EU domestically is not standard policy issues, Bartolini observes, but rather constitutive issues pertaining to the desirability of EU membership itself or certain fundamental aspects of its integration (e.g. the euro or the four freedoms). Providing increased democratic opportunities for political competition about the EU, he insists, runs the risk of putting European integration itself in question on a continuous basis. On this view, elite-level and public debates generated by specific Treaty changes or a significant policy issue going through the EU institutions are liable to be hijacked by Eurosceptics to question the EU's constitutive fundamentals that have little to do with the Treaty change or policy issue itself. In consequence, when democratic contestation over Europe issues is constantly charged with more fundamental debates about European integration itself, this will put a strain on community integration and make it more difficult to reach consensus on good policy outcomes.

In reflecting upon the relationship between citizen attitudes on politics beyond the state, de Vries et al. (2021: 8) observe the following:

> public opinion about international cooperation is ambivalent in nature. Attitude ambivalence is important because it makes citizens much more open to taking cues from political elites. This makes public opinion more malleable. In the absence of an international public sphere, citizens often rely on political elites or the mass media in forming opinions about international cooperation.

Such observations reinforce the case for democratic minimalism in the EU. They suggest that political entrepreneurs should be easily capable of exploiting ambivalent attitudes or indefinite volitions about European integration among the citizenry (cf. Moravcsik 2008: 338–40). By using democratic opportunity structures to politicise European integration, these entrepreneurs frame debates over Europe, helping to turn citizens who were either weakly supportive or apathetic about the EU into more definite Eurosceptics (de Vries and Hobolt 2020).

The case for a more participatory Europe has been variously made. Peter Mair (2007) reminds us that when there are too few opportunities to contest policy, those most frustrated with their lack of ability to democratically influence the political process will tend to establish an opposition to the very political system itself. In other words, contrary to Bartolini, Mair believes that it is the limited democratisation of the EU that provides ripe conditions for the development and deepening of anti-EU movements that would challenge the EU constitutively. The conclusion is that enhanced democratic opportunities are likely to make European integration more stable over time by mitigating some of the institutional drivers of anti-system politics. Others have gone further than Mair, arguing that the EU could also benefit from the community-building and epistemic virtues of greater opportunities for democratic contestation that have been traditionally highlighted by participatory democrats (Habermas 2015; White and Ypi 2016; Lacey 2017a; McNamara and Musgrave 2020).

My main purpose in this chapter is not to determine the merits of these claims. Instead, I aim to bolster the participatory case by focusing on a specific way that the theory of participatory democracy contradicts the minimalist theory. Participatory democracy does not take the above-mentioned ambivalence of citizens towards international cooperation as a given, but rather as a product of various factors, including the structure of political competition. On this view, the contestation afforded by democratic opportunity structures are necessary to mutually incentivise competing actors to present clear and distinct positions on important issues. In other words, democratic contestation motivates political actors to make their positions on important issues visible to citizens, so that these actors may secure stable and definite support for those issues over time. Simultaneously, to the extent that citizens feel like they have a say in the democratic process through their opportunities to participate, there are greater incentives for them to form definite individual volitions on key issues at stake in public debate. The failure of mainstream parties to go through the process of forming definite public support on important issues may facilitate political entrepreneurs who eventually do break through any constraining democratic opportunities for contestation. In the EU case, the job of political entrepreneurs to forge a Eurosceptical constituency naturally becomes easier when more traditional political actors have historically failed to develop a clear and convincing pro-European counter-frame, or if they remain reluctant to do so in the face of new challengers.

Contestation and Definite Political Support in the EU

In this section, I explore the merits of this argument for enhancing opportunities for contestation in the EU, in contrast to the challenge posed by the minimalist perspective previously outlined. Three types of democratic institutions relevant to European integration are analysed: national parliaments, the European Parliament and national referendums. Each case will begin with some examples of the kind of proposals typically favoured by those advocating for greater democratisation in the EU. Some of the potential trade-offs between democratisation and European integration implied by these proposals will then be fleshed out by an analysis of the dynamics of political behaviour within the existing institutionalisation of democratic structures in the EU.

National Parliaments

A common critique of democracy in the EU is that national executives become empowered by European integration at the expense of national parliaments, due to the direct role of these executives in the European Council and Council of Ministers. National parliaments, it is argued, have few institutional incentives to do the difficult work of scrutinising executive actions at the European level. This lack of domestic contestation results in a dearth of democratic debate pertaining to the EU during elections or during parliamentary terms (Hurrelmann and Debardeleben 2009). A potential solution is to go further in empowering national parliaments by, for example, giving them the collective right of legislative initiative (Bellamy and Kröger 2016). Such empowerment, it is believed, could provide the incentive structure necessary for national parliaments to engage more deeply on European issues and thereby drive more public domestic debates on the direction of European integration.

Largely in response to the sovereign debt crisis and the refugee crisis, Eurosceptical political entrepreneurs have been able to use the democratic opportunities provided by national elections to capitalise on these crises, dramatically increasing their electoral share and representation in national parliaments. Proposals to further empower national parliaments in Europe, such as by introducing the collective right of legislative initiative, clearly open up the potential for Eurosceptics to coordinate transnationally and to politicise the EU in ways that are favourable to a more disintegrative agenda. In line with Bartolini's fears, the potential for Eurosceptics to contribute towards setting the legislative agenda would allow them to select those policy issues that are most germane to rhetorically spilling over into constitutive issues.

The evident danger that national parliaments, and their further empowerment in European affairs, could present to European integration needs to be contextualised by considering the conditions that may have facilitated the emergence of Eurosceptics. Clearly, these actors have exploited political crises resulting from exogenous shocks. But is there anything about the operation of national democracy itself that may have affected the rise of Eurosceptics? Two factors are worth considering: 1) the perverse communicative incentives of national governments relying on the permissive consensus of their citizens pertaining to questions of European integration; and 2) the uncertainty exiting parties face over whether to accommodate or confront the demands of emergent challenger parties.

On the first point, as Habermas (2015: 551) complains: 'political elites have avoided turning European issues into topics of national public spheres for half a century'. It appears that a permissive consensus relieves pro-European parties of the need to build definite volitions in favour of European integration among their population. Given that the EU's political legitimacy has been substantially premised on its ability to deliver good outcomes (Schmidt 2013), the lack of positive communication about the

EU by national governments over time has been a missed opportunity for building a more robust and definite support. With the end of the permissive consensus, and the beginning of a constraining dissensus at least since the rejection of the Constitutional Treaty in 2004 in French and Dutch referendums, public support for European integration can no longer be taken for granted (Hooghe and Marks 2009).

On the second point, with the emergence of Eurosceptical political parties, many traditionally pro-European parties have been faced with an electoral conundrum that may make it more difficult for them to fully embrace and publicly defend their historically pro-European stance. If they become more visibly pro-European, just as political entrepreneurs are coaxing citizens towards a more Eurosceptical stance, then they may risk losing a substantial share of their support base to these entrepreneurs. There is therefore an electoral incentive for traditionally pro-European parties to either limit their pro-European rhetoric, or to even adopt some of the critical positions of Eurosceptics (Hooghe and Marks 2009: 21).

As Rauh et al. (2019) suggest, based on their analysis of executive public communication in the EU, whether national executives adopt an accommodative stance towards Eurosceptical challengers is largely determined by the level of the electoral threat. If the challenger party is credible and has a clear opportunity to mop up further votes in the future, then national executives tend to be more reticent or even negative in their communications about the EU. However, if the challenger party appears to have soaked up all the political support it can at the present time, national parties are more likely to cut their electoral losses and seek to shore up their pro-EU base with more positive public communications about the EU that directly confronts the Eurosceptical opposition. Plausibly, the authors believe that the unapologetically pro-EU position of Emanuel Macron during his 2017 electoral campaign and subsequent presidential term has been provoked by the intense Eurosceptical challenge of Marine Le Pen.

What lessons can we draw from these considerations concerning proposals to empower national parliaments in the EU legislative process? If they would simply serve as a further avenue to be exploited by Eurosceptical political entrepreneurs, then there may be little to be said in favour of such proposals from the perspective of supporting community integration and problem-solving effectiveness in the EU. However, this risk would appear to be counterbalanced by a different set of considerations. To the extent that Euroscepticism and the salience of European issues are likely to ebb and flow with crises or major events like Treaty ratification, the distinct possibility exists that pro-EU actors will fall back into relaxed public communicative habits concerning European integration during periods of low salience. This complacency can be exploited to maximum effect once again by political entrepreneurs during the next period of crisis.

Alternatively, by empowering national parliaments in the European legislative process, it is not just Eurosceptical political entrepreneurs, but also pro-European opposition parties that may seek to use their newfound powers to politicise European issues domestically on a more regular basis. Whether contestation proceeds from Eurosceptics or pro-European domestic opposition parties, the normalisation of political debate on European issues has the distinct advantage of creating the conditions for democratic communication about the EU. The politicisation of an issue by pro-EU national parties in opposition is less likely to spill over into constitutive issues, while nevertheless encouraging public discourse about European issues in more or less pro-European frames. When Eurosceptical representatives politicise an issue in a way that spills into constitutive issues, this in turn is more likely to put pro-EU parties in government and opposition in a position where they must discuss and justify their perspective on wider issues of European integration more publicly. Of course, there may still be evolving electoral calculi at play that determine just how reticent or vocal pro-EU parties are in facing down Eurosceptical challengers on any given issue at any given time. This is a disadvantage to proposals for empowering national parliaments in EU politics that appears difficult to expunge.

The European Parliament

Further democratising the European Parliament, while not incompatible with empowering national parliaments in European integration (see Lord, this volume), is a far more discussed option. Common reform proposals include expanding the EP's co-decision powers with the Council to other important areas, such as Common Defence and Security Policy (Cheneval and Schimmelfennig 2013). Most popular, however, is the proposal to make at least the appointment of the Commission president dependent upon the outcome of elections to the EP (Follesdal and Hix 2006; Bardi et al. 2010; Lacey 2017a). The standard rationale for such proposals runs as follows. By raising the stakes of European elections, making it in part about partisan control of executive office, the democratic visibility of the EP will be heightened and elections to the EP themselves will become first-order (in the sense that they will become mainly 'about' European issues and not second-order proxy contests run on domestic political issues).

Due to the second-order nature of EP elections (Hix and Marsh 2011; Schmitt and Teperoglou 2015) and the relatively low turnout for these elections over the last decades, the extent to which the EP has politicised the EU through its elections has been limited. However, insofar as the EP has managed to engender political debate over European issues, Bartolini's main fears appear to have been warranted. Studying three EP elections in four countries, Martin Dolezal (2012) found that European issues were indeed discussed with increasing attention over time, but that the majority of these were constitutional issues not within the ambit of the EP. Reinforcing the point, he observes that these debates were mainly framed between Eurosceptical challenger parties and more mainstream parties.

The way the EP facilitated the development of the kind of Euroscepticism that provoked the Brexit referendum provides an even more vivid illustration of the validity of Bartolini's fears. Despite the difficulty of arch-Eurosceptic Nigel Farage and his United Kingdom Independence Party (UKIP) to translate its support into seats at Westminster, due to the UK's first-past-the-post electoral system, UKIP has benefited from proportional representation in the EP, winning seats there in elections since 1999. When Farage ascended to the leadership of UKIP in 2006 and then created The Brexit Party in 2019, he was able to capitalise on the momentum of previous gains to become the British party leader with the largest share of seats in the EP. With a rhetorical gift for casting the media spotlight on the often-ignored daily affairs of the EP, Farage sought to do anything but illuminate policy debate. Instead, he used the public platform afforded by the EP to generate heat over constitutive issues associated with the EU (Lacey and Nicolaïdis 2020). The stated goal of Farage and his successive parties was for the UK to leave the EU and to do so without clinging on to any of its institutional structure or policy programmes. As such, all critiques of EU policy were in some way linked to an unreformable rottenness baked into the core of the EU system. All policy issues were, in effect, made into constitutive issues.

The ability of Farage to use the EP to politicise constitutive issues played no small role in motivating a British referendum on EU membership and subsequent victory for the leave campaign in that referendum in June 2016 (Lacey 2018). For a time, the shockwaves produced by the Brexit vote even emboldened anti-EU forces to argue more vocally for withdrawal of their nation-state from the EU, or at least from the Eurozone. Meanwhile, by the time of the 2014 elections, the EP had become stacked with all manner of Eurosceptical parties (Treib 2014). As a result of this trend, which continued in the 2019 EP elections (Treib 2020), pro-European actors have had to face down constitutive contestation, not just at the national level, but also at the European level due to the much-changed composition of the EP. Indeed, one study suggests that the cleavage over European integration has become a significantly better predictor of EP voting behaviour than the traditional left–right cleavage (Cheysson and Fraccoroli 2019).

The amplification of Eurosceptical voices in the EP and during EP elections has undoubtedly undermined community integration in the EU – as the Brexit case starkly demonstrates – though it is less clear that it has compromised the ability of the EP to serve as an effective legislator. It is the hardest Eurosceptics – with no desire to achieve anything in the EP except to use it as a platform to publicise disintegrative goals – that are most likely to serve as a threat in this regard. However, to the extent that these constitute a small minority in the European Parliament (Treib 2020) and among the European citizenry (de Vries 2018: 82) – even after several periods of heightened contestation during crises – the threat of Euroscepticism through the democratic opportunities provided by the EP is likely to remain relatively modest. As Bremberg and Norman indicate in their introduction to this volume, perhaps the greatest threat to European integration from within the EP is the ability of right-wing Members of the European Parliament (MEPs) to form a cohesive force dedicated to reforming the EU in an illiberal direction. In July 2021, right-wing national party leaders (including Marine Le Pen, Matteo Salvini and Victor Orban) declared an alliance with this very aim.[1] However, there remain serious doubts as to whether the stark differences between these national parties will allow them to both establish a European Political Group and sustain it over time.

When considering some of the potential benefits of proposals to expand the democratic reach of the EP from the perspective of European integration, the case for further democratisation appears to be strong. As we have seen, part of the problem with domestic politics for European integration are the various electoral incentives for pro-Europeans to limit or even downplay their positive communication messages about the EU. While these incentives may change or be overcome in certain circumstances, it appears that the EU is without a reliable set of actors with sufficient public visibility who are incentivised to communicate a pro-European message. To the extent that their political careers are directly tied up with the EP, MEPs and their political groups are likely to be less constrained than national representatives in their positive communications about the EU to citizens. Indeed, as Rauh et al. (2019) note in their previously mentioned analysis of executive communication in the EU, European commissioners are especially likely to adopt unambiguous pro-EU frames, even though they will sometimes resort to more ambiguous technocratic language on salient issues.

---

[1] See <https://www.politico.eu/article/viktor-orban-marine-le-pen-matteo-salvini-eu-integration-european-superstate-radical-forces/?utm_medium=Social&utm_source=Twitter#Echobox=1625252556> (last accessed 8 December 2022).

There appears to be no shortage of media coverage concerning commissioner statements in broadsheet newspapers, though the level of coverage is in general not matched by citizens' attention (Statham 2010). By making EP elections a contest over executive power, commissioners may increase their democratic visibility, both during elections and in the inter-electoral period. The expectant higher profile of EP elections undoubtedly provides the opportunity to amplify the voice of Eurosceptics. However, their contestation will in turn enhance the visibility of their pro-European opponents. Yet in this case, there will be few constraints on pro-European MEP or commissioner candidates attempting to contribute towards forming citizens' definite volitions on question of European integration. Counterfactually, given some of the negative consequences that the democratisation of the EP has had on European integration, the minimalist perspective on democracy in the EU may argue that the establishment of the EP as a directly elected body was mistaken. Whatever the merits of this position, to the extent that the EP has already been democratised and its abandonment as an electoral institution nigh on politically impossible, the relevant question is how the process of contestation for this institution can be best designed. From the perspective of sustainable European integration, using the process to mobilise those actors most likely to defend European integration is a distinctive advantage.

National Referendums

National referendums on questions of European integration are widely viewed as the riskiest form of democratic opportunity structure for European integration. Indeed, Schumpetarians have critiqued these devices as asking citizens to make decisions for which they are ill-equipped (Aachen and Bartels 2016: 302). Referendums on European integration that have resulted in a negative verdict have received far more scholarly attention than successful ones. In these studies, the referendum results have most often been explained by citizens' failure to understand what they are voting upon due to a range of factors, including the ability of political entrepreneurs to raise unfounded fears or to foreground untruths that are difficult to dispel (Offe 2017; Hansson and Kröger 2021). Historically, referendums on European integration have been about constitutive issues. As such, in this instance, the concern of minimalist democrats is less about the confusion of policy issues with constitutive issues. Rather, the primary concern is with the risk of citizens making a poor or misinformed judgement, likely to be at least in part the result of opportunistic actors confusing constitutive issues that are at stake in the referendum with others that are not. In this respect, wherever constitutionally possible, minimalist democrats tend to believe that referendums on European integration are best avoided.

Nevertheless, several proposals have been made to institutionalise referendums in the EU. These include a) requiring national referendums as a matter of course for states who are either entering or exiting the EU (Lacey 2017b); b) national referendums across all member states on all major integration steps or changes to the basic terms of membership (Cheneval 2007); c) optional referendums allowing citizens to launch European-wide popular votes to counter-measures passed by the European institutions (Abromeit 1998) and d) citizens' initiatives allowing citizens to propose new legislation for a European-wide popular vote (Papadopolous 2006). Putting aside the nuanced details of these proposals, some of the main arguments behind them are as follows.

In the case of national referendums (types a) and b)), the positive argument is that there are few better ways to legitimise a decision than through a referendum. As such, when the people(s) of Europe can be seen to validate European integration, its foundations will be stronger in the long term. The negative side of this argument employs Mair's perspective that unless citizens feel like they are in control of European integration, then they are more likely to develop opposition to it. Referendums, it is argued, can engender this sense of ownership far more impressively than either national or European elections. When it comes to European-wide referendums (types c) and d)), the previous arguments can be also applied. However, they apply in a weaker form because the optional referendum and citizens' initiative are popular devices aimed at improving democratic inputs on policy issues only. There would be therefore less at stake in referendums of this kind, compared to membership or Treaty referendums, making their legitimating potential less dramatic. An added virtue of these policy referendums is their potential to draw attention to actors who are directly implicated by European policy debates and who face few obstacles to couching their discourse in pro-European frames. As we have already seen, these actors include pro-EU MEPs and their political groups, as well as European Commissioners. Plausibly, European political groups may be incentivised to become actively involved in coordinating a competing transnational campaign, helping to ensure that the debate maintains a European focus.

When considering the French and Dutch rejection of the Constitutional Treaty by referendum, or the Irish rejections of the Nice and Lisbon Treaties by referendum, or the UK rejection of EU membership by the Brexit referendum, the risks to European integration posed by referendums are hard to deny. Some of the dynamics most feared by minimalist democrats are most evidently at play in the Dutch rejection of the Constitutional Treaty in 2005 and the Brexit referendum in 2016.

In the Dutch case, the emergence of the charismatic national populist figure Geert Wilders in 2004 played a substantial role in transforming European integration into a salient issue for the Dutch. According to the Eurobarometer (2004) survey, in autumn 2004 70 per cent of Dutch citizens supported the idea of a European Constitution. This reflected broad support for the Treaty by the dominant government and opposition parties. However, by the time of the actual vote, 61.5 per cent of Dutch citizens had rejected the Treaty. Part of the success of the No campaign, primarily driven by Wilders, related to his ability to use the Treaty as a means of fearmongering about the erosion of Dutch culture in a cosmopolitan EU that was opening its arms to Turkish membership (Aarts and van der Kolk 2006).

In the Brexit case, we have already seen that the referendum itself was in part a response to electoral pressure by Nigel Farage and UKIP. To this we may add that it was also a response to decades of pressure by a Eurosceptical wing of the Conservative Party. Rather than confront these challenges head-on by consolidating a pro-European narrative, the decision of Prime Minister David Cameron to hold a referendum was an attempt to accommodate the demands of Eurosceptics internal and external to his party. With the expectation that British citizens would vote to remain in the EU, as they had overwhelmingly done in 1973, Cameron hoped to settle 'the Europe question' for at least a generation, silencing internal party critics and neutralising the electoral threat of UKIP. Some of the campaign dynamics during the Brexit referendum were similar to that of the Dutch case. In particular, the part of the leave campaign led by Farage raised fears of Turkish membership and the potential influx of refugees from Syria if Britain remained in the EU.

At first glance, these referendums appear to impressively confirm the worries motivating the minimalist perspective on referendums in the EU. Issues that were irrelevant to the referendums played major roles in determining their outcome, while substantial portions of the population appeared to be unable to rationally navigate the misleading information and speculative arguments to which they were being exposed. However, the story concerning referendums and European integration is not so straightforward. It appears that in both cases political entrepreneurs were able to take advantage of the same lack of positive communication about the EU that we found in the case of national elections.

In both cases, national parties had limited incentives to forge more definite and positive individual volitions on European integration among their citizenries. While Dutch complacency may have benignly demotivated mainstream parties to actively communicate to citizens about the EU by the historical permissive consensus, British parties have been strongly disincentivised to build pro-European narratives. For the Conservatives to do so, it would involve an internal party dispute. This was also true for much of the modern history of the Labour Party who had its own Eurosceptics, due to fears over the neoliberal orientation baked into the four freedoms defining the single market.

The complacency of mainstream Dutch parties helps to explain why debate about the Constitutional Treaty only really began just one month prior to the referendum. In the UK, by contrast, the awareness that any permissive consensus had eroded ensured a much more intense and long-drawn-out debate. Despite this, in both campaigns, pro-European parties struggled to set the agenda and make their pro-integration case, either being outstripped by the ability of Eurosceptics to drive media coverage (Levy et al. 2016) or being forced into a more defensive role, attempting to dispel the claims made by their opponents (Hobolt and Brouard 2011: 313). Indeed, to the extent that mainstream parties had neglected to build a more definite support for European integration over previous decades through a positive communication strategy, their communicative resources for making this case were more limited than they may otherwise have been.

Considering the dynamics of two referendums on major questions can only tell us so much about the potential costs and benefits to direct democracy in the EU. It is therefore worth considering other cases that may shed further light. Simon Hix (2014) notes a curious contrast between the development of public attitudes towards the EU in both the UK and Denmark. Both joined the EU at the same time and with similar levels of enthusiasm among their publics. Yet since the 1990s, public opinion in Denmark has become more positive towards the EU, while it has been on a consistent downward trend in the UK. Hix believes that part of the explanation for this divergence in public opinions has to do with the regular use of referendums in Denmark to decide their nation's stance with respect to issues of European integration. This compares with just two blunt in/out referendums on EU membership in the UK in 1975 and 2016. Following some key assumptions of participatory democracy, Hix (2014: 193) observes that the various referendums on European integration in Denmark (on issues such as Eurozone membership, inclusion in EU Justice and Home Affairs, accession to the authority of the Patent Court, etc.) appear to have given Danish citizens a sense of agency over their EU membership. When they have popularly rejected or accepted some aspect of European integration, they can visibly see their will being implemented.

Relevant here is a corollary of Mair's argument that a lack of democratic opportunities for opposition within the system will lead to opposition to the system itself. Specifically, when there are too few opportunities for opposition, the opportunities that are available are more likely to become a channel for myriad grievances. Indeed, one thing that referendum results against European integration have shown is that they are only partly based on anti-EU sentiment. More broadly, the results are also explained by pro-Europeans that have (well-founded or unfounded) concerns about aspects of European integration (Hobolt and Brouard 2011). Indeed, in her analysis of public opinion on European integration, Catherine de Vries (2018: 82) finds that only 18 per cent of European citizens can be classified as exit sceptics (wishing for the withdrawal of their state from the EU). Meanwhile, 23 per cent of citizens can be considered regime sceptics (wishing for some improvement in the legitimacy of EU institutions and procedures) and 16 per cent are best thought of as policy sceptics (generally wishing for a return of certain competences to their member state).

Those advocating national or European-wide referendums on European issues believe that, with more regular and diverse opportunities to express a view on the direction of Europe, citizens can afford to be more nuanced in how they vote about European integration. Bundling all concerns that they may have about European integration into one exceedingly rare referendum is expected to be less of a temptation when citizens can be sure that they will be regularly and directly consulted on the future of Europe through a direct democratic opportunity structure. This does not mean that pro-integration measures would always pass such referendum tests. However, the democratic visibility of the EU provided by referendums is expected to have a community integration function that helps to stabilise support for European integration over time. The mechanisms of such polity-building are the sense of inclusion and ownership over the European project felt by citizens, in addition to the incentive structure for pro-European national parties and EU level actors to more frequently and publicly develop their positive arguments for European integration.

Conclusion

The purpose of this chapter has not been to discredit the concerns of the minimalist perspective on democratic contestation in the EU. We have seen time and again that their central worries are not without merit: opportunities for contestation have posed risks to European integration, thus validating the tension at the heart of the democratic dilemma facing deeply divided societies. Neither has the chapter attempted to be comprehensive in thinking about all the possible trade-offs between democratic contestation and European integration. For example, it does not systematically discuss the effects of contestatory institutions or the lack thereof on European citizenship or on the democratic legitimacy of the Union (which will include, but is not limited to, the kinds of democratic goods discussed in this chapter). Sandra Seubert's contribution to this volume on what she calls the 'democratic minimum' of European citizenship and Chris Lord's considerations of the trade-offs related to direct and indirect forms of legitimation outline the kind of considerations that would need to be countenanced in such analyses. Instead, the chapter has attempted to make the more general argument that the risks to European integration from a lack of democratisation may be higher than the risks commonly associated with democratisation. Given the fact that the EU has faced several crises in recent years, and is likely to do so again in the future, the potential for political entrepreneurs to ride the wave of these crises by using the existing national and European democratic opportunity structures is an ever present threat to European integration. But what exacerbates this risk is when pro-European actors lack the incentives or institutional mechanisms to make a vigorous case for European integration, both in crisis and non-crisis periods.

By further democratising the EU in some significant way(s), enhanced opportunities for contestation between partisan actors are a means of allowing for and incentivising pro-European political actors to make their pro-EU arguments on a more continuous basis. When political elites are well-experienced in communicating about Europe, they will be better able to deploy these communicative capacities when challenged on questions of European integration, most importantly in times of crisis. Furthermore, when citizens are familiar with the contours of these communications through regular exposure, the capacity of Eurosceptics to exploit ambivalence in public attitudes or to prey on unfounded fears is likely to be significantly reduced.

The chapter has not taken a position on which kind of democratisation may be most desirable from the perspective of preserving and facilitating community integration and problem-solving effectiveness in the EU. To make such a case, a far more elaborate account would be required. One consideration, however, has been highlighted. If one of the key benefits of proposals to further democratise the EU is to incentivise and make publicly visible more vigorous and regular pro-European claims by political actors, then proposals for connecting EP elections to executive office and for European-wide referendums have an advantage over empowering national parliaments in the integration process. Specifically, as the former proposals have transnational reach, they improve the conditions of democratic visibility for commissioners and MEPs and their political groups. These actors, to the extent that their careers and strategic interests are bound up with European integration, will have a strong incentive to communicate positively about European integration. Furthermore, to the extent that they are not mired in domestic party politics, they will have fewer obstacles to communicating as such.

Whatever may be the optimal way to democratise the EU, there are clear obstacles to such reforms. Most obvious is the need for Treaty reform and the condition of unanimous consent to make such changes. This hurdle, in turn, demotivates political actors to even consider pursuing reforms. Related to the unanimity requirement is what kind of reforms citizens would be most likely to support. The problem is that it can be difficult to reliably draw conclusions about what forms of democratisation citizens are most likely to support from existing data. For example, in exploring the regime and policy preferences of various kinds of Eurosceptics and EU loyalists, de Vries (2018: 190–4) finds that there is strong support for strengthening the EP and little appetite for strengthening the Commission. Furthermore, the idea of a European president is deeply unpopular. From this data, it is unclear what exactly citizens are imagining by a 'European president' or the empowerment of the EP, and therefore whether connecting EP elections to the Commission presidency would have popular appeal.

A clearer signal from de Vries' data is unambiguous support for the greater involvement of citizens in European decision-making through referendums. Intriguingly, this proposal is by far the most popular of all regime and policy proposals considered by citizens in the survey. Furthermore, referendums are supported by both EU loyalists and all categories of Eurosceptic mentioned above. What kind of direct democratic opportunities would satisfy the clear appetite for referendums is not entirely obvious. Another study fills out at least part of what it might mean. Using EUVox data measuring public attitudes in twenty-two EU countries, Mendez and Mendez (2017: 43–4) find that there are majorities in almost all member states (except Czech Republic and Slovenia) that Treaties should be decided by referendum. However, there is no majority in any population for the idea that a single member state on its own should be able to veto a Treaty. None of this can be taken as direct support for a scheme of European-wide referendums on non-Treaty or secondary legislation, whether it be the optional referendum or citizens' initiative. However, to the extent that citizens appear to be broadly supportive of increased referendum opportunities in the EU, while being willing to relax the unanimity requirement even for Treaty change, then the prospects of a (super-)majoritarian form of European-wide direct democracy on secondary legislation is worth exploring.

References

Aachen, Christopher H. and Bartels, Larry M. (2016) *Democracy for Realists: Why Elections Do Not Produce Responsive Government*. Princeton: Princeton University Press.

Aarts, Kees and van der Kolk, Henk (2006) Understanding the Dutch 'No': The Euro, the East and the Elite. *PS: Political Science and Politics*, 39: 243–6.

Abromeit, Heidrun. (1998) *Democracy in Europe: Legitimising Politics in a Non-State Polity.* Oxford: Berghahn Books.

Barber, Benjamin. (1984) *Strong Democracy. Participatory Politics for a New Age.* Berkeley: University of California Press.

Bardi, Luciano, Bressanelli, Edoardo, Calossi, Enrico, Gagatek, Wojciech, Mair, Peter and Pizzimenti, Eugenio (2010) *How to Create a Transnational Party System.* European Parliament Directorate-General for Internal Policies, <http://www.eui.eu/Projects/EUDO-OPPR/Documents/StudyOPPR-PE.pdf> (last accessed 18 March 2012).

Bartolini, Stefano (2006) Should the Union be 'Politicized'? Prospects and Risks. Politics: The Right or the Wrong Sort of Medicine for the EU? Notre Europe, Policy Paper No. 19.

Bellamy, Richard (2019) *A Republican Europe of States: Cosmopolitanism, Intergovernmentalism and Democracy in the EU.* Cambridge: Cambridge University Press.

Bellamy, Richard and Kröger, Sandra (2016) Beyond a Constraining Dissensus: The Role of National Parliaments in Domesticating and Normalising the Politicization of European Integration. *Comparative European Politics*, 14: 131–53.

Bellamy, Richard, Bonnotti, Matteo, Castiglione, Dario, Lacey, Joseph, Owen, David, Nasstrom, Sofia and White, Jonathan (2019) The Democratic Production of Political Cohesion: Partisanship, Institutional Design and Life Form. *Contemporary Political Theory*, 18(2): 282–310.

Cheneval, Francis (2007) *Caminante, no hay camino, se hace camino al andar*: EU Citizenship, Direct Democracy and Treaty Ratification. *European Law Journal*, 13(5): 647–63.

Cheneval, Francis and Schimmelfennig, Frank (2013) The Case for Demoi-cracy in the European Union. *Journal of Common Market Studies*, 51(2): 334–50.

Cheysson, Anatole and Fraccoroli, Nicolo (2019) Ideology in Times of Crisis: A Principal Component Analysis of Votes in the European Parliament, 2004-2019. CEIS Tor Vergata Research Paper Series, Vol. 17, Issue 5, No. 461.

De Vries, Catherine (2018) *Euroscepticism and the Future of European Integration.* Oxford: Oxford University Press.

De Vries, Catherine and Hobolt, Sara B. (2020) *Political Entrepreneurs: The Rise of Challenger Parties in Europe.* Princeton: Princeton University Press.

De Vries, Catherine E., Hobolt, Sara B. and Walter, Stefanie (2021) Politicizing International Cooperation: The Mass Public, Political Entrepreneurs, and Political Opportunity Structures. *International Organization*, 7 (2): 306–32.

Dolezal, Martin (2012) Restructuring the European Political Space: The Supply Side of Eurobarometer (2004) Standard Eurobarometer 62 – Autumn 2004. <https://europa.eu/eurobarometer/surveys/detail/455> (last accessed 15 January 2022).

European Electoral Politics. In Kriesi, Hanspeter, Grande, Edgar, Dolezal, Martin, Helbling, Marc, Höglinger, Dominic, Hutter, Swen and Wüest, Bruno (eds) *Political Conflict in Western Europe.* Cambridge: Cambridge University Press, pp. 127–50.

Featherstone, Kevin (1994) Jean Monnet and the 'Democratic Deficit' in the European Union. *Journal of Common Market Studies*, 32(2): 149–70.

Follesdal, Andreas and Hix, Simon (2006) Why There is a Democratic Deficit in the EU: A Response to Majone and Moravcsik. *Journal of Common Market Studies,* 44(3), 533–62.

Habermas, Jürgen (2015) Democracy in Europe: Why the Development of the EU into a Transnational Democracy is Necessary and How it is Possible. *European Law Journal,* 21(4): 546–57.

Hansson, Sten and Kröger, Sandra (2021) How a Lack of Truthfulness Can Undermine Democratic Representation: The Case of Post-referendum Brexit Discourses. *The British Journal of Politics and International Relation,* 23(4): 609–26.

Hix, Simon. (2014) Democratizing a Macroeconomic Union in Europe. In Cramme, Olaf and Hobolt, Sara B. (eds) *Democratic Politics in a European Union Under Stress.* Oxford: Oxford University Press, pp. 180–98.

Hix, Simon and Marsh, Michael (2011) Second-order Effects Plus Pan-European Political Swings: An Analysis of European Parliament Elections across Time. *Electoral Studies,* 30: 4–15.

Hobolt, Sara Binzer and Brouard, Sylvian (2011) Contesting the European Union? Why the Dutch and the French Rejected the European Constitution. *Political Research Quarterly,* 64(2): 309–22.

Hooghe, Liesbet and Marks, Gary (2009) A Postfunctionalist Theory of European Integration: From Permissive Consensus to Constraining Dissensus. *British Journal of Political Science,* 39(1): 1–23.

Hurrelmann, Achim and Debardeleben, Joan (2009) Democratic Dilemmas in EU Multilevel Governance: Untying the Gordian Knot. *European Political Science Review,* 1(2), 229–47.

Isiksel, Turkuler (2017) *Europe's Functional Constitution: A Theory of Constitutionalism Beyond the State.* Oxford: Oxford University Press.

Lacey, Joseph (2016) Conceptually Mapping the European Union: A Demoi-cratic Analysis. *Journal of European Integration,* 38(1): 61–77.

Lacey, Joseph (2017a) *Centripetal Democracy: Democratic Legitimacy and Political Identity in Belgium, Switzerland and the European Union.* Oxford: Oxford University Press.

Lacey, Joseph (2017b) National Autonomy and Democratic Standardization: Should Popular Votes on European Integration be Regulated by the European Union? *European Law Journal,* 23(6): 523–35.

Lacey, Joseph (2018) Populist Nationalism and Ontological Security. On the Construction of Moral Antagonisms in the UK, Switzerland and Belgium. In Herman, Lise and Muldoon, James (eds) *Trumping the Mainstream: The Conquest of Mainstream Democratic Politics by Far-Right Populism.* London: Routledge.

Lacey, Joseph and Nicolaïdis, Kalypso (2020) Democracy and Disintegration: Does the State of Democracy in the EU Put the Integrity of the Union at Risk? In Coman, Ramona, Crespy, Amandine and Schmidt, Vivien A. (eds) *Governance and Politics in the Post-crisis European Union.* Cambridge: Cambridge University Press.

Levy, David A. L., Aslan, Billur and Bironzo, Diego (2016) The UK Press Coverage of the EU Referendum. Reuters Institute for the Study of Journalism, <https://ora.ox.ac.uk/objects/uuid:8a0aac1f-8805-4ce4-96a8-207c1479c0c6> (last accessed 12 March 2021).

Lijphart, Arend (1977) *Democracy in Plural Societies*. New Haven: Yale University Press.
McNamara, Kathleen R. and Musgrave, Paul (2020) Democracy and Collective Identity in the European Union and the United States. *Journal of Common Market Studies*, 58(1): 172–88.
Mair, Peter (2007) Political Opposition and the European Union. *Government and Opposition*, 42(1): 1–17.
Mendez, Fernando and Mendez, Mario (2017) *Referendums on EU Matters*. European Parliament.
Miller, David (1995) *On Nationality*. Oxford: Oxford University Press.
Mitrany, David [1943] (1966) *A Working Peace System*. Chicago: Quadrangle Books, pp. 25–99.
Moore, Gavin, Loizides, Neophytos, Sandal, Nukhet A. and Lordos, Alexandros (2014) Winning Peace Frames: Intra-Ethnic Outbidding in Northern Ireland and Cyprus. *West European Politics*, 37(1): 159–81.
Moravcsik, Andrew (2008) The Myth of Europe's 'Democratic Deficit'. *Intereconomics*, 43(6): 331–40.
Norman, Ludwig (2021) To Democratize or to Protect? How the Response to Anti-System Parties Reshapes the EU's Transnational Party System. *Journal of Common Market Studies*, 59(3): 721–37.
Offe, Clause (2017) Referendum Versus Institutionalized Deliberation: What Democratic Theorists Can Learn from the 2016 Brexit Decision. *Daedalus*, 146(3): 14–27.
Papadopolous, Yannis (2006) Implementing (and Radicalizing) Art. I-47.4 of the Constitution: Is the Addition of Some (Semi-)Direct Democracy to the Nascent Consociational European Federation Just Swiss Folklore? *Journal of European Public Policy*, 12(3): 448–67.
Papadopoulos, Yannis and Magnette, Paul (2010) On the Politicisation of the EU: Lessons from Consociational National Polities. *West European Politics*, 3 (4), 711–29.
Pateman, Carole (1970) *Participation and Democratic Theory*. Cambridge: Cambridge University Press.
Pateman, Carole (2012) Participatory Democracy Revisited. *Perspectives on Politics*, 10(1): 7–19.
Rauh, Christian, Bes, Bart Joachim and Schoonevelde, Martijn (2019) Undermining, Defusing, or Defending European Integration? Assessing Public Communication of European Executives in Times of EU Politicization. *European Journal of Political Research*, 59(2): 397–423.
Reilly, Benjamin (2012) Institutional Designs for Diverse Democracies: Consociationalism, Centripetalism and Communalism Compared. *European Political Science*, 11: 259–70.
Schmidt, Vivian A. (2013) Democracy and Legitimacy in the European Union Revisited: Input, Output and Throughput. *Political Studies*, 61: 2–22.
Schmitt, Hermann and Teperoglou, Eftichia (2015) The 2014 European Parliament Elections in Southern Europe: Second-Order or Critical Elections? *South European Society and Politics*, 20(3): 287–309.

Schumpeter, Joseph [1943] (2003) *Capitalism, Socialism & Democracy*. London: Routledge.
Statham, Paul (2010) What Kind of Europeanized Public Politics? In Koopmans, Ruud and Statham, Paul (eds) *The Making of a European Public Sphere: Media Discourse and Political Contention*. Cambridge: Cambridge University Press.
Stojanović, Nenad (2019) Democracy, Ethnoicracy and Consociational Demoicracy. *International Political Science Review*, 41(1): 30–43.
Taylor, Charles (1993) *Reconciling the Solitudes: Essays on Canadian Federalism and Nationalism*. Quebec: McGill-Queens University Press.
Treib, Oliver (2014) The Voter Says No, But Nobody Listens: Causes and Consequences of the Eurosceptic Vote in the 2014 European Elections. *Journal of European Public Policy*, 21(10): 1541–54.
Treib, Oliver (2020) Euroscepticism is Here to Stay: What Cleavage Theory Can Teach Us about the 2019 European Parliament Elections. *Journal of European Public Policy*, 28(2): 174–89. DOI: 10.1080/13501763.2020.1737881.
White, Jonathan (2019) *Politics of Last Resort*. Oxford: Oxford University Press.
White, Jonathan and Ypi, Lea (2016) *The Meaning of Partisanship*. Oxford: Oxford University Press.

SEVEN

Europe's Democratic Dilemmas in Historical Perspective

Sheri Berman

We are living in a time when democracy in the West is facing its greatest challenges since the 1960s and perhaps even since the end of the Second World War. The chapters in this book address various challenges confronting European democracy at the national and regional levels. As Niklas Bremberg and Ludvig Norman note in their introduction to the volume 'The European political order has an ambivalent relationship with democracy. Democratic concerns have been part of the discussions on European [postwar] cooperation since its inception.' It is now perhaps worth stepping back and reminding ourselves how recent and difficult to achieve stable consolidated democracy actually was in Europe.

During the nineteenth and first half of the twentieth century, Europe was convulsed by political upheaval; despite myriad attempts since the French Revolution, stable democracy proved elusive. Most tragically, during the interwar period failed democratic experiments led to the rise of the most brutal regime and deadliest war the world had ever experienced. Yet after the Second World War, the western half of the continent was transformed: political stability became the norm. It is against the backdrop of the decades of democracy Western Europe has enjoyed since 1945 that the democratic dilemmas and challenges examined in this volume emerged. Understanding and addressing these dilemmas should, accordingly, be facilitated by an examination of what it took to finally make democracy work in Europe.

There were many reasons, of course, for Western Europe's post-1945 transformation, but essential were changes that occurred at the war's end (Berman 2019). In particular, actors across the political spectrum and on both sides of the Atlantic recognised that stabilising democracy would require more than merely getting rid of existing dictatorships; it would necessitate a new understanding of the relationship among states, markets and societies. As a result, after 1945 Europeans, with the cooperation of the United States, constructed a new order designed to promote peace and democratic consolidation. At the heart of this order was a recognition, as other authors in this volume note, of the tension between capitalism and democracy. This is a tension, of course, that scholars and citizens have grown increasingly concerned about in our era of rapid economic change and in light of the fallout from the 2008 financial crisis. After the Second World War, actors across the political spectrum and on both sides of the Atlantic accepted the need for a new social contract between governments and their citizens, with the former promising to protect the latter from the destructive and destabilising effects of capitalism. This was understood as necessary to avoid the economic crises, extremism and democratic failures that had plagued Europe during the interwar years.

European integration was the regional pillar of this postwar order, complimenting new international and domestic institutions. During the last decades of the twentieth century, however, the regional, international and domestic pillars of the postwar order deteriorated. With regard to European integration, the authors in this volume stress how the process veered away from many of the insights motivating the architects of the postwar order. In particular, economic integration outpaced political integration, particularly after the transition to European monetary union and the shift towards a neoliberal economic order at the end of the twentieth century, contributing to a situation where neither national nor European-level institutions were capable of dealing with the destructive and destabilising consequences of capitalism. As architects of the postwar order might have predicted, this had problematic consequences for democracy. In order to fully understand how and why this was the case, it is necessary to re-examine the insights and institutions the postwar order was based on. A recognition of the need to forthrightly recognise and address the tension between capitalism and democracy or free markets and democratic stability was at the heart of this order, just as it is at the heart of many of the dilemmas and challenges facing Europe today.

The Postwar Order

It was only after the most destructive war in history that Western Europe finally put an end to the political, social and international conflicts it had suffered through since 1789. One consequence of the tragedies of the 1930s and 1940s was that the leaders who survived emerged devoted to ensuring peace and democracy and more knowledgeable about what it would take to make those a reality. After 1945 actors across the political spectrum understood that successful liberal democracy required more than changing political institutions and procedures; it also required new social and economic arrangements and relationships capable of taming capitalism and protecting citizens from its negative economic and social consequences. Such views had long been championed by social democrats (Berman 2006); what changed after 1945 is that they were embraced by liberals, Christian Democrats and others.

Liberals, for example, had long been wary of democracy, fearing providing the 'masses' with the vote would inevitably lead to threats to private property in particular and capitalism in general. Liberals also, of course, did not view capitalism as dangerous nor did they believe the state could or should intervene regularly to tame it. (Late nineteenth and early twentieth-century progressive liberals did recognise social and political problems with capitalism, but they generally favoured dealing with these after the fact, rather than by governments directly intervening to prevent problems.) Christian Democratic parties, meanwhile, had a mixed record on democracy during the pre-Second World War period, and while they did recognise capitalism's negative effects, they generally focused on its tendency to undermine religious beliefs and 'traditional' values and favoured corporate, illiberal arrangements over liberal democratic ones.

This changed, however, after the war. Liberal parties accepted democracy and the need for governments to do more to protect citizens from capitalism's downsides. Christian Democrats also accepted democracy as well as the need to counteract capitalism's negative effects within a democratic framework. And on the other side of the Atlantic, the United States, which was most committed to the restoration of a global free-trade order after the war, nonetheless also recognised that ensuring political stability and liberal democracy in Europe required limiting capitalism's destabilising and destructive effects. Reflecting this, in his opening speech to the Bretton Woods conference, US Treasury Secretary Henry Morgenthau noted, 'All of us have seen the great economic tragedy of our time. We saw the worldwide depression of the 1930s . . . We saw bewilderment and bitterness become the breeders of fascism and finally of war.' To prevent a recurrence of this phenomenon, Morgenthau argued, national governments would have to be able to do more to protect people from capitalism's 'malign effects' (Ikenberry 1992).

The postwar order that emerged in Western Europe was accordingly based on a recognition of the tension between capitalism and democracy and that new institutions and relationships would be needed if it was to be overcome. More particularly, European and American leaders recognised that for democracy to work, the economic crises, inequality and social divisions that had generated political extremism and undermined democracy in the past had to be avoided. This order entailed, in other words, a social democratic contract between governments and citizens (Berman 2006), with the former committing to protecting the latter from capitalism's negative effects.

With regard to policy changes at the domestic level, the two most obvious reflections of this change were Keynesianism and the welfare state. Keynesianism rejected the view that markets operate best when left alone and accepted that substantial state intervention might be necessary to avoid economic crises that could threaten democracy and the capitalist system itself. Critical was that Keynes, having experienced the rise of the Soviet Union and the Great Depression, understood that unchecked markets were socially and politically dangerous. As his biographer Robert Skidelsky noted, 'Keynes was quite conscious in seeking an alternative to dictatorship . . . a programme on which to fight back against fascism and communism' (Skidelsky 1989: 35–6; Katzenstein and Kirshner 2022). That Keynes favoured a more active role for the state for economic as well as political reasons is important to remember: he understood the power of communism's insistence that capitalism could not be rescued from its flaws and that a large part of fascism's appeal had stemmed from its critique of liberalism's ineffectiveness in the face of economic crisis combined with its own illiberal, undemocratic solutions to the Great Depression (Skidelsky 1989: 35–6). Keynes hoped that by designing a 'system that held out the prospect that the state could reconcile the private ownership of the means of production with democratic management of the economy' (Przeworksi 1985: 207) he could convince people that democracy was capable of tackling capitalism's problems.

Like Keynesianism, the welfare state reflected a transformed understanding of the correct relationship among states, markets and societies. As C. A. R. Crosland noted, after 1945 'it was increasingly regarded as a proper function and indeed obligation of Government to ward off distress and strain not only among the poor but almost all classes of society' (Crosland 1967: 98). West European welfare states were designed not only to protect citizens from economic distress; they were also designed to promote social solidarity, since welfare states required and fostered a sense of kinship and solidarity among citizens. In T. H. Marshall's formulation, welfare states provided the foundation for a new, 'social' understanding of citizenship whereby it became the government's obligation to ensure 'an equalization between the more and the less fortunate' and that all citizens enjoyed a level of 'economic welfare and security' that would enable them to 'share to the full in the social heritage' and 'civilized life' of their nation (Marshall 1950: 113, 115, 120). Like Keynesianism, the expansion of welfare states reflected the postwar order's political goal of undercutting support for left and right-wing extremism, both of which had fed off the social and economic dislocations and divisions generated by capitalism.

Keynesianism and expanded welfare states were not the only changes characterising European political economies during the postwar period – nor, in the case of Keynesianism, were they equally embraced by all West European nations. Each West European country developed its own particular mix of policies designed to protect its citizens from the downsides of markets. This reshaping of postwar domestic political economies along social democratic lines and the 'social' understanding of citizenship that developed along with it, reshaped the relationship between states, markets and society in a way that contributed significantly to social peace and the consolidation of democracy in Western Europe after 1945. But the architects of the postwar order understood that the maintenance of peace, prosperity and democracy would require more than changes at the domestic level; new international and regional institutions would be necessary as well.

At the international level the United States helped to create new international security and economic institutions to help stabilise postwar Western Europe. The Truman doctrine committed the United States to defending Western Europe's fledgling democracies from the Soviet threat, and the North Atlantic Treaty Organization (NATO) linked Western Europe to the United States and integrated Germany into the Western security bloc. Economically, the United States helped to construct the Bretton Woods system, the General Agreement on Tariffs and Trade (GATT), the International Monetary Fund (IMF) and more, to support Western Europe's postwar economic reconstruction and the growth that would be necessary to build support for democracy. The regional pillar of the postwar order – European integration – stemmed from a recognition by European and American leaders that successful democracy required overcoming challenges that could not be achieved by individual European governments acting alone. Postwar economic reconstruction, for example, could not be achieved without coordination and cooperation among European countries. As Robert Schuman (1950) put it, if 'Europe' were 'to exist . . . It will be a Europe where the standard of living will rise and [France and Germany] work together for common goals.' Reconstruction had to be complemented by peace, moreover, which meant finding a way to reconcile Germany with Europe and vice versa. In Churchill's words, 'to bring [Europe's horrible history] to an end, it would be necessary to re-create the European family . . . and provide it with a structure under which it can dwell in peace, safety and freedom'.

The goal had to be the creation of a 'continent so integrated, so connected that war would be impossible' (Churchill 1946).

In general, the postwar order worked remarkably well. Western Europe recovered more rapidly from the destruction of the war than almost anyone initially thought possible and the three decades following the war's end were Europe's fastest period of growth ever. Alongside rapid economic growth came a dramatic rise in living standards and a dramatic decline in inequality: the economic pie grew and became more evenly distributed. These socio-economic changes had profound political consequences. The combination of growth and equity undercut liberal and conservative fears of the lower classes' political power as well as communists' insistence on capitalism's ineluctable inequities and demise. The order's success concomitantly de-radicalised workers and employers, making both more willing to compromise (Offe 1983; Maier 1981). West European party systems also de-radicalised, becoming dominated by moderate parties of the centre-left (social democratic or Labour) and centre-right (Christian Democratic, liberal, conservative), as opposed to the pre-war pattern where most European party systems were pulled apart by right and left-wing extremism (Kirchheimer 1966). Alongside changed domestic dynamics, European integration and American-led security and economic arrangements facilitated Germany's incorporation into the European community and the Atlantic alliance, enabling Western Europe to achieve a degree of peace and political stability unmatched in its modern history.

The Unravelling of the Postwar Order

Despite the postwar order's success, it began deteriorating during the 1970s. As many authors in this volume discuss, with regard to the order's regional component, European integration, despite originating as part of a multi-pronged effort to promote stable democracy, the way European integration proceeded ended up generating myriad political problems. Most obviously, Europe developed a highly integrated and interdependent economy, but no corresponding political authority capable of tempering or taming it.

A political deficit appeared during the earliest stages of the integration process. The foundation of the European project – the 1951 European Coal and Steel community (ECSC) – set a pattern whereby European economic integration outpaced the development of European political institutions. The goals of the ECSC were explicitly political – ensuring peace and stability in Europe by binding France and Germany so closely together so as to make conflict between them unthinkable. But the means chosen to achieve these ends were economic – the creation of a common market for coal and steel. As Europe's common market expanded to include more countries and more sectors of the economy, the pattern continued. In the 1957 Treaty of Rome, for example, France, Germany, Italy, Belgium, Luxembourg and the Netherlands agreed to remove all restrictions on trade, institute common external tariffs, reduce barriers to the free movement of people, services and capital, and develop common agricultural policies, but did little to integrate political decision-making. The result was that by the 1960s, European economic integration had probably gone further than even early architects of the process had imagined, while political integration lagged further and further behind. Accompanying this, as Sandra Seubert discusses in her chapter, was the development of a type of European citizenship that was primarily economic in nature, to use T. H. Marshall's categories, based on economic rights like freedom of movement and economic non-discrimination, rather than political and social rights, as national-level citizenship regimes had come to entail.

Problems or dilemmas stemming from these developments became increasingly clear during the last decades of the twentieth century. By the late 1970s, Europe's postwar period of growth was coming to an end as Western countries experienced a toxic mix of unemployment and inflation. Partially in response, the United States abandoned the gold standard, throwing the postwar monetary order into chaos. European governments responded to these developments with various policies, none of which worked well and some of which, like floating currencies, threatened to lead to conflict among them. In response, European leaders decided to move forward with monetary cooperation and, eventually, integration (Economic and Monetary Union (EMU)) (McNamara 1997).

At the time, many viewed this as the next logical step in the process of economic integration. But as many in this volume point out, monetary integration along with the rise of neoliberalism deepened the divergence between European economic and political integration, sowing the seeds of myriad contemporary political problems. Most obviously, EMU and neoliberalism furthered and deepened the democratic deficit already embedded in the European project. The economic problems confronting the West during the last decades of the twentieth century combined with the collapse of communism in 1989–90 opened up a space for the rise of neoliberalism.

In the decades after 1945 neoliberals had been thinking about what they viewed as the downsides of the postwar order and what to do about it (Slobodian 2018). This neoliberalism didn't gain much traction when the postwar order was working well but when problems appeared beginning in the 1970s, neoliberals were prepared with critiques of the existing order and an alternative to it. Neoliberalism's success was further promoted by the collapse of communism which removed a threat that had led many on the right to accept the social democratic consensus as the 'lesser evil'. The collapse of communism also led, particularly within the economics profession (Appelbaum 2019) and among the technocrats dominating many European political parties, including social democratic and Labour ones (Mudge 2018; Fourcade and Babb 2002), to a sort of market triumphalism, a sense that capitalism's problems had been solved – that experts now fully understood how markets worked and how to ensure that they continued to do so smoothly

Neoliberalism's goal was to unshackle markets from the oversight of political authorities in general and roll back many of the postwar order's restrictions on markets in particular. Not fully achievable on the domestic level thanks to deeply rooted social democratic norms and institutions, neoliberal thinking and policies gained more success at the regional level, most notably with the development of European monetary union which deprived national governments of a critical economic policy tool and shifted authority to a central bank free from political, let alone democratic, oversight.

As Kathleen McNamara, for example, notes in her chapter in this volume, EMU made even clearer the negative consequences of the development of a 'European capitalism without European democracy'. McNamara stresses the long-term, historical tension between free-market capitalism and democracy; indeed, as noted above, a key goal of the postwar order was alleviating this tension. Yet by the late twentieth century, those driving the process of European integration had either forgotten about this tension or believed it had been overcome, since the European Community/Union's development during this period was characterised by increasing economic integration and marketisation, but not a concomitant development of national or regional authorities capable of regulating or alleviating the disruptive consequences of economic integration and marketisation. Neither, relatedly, did the nature of European Union (EU) citizenship change greatly during this period. It instead, remained, as Sandra Seubert puts it in her chapter in this volume, 'substantially thin', with economic rights still largely detached from the 'privileges of political membership ... and collective identity', thereby potentially hindering the formation of the type of pan-European social solidarity and identity that might have contributed to overcoming the divergence between the EU's economic and political development.

It is for these reasons, of course, as almost all the chapters in this volume point out, that discussions of Europe's democratic deficit heated up during the late twentieth and early twenty-first centuries. The deepening of economic integration, European monetary union and the spread of neoliberal capitalism throughout Western and then, after the collapse of the Soviet Union, to the newly democratised countries of Eastern Europe occurred, while little progress was made on increasing the EU's political capacity and hence its ability to deal with the downsides stemming from the spread of a neoliberal version of capitalism. More generally, the underdevelopment of European-level political institutions, combined with the diminished economic control enjoyed by national-level governments due to EMU and neoliberalism, contributed to what Peter Mair and other scholars (Mair 2013; Bickerton 2012) refer to as the hollowing out of European democracy – a decline in the ability of political actors and institutions to recognise and respond to the needs of citizens.

This was made most obvious in the economic sphere in the aftermath of the 2008 financial crisis. The lack of authoritative, democratic political institutions at the regional level robbed the EU of the ability to respond forcefully to the crisis, fanning the flames of nationalism and contributing to a populist backlash. Brexit, of course, was the most dramatic consequence of a perception that European integration no longer benefited many citizens. Similarly tragic has been the development of Eastern Europe over the past decades. East European nations were integrated into the European Union during a period of neoliberal market enthusiasm. Although there were many reasons for the particular type of economic transition that occurred in Eastern Europe, the strictures, norms and requirements of European Union membership were a crucial determinant. The neoliberal version of capitalism introduced into Eastern Europe generated immense economic suffering and deep social and geographic inequalities (Ghodsee and Orenstein 2021) that nationalist, illiberal populists exploited to garner support, generate resentment against the EU and undermine the foundations of democracy. The EU's overall political weakness then made it difficult to respond forcefully to the democratic backsliding promoted by national, illiberal populists in the East, thereby tragically bringing the European project full circle – from one designed to strengthen democracy in Western Europe to one that stood by impotently while it was undermined in its Eastern half.

Conclusions

Consolidated well-functioning democracy only became the norm in Western Europe after 1945. The political and economic success of Western Europe after 1945 was built on the foundation of the postwar order. This order had domestic, regional and international pillars, all of which were designed to help Europe overcome the challenges that had hindered peace and political stability in the past, perhaps the most obvious of which was the tension between capitalism and democracy. The postwar order, accordingly, was designed to tame or counteract the destabilising and destructive social and political consequences of capitalism and thereby avoid the economic crises, extremism and democratic failures that had plagued Europe through the interwar years.

So successful was this order that stable democracy came to be taken for granted in Europe. By the late twentieth century, European and American leaders seemed to have forgotten how long it took and how difficult it was to achieve stable, consolidated democracy in the first place. The historical tension between capitalism and democracy that had played such a large role in scuttling democratic experiments in the past, and whose overcoming was a key goal of the postwar order's architects, seemed to be either forgotten about or believed to have been overcome. As a result, during the last decades of the twentieth century the rise of neoliberalism in general and the transition to European monetary union in particular dramatically increased the divergence between the negative and differential impact of neoliberal capitalism on certain European citizens and populations and the ability of national and European-level political institutions to recognise and respond to these citizens' and populations' concerns and needs. Europe accordingly ended up during the early twenty-first century not only with serious economic problems, like rising socio-economic and geographical inequality, but also myriad political ones as well, most notably rising nationalism and populism in Western Europe and illiberalism and democratic backsliding in Eastern Europe.

Understanding and perhaps addressing Europe's democratic dilemmas requires understanding what it takes to make democracy work – at the national and European levels – in the first place. What Europe's own history makes clear, is that making democracy work requires forthrightly recognising and dealing with the long-standing historical tension between capitalism and democracy. If left untamed and unregulated, capitalism generates socio-economic and geographic inequalities, economic crises, unemployment, poverty and more – all of which provide fertile ground for extremism, racism and xenophobia, and civil as well as international conflicts. Even with the growth of populism in Western Europe and democratic backsliding in Eastern Europe, contemporary Europe does not face the type of challenges it did in the interwar years. But developments over the past decade or two should give democracy's supporters pause – dealing with Europe's democratic dilemmas will require that national and regional-level political institutions (re)develop the ability to deal with contemporary social and economic challenges. While this will not be easy – as authors in this volume note, European countries have different views about the type of political and social reforms necessary to revitalise European democracy and the European Union – problems cannot be solved until they are confronted head-on. If they are not, discontent and disillusionment with democracy and the EU will grow and, with it, the potential for further democratic decay.

References

Appelbaum, Binyamin (2019) *The Economists' Hour. False Prophets, Free Markets, and the Fracture of Society*. New York: Little Brown and Company.

Berman, Sheri (2006) *The Primacy of Politics. Social Democracy and the Making of Europe's Twentieth Century*. New York: Cambridge University Press.

Berman, Sheri (2019) *Democracy and Dictatorship in Europe. From the Ancien Régime to the Present Day*. New York: Oxford University Press.

Bickerton, Chris (2012) *European Integration. From Nation-States to Member States*. London: Oxford University Press.

Churchill, Winston (1946) I Wish to Speak to You Today About the Tragedy of Europe, Zurich, 19 September, <https://www.open.edu/openlearn/ocw/pluginfile.php/614782/mod_resource/content/1/ReadingsBCD.pdf> (last accessed 5 December 2022).

Crosland, C. A. R. (1967) *The Future of Socialism*. London: Fletcher and Son.

Fourcade, Marion and Babb, Sarah (2002) The Rebirth of the Liberal Creed. Paths to Neoliberalism in Four Countries. *American Journal of Sociology*, 108(3): 533–79.

Ghodsee, Kristen and Orenstein, Mitchell (2021) *Taking Stock of Shock. Social Consequences of the 1989 Revolutions*. New York: Oxford University Press.

Ikenberry, G. John (1992) A World Economy Restored. *International Organization*, 46(1): 289–321.

Katzenstein, Peter J. and Kirshner, Jonathan (eds) (2022) *The Downfall of the American Order*. Ithaca: Cornell University Press.

Kirchheimer, Otto (1966) The Transformation of West European Party Systems. In LaPolombara, Joseph and Weiner, Myron (eds) *Political Parties and Political Development*. Princeton: Princeton University Press.

McNamara, Kathleen (1997) *The Currency of Ideas. Monetary Politics in the European Union*. Ithaca: Cornell University Press.

Maier, Charles (1981) The Two Postwar Eras and the Conditions for Stability in Twentieth-Century Western Europe. *The American Historical Review*, 86(2): 327–52.

Mair, Peter (2013) *Ruling the Void. The Hollowing of Western Democracy*. New York: Verso.

Marshall, T. H. (1950) *Citizenship and Social Class*. New York: Cambridge University Press.

Mudge, Stephanie (2018) *Leftism Reinvented: Western Parties from Socialism to Neoliberalism*. Cambridge, MA: Harvard University Press.

Offe, Clas (1983) Competitive Party Democracy and the Keynesian Welfare State. Factors of Stability and Disintegration. *Policy Sciences*, 15: 225–46.

Przeworksi, Adam (1985) *Capitalism and Social Democracy.* New York: Cambridge University Press.
Schuman, Robert (1950) The Schuman Declaration, <https://europa.eu/european-union/about-eu/symbols/europe-day/schuman-declaration_en> (last accessed 5 December 2022).
Skidelsky, Robert (1989) The Political Meaning of Keynesianism. In Hall, Peter (ed.) *The Political Power of Economic Ideas.* Princeton: Princeton University Press.
Slobodian, Quinn (2018) *Globalists: The End of Empire and the Birth of Neoliberalism.* Cambridge, MA: Harvard University Press.

EIGHT

The European Union's Main Democratic Deficits in Comparative Perspective

R. Daniel Kelemen

This excellent volume edited by Niklas Bremberg and Ludvig Norman seeks to foster debate about the trade-offs and dilemmas policymakers face in trying to build a democratic European Union (EU) and the challenges that scholars face in trying to assess the EU's democratic credentials. The contributors examine a number of key dilemmas of European democracy – including legitimate representation in the absence of a shared identity (Lord), the potential for citizen participation and deliberative democracy in the EU (Cengiz), the importance of enhancing contestation over EU policies (Lacey), the tensions between market logics and democracy (McNamara), the challenges of sustaining democracy as the territorial scale at which collective action is needed shifts (Keating) and the content of democratic citizenship (Seubert). The erudite contributions deliver on the editors' aim, which was not to provide a conclusive set of answers to Europe's democratic dilemmas but rather to offer 'fresh insights into EU democracy [and highlight] new ways to understand the tensions and trade-offs inherent in the application of democratic concepts to the European political order'.

In offering my reflections, I will explore some cross cutting issues concerning the democratic dimensions of Europe's political order that have implications for themes that come up across the contributions to the volume. My modus operandi is, following McNamara's advice in her chapter, to '[situate] the EU case within the broader history of comparative political development' – specifically through comparisons with the development and functioning of democratic polities. Debates over the democratic dilemmas of European Union politics have long suffered from a lack of comparative and historical perspective. The EU is often judged against a kind of platonic ideal of democracy and found wanting. But the EU might be assessed much more sympathetically if compared to the flawed democratic federations of the real world. Likewise, the development of EU democracy is often treated ahistorically and atemporally, without appreciating what a new polity the EU is and how long it took many real, existing democracies to develop crucial democratic institutions. This lack of perspective has led many analysts to misjudge EU democracy – to convict it of crimes it did not commit, while ignoring those of which it is actually guilty.

In particular, I will emphasise that much of the debate about EU democracy has been focusing on the wrong democratic deficits. The EU is most often critiqued for alleged democratic deficits of EU-level institutions in Brussels and Strasbourg that – when viewed comparatively and historically – do not appear particularly problematic. Meanwhile, EU scholars have ignored or underestimated democratic deficits in member state governments and the threats these pose to EU democracy. Applying a comparative perspective helps us to rectify this imbalance. It helps us to see that, for all their shortcomings, the EU's central institutions do not suffer from grave democratic deficits compared to the central institutions of some well-established federal democracies. Simultaneously, the comparative perspective reminds us that in large, diverse, federal polities like the EU, some of the greatest threats to democracy can come from the emergence of autocratic regimes at the member state level – and helps us to see that this is precisely what has happened in the EU.

The EU's Alleged Democratic Deficits in Comparative Perspective

Democracy is a political system in which leaders are chosen through regular, free and fair elections based on near universal adult suffrage. So is the EU democratic? My main claim is that EU institutions are quite democratic compared to real, existing federal democracies (Zweifel 2002), and that while the EU does have some serious democratic shortcomings, they are very different ones from those emphasised by most of the democratic deficit literature. The EU's main democratic deficits stem from the way its half-baked institutions contribute to an 'authoritarian equilibrium' (Kelemen 2017, 2020), supporting the consolidation of authoritarian governments in some EU member states and enabling them to infiltrate and poison the Union.

First let us review the usual charge sheet against the EU when it comes to its supposed democratic deficit, and consider how the EU's democratic credentials stack up against those of real world democracies. The four most common democratic deficit critiques of the EU are as follows: 1) the EU lacks a demos and common public sphere, so it can't be a democracy; 2) the EU lacks accountability and transparency because too much power lies in the hands of unelected bureaucrats (the Commission) and judges (the European Court of Justice (ECJ)) and too much decision-making happens behind closed doors in the Council out of sight of national parliaments; 3) the main EU institution designed to address the EU's democratic deficit, the European Parliament, cannot do so effectively because it is too distant from the people and attracts little interest or engagement; and finally 4) citizens do not have the sense that they can change the direction of EU policy through replacing one set of leaders with another in truly pan-European elections. In other words, in EU politics citizens cannot really 'vote the bastards out' – replacing one government with another. Therefore, scholars like Sheri Berman (2017), Cas Mudde (2015) and Yascha Mounk (2016) have critiqued the EU as a system of undemocratic liberalism: a polity that promotes liberal policies, but one in which voters cannot really exert democratic control over policy through elections. From this follows the accusation that through its 'undemocratic liberalism' the EU has provoked a backlash of 'illiberal democracy'. In other words, because voters found their countries constrained by EU policies that limited their elected leaders' freedom of choice, they turned to illiberal populists who promised to ignore European legal requirements (as well as national constitutional requirements) in order to deliver on 'the will of the people'.

Certainly, there is some truth to all of these critiques. But how bad does the EU look in these terms when we compare it to actual democracies – especially to the sorts of large, heterogenous federal democracies to which it is most plausibly comparable? As Zweifel (2002) notes, the EU compares favourably to leading models of federal democracy (the US and Switzerland) on many major measures of democracy. Before we assess the democratic character of EU institutions, let us briefly consider those of the contemporary United States – a polity which the EU is often compared to and contrasted with. Even prior to its recent bout of democratic backsliding under the aspiring authoritarian populist Donald Trump, the US's democratic credentials did not look particularly more impressive than the EU's (Mickey et al. 2017; Mounk 2018).

We can begin with arguably the US's most undemocratic institution: the US Senate. Though many legislatures (particularly upper chambers) in democracies are malapportioned, the degree of malapportionment in the US Senate is shocking. California has nearly seventy times more residents than Wyoming, but each state is represented by two senators. Indeed, the 39 million citizens who live in California are represented by two senators, while the roughly 39 million citizens who live in America's 22 smallest states are represented by 44 senators. Given the distribution of Republican and Democratic voters (and the Senate's supermajority filibuster decision-making procedures), these discrepancies give a huge advantage to the Republican Party in national politics. Small minorities of Republican voters can and do block policy change in the US. It is common for senators representing a minority of voters to block legislation favoured by a large majority.

Things do not look much better in the lower chamber (the House of Representatives) or in the executive (the Presidency). Due to gerrymandering of congressional districts (and the geographic distribution of voters for the two main parties) and due to the structure of the Electoral College system, the outcome of American congressional and presidential elections sometimes does not reflect the will of the majority of voters. For instance, in the 2012 congressional election, Democratic candidates won 1.4 million more votes than Republicans, yet Republicans won a 33-seat majority in the House of Representatives. Famously, in the 2016 presidential election, Hillary Clinton won the popular vote by a margin of nearly 3 million votes, yet Donald Trump won decisively in the Electoral College and became president. Taken together, these anti-democratic features of the US Constitution help to explain why federal policies do not reflect the preferences of the majority of Americans on so many issues, and why citizens are so dissatisfied with their government's performance. For our purposes, this review of the shortcomings of the US as a democracy serves to remind us that the EU is hardly alone among large, heterogenous democratic federations in falling short of democratic ideals. So how do the EU's institutions stack up?

Let us begin with the EU's most powerful legislative body: the Council of Ministers. The Council is composed of representatives of democratically elected governments – and in that respect it is designed much like the German Bundesrat. Critics rightly argue that the Council operates without transparency. Indeed, many have suggested that national governments take advantage of this opacity in order to avoid scrutiny from and accountability to their national parliaments, thus undermining national democracies. But this critique gets things backwards. The lack of transparency in the Council – and the failure of governments represented there to respond to demands from their national parliaments – is a product of the weakness of national parliaments in domestic politics – not a product of EU politics. In short, many parliaments in Europe are thoroughly dominated by their executives as a result of the dynamics of party discipline and other domestic institutions. There are of course a few exceptions, such as the Danish Folketing and the Swedish Riksdag. However, the success the few powerful parliaments have in holding their governments accountable for their actions in Brussels only serves to underscore the weakness of many other national parliaments in safeguarding democratic standards within the Council.[1] To be clear, the Council does have important democratic shortcomings: its informal practices lack transparency and its culture of seeking unanimity – rather than voting as prescribed by the treaties – often allows small minorities of states to block initiatives favoured by large majorities. But these faults lie not with the EU per se, but with the member state governments themselves.

The EU's second legislative chamber is of course the European Parliament. Though it is directly elected, and therefore ostensibly democratic, critics point to low turnout – which fell from just over 60 per cent in 1979 to just over 40 per cent in 2014 before rebounding to 50 per cent in 2019 – as a problem reflecting voters' lack of interest. The turnout could certainly be much better, but in fact it compares favourably to voter turnout in US Congressional midterm elections and Swiss Parliamentary elections – to take two examples of federal democracies. More generally, as to whether voters feel alienated from the European Parliament, it is worth noting that Eurobarometer surveys regularly reveal that EU citizens on average have higher levels of trust in the European Parliament than they do in their national parliaments.

The EU's executive, the European Commission, does seem more problematic from a democratic standpoint, in that it is composed of leaders that lack a clear democratic mandate. Historically of course, the Commission was composed of bureaucrats appointed by their (democratically elected) national governments. Over the past two decades, a series of EU Treaty reforms sought to enhance the Commission's democratic legitimacy by giving the European Parliament a greater say in its appointment. Most recently, the Lisbon Treaty (Art. 17(7)) provided that the Council shall propose a candidate for Commission president, 'taking into account the elections to the European Parliament' and that the candidate must then be 'elected' by a majority of Members of the European Parliament (MEPs). In other words, Lisbon was more explicit about democratising the selection of the Commission president by linking it to the outcome European Parliament elections. The Parliament then took this even a step further by establishing the so-called *Spitzenkandidaten* process in the run up to the 2014 European Parliament elections. In short, each Europarty put forward

---

[1] Incidentally, this helps to explain why the 'yellow card' Early Warning System established in the 2009 Lisbon Treaty to empower national parliaments in the EU legislative process has been so rarely used. Because the weakness of national parliaments is rooted in domestic dynamics, it must be addressed with reform of flawed national democracies, and cannot be resolved by tinkering with EU institutions. See Kelemen (2019).

a candidate for the Commission presidency ahead of the Parliamentary elections, and the Parliament demanded governments in the Council nominate the candidate whose party won the most votes. This bold gambit succeeded in 2014, leading to the election of Jean Claude Juncker, but it spectacularly failed in 2019, when the European Council rejected the *Spitzenkandidat* of the party that had won the most seats in the election (the European People's Party's (EPP's) Manfred Weber) and, after secretive negotiations, nominated German Defence Minister Ursula von der Leyen, who had not been a candidate.

In effect, the Parliament sought to leverage its Treaty power to approve the Council's nominee in order to transform the Commission president into a kind of prime minister selected by the Parliament and serving with the backing of a parliamentary majority. The Parliament argued that the *Spitzenkandidaten* process would strengthen EU democracy by increasing public engagement in European elections and enhancing the legitimacy of the EU by giving voters the sense that European elections mattered for determining the policy direction of the EU. However, the (democratically elected) leaders in the European Council saw it as an illegitimate power grab by the Parliament and put a stop to it in 2019. Whether the *Spitzenkandidaten* process will be resuscitated in future election cycles remains to be seen.

In a larger sense, the battle over the *Spitzenkandidaten* process highlights a crucial point about the character of EU democracy. It is certainly true, as critics emphasise, that the EU's institutional order does not give citizens the sense that they can, in one election, shift the direction of EU politics by 'throwing the bastards out'. However, we should keep in mind that the extreme of that version of democracy is based on the notion of a Westminster-style majoritarian democracy that consolidates power in the hands of a single parliamentary majority. But as Lijphart (1999) taught us long ago, many democracies are not majoritarian but are consensual, dividing power (horizontally and vertically) among multiple veto players – elected and unelected – and constraining fleeting majorities from shifting policy too radically. Indeed, many forget that in his 1999 book on *Patterns of Democracy* Lijphart used the EU as one of his models of a consensus democracy. Arguably, the *Spitzenkandidaten* process is based on a misconception that the EU is or could become a majoritarian democracy in which the party or coalition of parties that 'wins' the European elections governs the EU. Indeed, the *Spitzenkandidaten* process discounted the role the Treaties gave to the European Council in the appointment of the Commission president, and ignored the fact that partisan composition of the Council may be quite different from that of the Parliament.

However much the EU develops democratically, it will always be a consensus democracy that ensures a wide representation of diverse interests and does not let a single voting majority dramatically change policy in one fell swoop. That can be very frustrating for voters of course, but it has other benefits that one can argue outweigh its costs. In any event, any sober assessment of EU democracy must get away from majoritarian thinking and accept the EU for the consensus democracy it is. Moreover, the EU is not just any consensus democracy – it is a particular kind – a federal or quasi-federal one, and that bring its own unique set of problems. As Bremberg and Norman state in their introduction, many debates on EU democracy gloss over the multiple 'tensions and trade-offs inherent in the application of democratic concepts to the European political order'. They emphasise a key point here. When we view the EU in this light and apply a comparative perspective, we start to see the EU's democratic dilemmas differently.

As discussed above, when we apply a comparative perspective, we recognise that many of the EU's democratic dilemmas are common to multilevel federal democracies. Indeed, there is an inherent tension between federalism and democracy. From the perspective of the states that make up a federation, federalism constrains democracy because federal laws may limit their ability to adopt policies consistent with their citizens' preferences. At the same time, from the perspective of the federation as a whole, federalism constrains democracy because on certain issues state governments may be in the position to block policies favoured by majorities at the federal level. Whether local majorities constrain federal ones, or vice versa, one group will feel aggrieved and claim their democratic will has been violated. Indeed, US scholar of federalism Martha Derthick put it once, 'Federalism is an arrangement that is chosen by people who cannot decide whether they want to be one community or many' (Derthick 1999: 125). In this sort of context, the tensions and the trade-offs between trying to satisfy the preferences of various communities aggregated at different levels are inescapable. Finally, considering the shortcomings of federal democracies also underscores a problem I have highlighted in my recent work, a problem that the EU democratic deficit literature had almost completely ignored: democratic deficits at the member state level. It turns out that while EU politics scholars were lamenting the various democratic shortcomings of EU institutions in Brussels and Strasbourg, much more profound attacks on democracy emerged in member state capitals.

Europe's Real Democratic Deficit

Over the past several years, a number of EU member states have experienced democratic backsliding. Hungary was the first mover in this regard and has descended the furthest. Viktor Orbán's Fidesz regime came to power through a free and fair election in 2010, but once in office proceeded to dismantle Hungary's democracy and to replace it with a form of 'competitive authoritarianism' (Levitsky and Way 2010). Now major ratings bodies such as Freedom House and the V-Dem Institute, and leading scholars, categorise Hungary as a hybrid or electoral authoritarian regime, making it the EU's first non-democratic state. Next came the Law & Justice (PiS) regime in Poland, which very self-consciously followed Orbán's example after they came to power in 2015 and set about rolling back the rule of law and democracy. In its latest report, the V-Dem Institute (2021) found Poland to be the most rapidly autocratising country in the world; it has slipped from the category of liberal democracy to electoral democracy, though it has not yet sunk into the category of electoral autocracy like Hungary. Other EU member state governments have followed suit more recently, seeking to roll back the rule of law and democracy, for instance in Bulgaria, Slovenia and Malta, with varying degrees of success.

Many EU scholars find these developments shocking, but the literature on comparative federalism suggests that we should not be in the least surprised. A large literature on 'regime juxtaposition' and 'subnational authoritarianism' demonstrates that the existence of authoritarian member states within broadly democratic unions is common in large heterogenous federations and can sometimes persist for decades (see e.g., Gibson 2005; Gervasoni 2010; Giraudy 2015; Mickey 2015). In my recent work, I have demonstrated how insights from this literature can shed light on the EU (Kelemen 2017, 2020). In short, I show that many of the same factors that have sustained local authoritarian enclaves in other federations – such as national parties supporting local autocrats who deliver votes to them, the emigration of dissatisfied citizens to other states in the federation, and funding from the centre that sustains local autocrats – are also at work in the EU. And in fact, I show that the situation is worse in the EU than in other federations, because the underdeveloped character of EU-level democracy in fact makes it less likely the EU will confront authoritarian member states (Kelemen 2020).

The EU's half-baked democratic institutions not only make it more likely that national autocratic governments will persist, they make it more likely they will eventually infiltrate the Union and poison its institutions. Consider for instance Europarties – the EU-level political groups that bring together national member parties to collaborate on a pan-European basis, to run candidates for European Parliament elections, and to seek to place their members in positions of influence throughout the EU's institutions. In the EU, as in other federations, democratic parties and leaders at the federal level sometimes protect local autocrats for partisan gain – because the autocrat delivers votes to their party at the national level. So just as the Democratic Party protected autocratic governments in the US South because they delivered them votes, so too did the (supposedly 'centre right') EPP protect Orbán's autocracy for a decade because he delivered them votes in the European Parliament and the Council. Likewise, other Europarties protect their own pet autocrats – with the Party of European Socialists protecting the likes of the Labour Party of Malta, and the European Liberals (ALDE) protecting the ANO Party of Czech Prime Minister Andrej Babiš, despite their autocratic tendencies.

While this comparative politics literature shows us how federal partisan politics may help to enable local authoritarians, it also highlights the conditions under which partisan politics may finally help to oust them – and makes it clear why these conditions are unlikely to be met in the contemporary EU. The literature suggests that if the local autocrat's bad behaviour begins to damage the reputation of his federal party, then the party's leaders may withdraw their support and push for democratisation in the state (Giraudy 2010: 72). Likewise, if federal parties who oppose the local authoritarian party manage to provide local opposition parties with adequate resources, they may manage to break the local authoritarian's hold on power (Gibson 2005). Unfortunately, neither of these dynamics seems likely to play out in the EU's half-baked Europarties.

First, Europarties pay no political price for allying with and enabling pet autocrats. Voters' awareness of Europarties is minimal, and their knowledge of which national parties are members of any given Europarty is even more scant. Therefore, Europarties can make their groupings larger and more powerful by allying with pet autocrats, while paying no political price for doing so with their supporters. Consider this contrast: the Christian Democratic Union (CDU) has consistently maintained a cordon santitaire, prohibiting cooperation with the far-right Alternative for Germany (AfD). Indeed, Merkel's anointed successor Annegret Kramp-Karrenbauer was pressured by public protests to step down as CDU leader after the CDU in Thuringia cooperated for one day with the AfD. To have allowed for such cooperation with the far-right was seen as an unacceptable failure and indeed prompted mass protests. Meanwhile, the very same CDU was in coalition with Orbán's Fidesz party for ten years at the EU level. Fidesz espouses the same far-right ideology and rhetoric as the AfD and in addition established the first autocratic government in the EU, and yet no voters seemed to care, and certainly no CDU politicians paid a price for this collaboration. Indeed, Merkel's candidate for the Commission presidency, German Defence Minister and fellow CDU member Ursula von der Leyen, relied on Orbán's support (along with that of the far-right PiS regime in Poland) to become president – and it caused almost no controversy at all. If voters became more aware of Europarties – and of the national member parties that make them up – then these groupings might be more likely to cut off ties with and stop supporting pet autocrats; but in the current underdeveloped state of Europarty politics, there is little reason to expect this will happen.

Likewise, where the comparative politics literature highlights the role that federal opposition parties can play in supporting the opposition in an authoritarian enclave so that it can finally dislodge the local autocrat, in the contemporary EU context, such intervention seems unlikely. Europarties are prohibited from providing direct material support to national member parties, and even beyond this prohibition, there are strong norms against 'foreign' intervention in domestic politics that would discourage outside allies from stepping in to provide other softer forms of support to opposition parties.

In short, the underdevelopment of Europarties is poisonous to EU-level politics. As McNamara emphasises in her contribution, electoral competition between parties with rival programmes is essential for a functioning democracy. Though the mechanism I emphasise here is slightly different, like her I find that the limited nature of EU democracy feeds the growth of anti-system (or even authoritarian) parties, and that therefore, as she puts it, 'what is needed is a new commitment to building pan-European political parties and mechanisms of contestation and representation'.

Just as the underdeveloped character of Europarties helps to perpetuate autocratic member governments, so too does the underdeveloped character of EU citizenship. Though EU citizenship entails a right to vote in local elections and in European Parliament elections in a citizens' member state of residence, this right does not extend to voting rights in national elections. More generally, the EU essentially takes for granted that national elections in its member states will be free and fair, and does nothing to regulate them or to guarantee the voting rights of European citizens. As Seubert emphasises in her contribution in this volume, the EU offers a constrained version of citizenship that is still based primarily on an economic logic, rather than on membership in a social and political space. If the EU had a more fully developed concept of citizenship that included a clearly established right to vote in free and fair national elections, then there might be more basis for the EU to challenge undemocratic electoral practices that backsliding governments regularly engage in – from attacks on opposition parties, to manipulation of media markets, to use of state resources to advantage the ruling party. But there is no prospect of this happening in the contemporary EU. As Sandra Seubert puts it in her chapter in this volume, 'EU citizenship is not a full status of political empowerment'. Under these conditions, governments that wish to transform their countries from democracies into electoral autocracies face little prospect that the EU will intervene to defend the democratic voting rights of 'EU citizens'.

As a result of such shortcomings, the EU now finds itself mired in an authoritarian equilibrium (Kelemen 2020), in which increasingly authoritarian member state regimes are able to endure within the EU, even benefiting from its subsidies while flouting its professed values. The EU's responses to date have been feckless. The autocratic cancer is spreading as aspiring authoritarians in other member states see what the likes of Orbán in Hungary and Jarosław Kaczyński in Poland have gotten away with, and follow their playbook. Clearly, the greatest threats to democracy in the EU today are emerging at the national level in backsliding member states. While these dangers emerge at the national level, eventually they affect the Union as a whole. Today's nascent autocrats in the EU may spout Eurosceptic rhetoric, but they have no interest in leaving the EU: instead, they want to transform it from within. In their book *Southern Nation*, Lapinsky et al. (2018) explain how white supremacists who ran authoritarian regimes in southern states managed to transform national politics in the US as their representatives came to control powerful positions in Congress. The EU's nascent autocrats hope to achieve something similar, by placing their minions in committees of the European Parliament and in the European Commission bureaucracy. The democratic deficits that have emerged in national capitals are thus seeping into the European level, and as a result there is a risk, as Bremberg and Norman suggest in their introduction, that a 'distinctively less democratic, kind of European political order could emerge'. Indeed, legal scholar John Cotter (2020) has pointed out that the EU is already operating in clear violation of its own democratic requirements as set out in Article 10 of the Treaty on European Union (TEU). Article 10(1) TEU provides, 'The functioning of the Union shall be founded on representative democracy'; and Article 10(2) TEU provides, 'Member States are represented in the European Council by their Heads of State or Government and in the Council by their governments, themselves democratically accountable either to their national Parliaments, or to their citizens.' Since the Council already contains one non-democratic member government, it is already operating in violation of its democratic mandate.

To confront the threats posed by democratic deficits at the national level, the EU will have to become far more assertive in standing up to the autocrats in its midst. It faces dilemmas similar to those that other democratic polities have confronted historically in deciding how to deal with actors who seek to subvert their democracies from within (Capoccia 2005; Mickey 2015). On top of the usual dilemmas involved in decisions over sanctioning or excluding non-democratic actors from democratic processes, EU leaders must overcome the strong sovereignty norms that have discouraged them from intervening in what have widely (but incorrectly) been seen as strictly domestic affairs. Ironically, the years of debate about the EU's democratic deficit plagued its leaders with so much self-doubt about the Union's democratic *bona fides* that when truly existential threats to democracy emerged within some member states, many EU leaders questioned whether they had the legitimacy to intervene. Some scholars even agree with this view (Weiler 2016; von Bogdandy 2019). However, as others have convincingly demonstrated, the EU certainly does have the legitimacy – indeed the duty – to require states to respect the fundamental values they committed to uphold when joining the Union (Müller 2015). Arguments proffered by some to suggest the EU should sit idly by as autocracy spreads within the Union are not only untenable, they are dangerous (Kelemen et al. 2019). If EU leaders fail to confront the rise of autocracy in the Union, the cancer of autocracy will spread to more member states, and they will eventually poison EU institutions and unravel the legal order that holds the Union together (Kelemen 2022: 79). Fortunately, there have been recent signs that the European Commission may finally be preparing to take more forceful action in defence of its democratic values. As of this writing the Commission has withheld the release of the EU's pandemic recovery funds to Hungary and Poland citing rule of law concerns, and there have been signals it may trigger the rule of law conditionality regulation (Regulation (EU) 2020/2092) to suspend even more funds to these regimes. But for now, it remains to be seen whether EU leaders will ultimately use the many tools at their disposal to defend the Union's democratic values. Until they do, the authoritarian rot emanating from some national capitals will continue to spread and to poison the EU's democratic political order.

References

Berman, Sheri (2017) The Pipe Dream of Undemocratic Liberalism. *Journal of Democracy*, 28(3): 37.

Capoccia, Giovanni (2005) *Defending Democracy: Reactions to Extremism in Interwar Europe*. Baltimore: The Johns Hopkins University Press.

Cotter, John (2020) The Last Chance Saloon. Verfassungsblog, 19 May, <https://verfassungsblog.de/the-last-chance-saloon/> (last accessed 5 December 2022).

Derthick, Martha (1999) How Many Communities? The Evolution of American Federalism. In Derthick, M. (ed.) *Dilemmas of Scale in America's Federal Democracy*. Washington, DC: Woodrow Wilson Center Press, pp. 125–53.

Gervasoni, Carlos (2010) A Rentier Theory of Subnational Regimes. *World Politics*, 62: 302.

Gibson, Edward (2005) Boundary Control: Subnational Authoritarianism in Democratic Countries. *World Politics*, 58: 101.

Giraudy, Agustina (2010) The Politics of Subnational Undemocratic Regime Reproduction in Argentina and Mexico. *Journal of Politics in Latin America*, 2(2): 53–84.
Giraudy, Agustina (2015) *Democrats and Autocrats: Pathways of Subnational Undemocratic Regime Continuity within Democratic Countries*. Oxford: Oxford University Press.
Kelemen, R. Daniel (2017) Europe's Other Democratic Deficit. *Government & Opposition*, 52(2): 211–38.
Kelemen, R. Daniel (2019) The Impact of the Lisbon Treaty. In Södersten, Anna (ed.) *The Lisbon Treaty 10 Years on: Success or Failure?* Stockholm: Swedish Institute of European Policy Studies (SIEPS), pp. 45–62.
Kelemen, R. Daniel (2020) The European Union's Authoritarian Equilibrium. *Journal of European Public Policy*, 27(3): 481–99.
Kelemen, R. Daniel (2022) Europe's Authoritarian Cancer: Diagnosis, Prognosis, and Treatment. In Andor, L., Skrzypek, A. and Giusto, H. (eds) *Progressive Yearbook 2022*. Brussels: FEPS – Foundation for European Progressive Studies, pp. 73–82, <https://www.feps-europe.eu/attachments/publications/progressive%20yearbook%202022%20v9.pdf> (last accessed 5 December 2022).
Kelemen, R. Daniel, Pavone, Tommaso and Emmons, Cassandra (2019) The Perils of Passivity in the Rule of Law Crisis: A Response to von Bogdandy. Verfassungsblog, 26 November, <https://verfassungsblog.de/the-perils-of-passivity-in-the-rule-of-law-crisis-a-response-to-von-bogdandy/> (last accessed 5 December 2022).
Lapinsky, John, Bateman, David and Katznelson, Ira (2018) *Southern Nation: Congress and White Supremacy after Reconstruction*. Princeton: Princeton University Press.
Levitsky, Steven and Way, Lucan (2010) *Competitive Authoritarianism*. New York: Cambridge University Press.
Lijphart, Arend (1999) *Patterns of Democracy*. New Haven: Yale University Press.
Mickey, Robert (2015) *Paths out of Dixie*. Princeton: Princeton University Press.
Mickey, Rob, Levitsky, Steven and Way, Lucan (2017) Is America Still Safe for Democracy? *Foreign Affairs*, 96(3): 22.
Mounk, Yascha (2016) Illiberal Democracy or Undemocratic Liberalism?, Project Syndicate, 9 June, <https://www.project-syndicate.org/commentary/trump-european-populism-technocracy-by-yascha-mounk-1-2016-06> (last accessed 5 December 2022).
Mounk, Yascha (2018) America Is Not a Democracy. *The Atlantic*, March.
Mudde, Cas (2015) The Problem with Populism. *The Guardian*, 17 February, <https://www.theguardian.com/commentisfree/2015/feb/17/problem-populism-syriza-podemos-dark-side-europe> (last accessed 5 December 2022).
Müller, Jan-Werner (2015) Should the EU Protect Democracy and the Rule of Law Inside Member States? *European Law Journal*, 21(2): 141–60.
V-Dem Institute (2021) Autocratization Turns Viral: Democracy Report 2021, <https://www.v-dem.net/static/website/files/dr/dr_2021.pdf> (last accessed 5 December 2022).
Von Bogdandy, Armin (2019) Fundamentals on Defending European Values. Verfassungsblog, 12 November, <https://verfassungsblog.de/fundamentals-on-defending-european-values/> (last accessed 5 December 2022).

Weiler, Joseph (2016) Epilogue: Living in a Glass House: Europe, Democracy and the Rule of Law. In Closa, Carlos and Kochenov, Dimitry (eds) *Reinforcing Rule of Law Oversight in the European Union*. Cambridge: Cambridge University Press, 2016, pp. 313–26.

Zweifel, Thomas (2002) Who is Without Sin Cast the First Stone: The EU's Democratic Deficit in Comparison. *Journal of European Public Policy*, 9: 812

CONCLUSION

The Dilemmatic Perspective on European Democracy

Niklas Bremberg and Ludvig Norman

We started off this volume by highlighting the European political order's ambivalent relationship with democracy. This ambivalence is also mirrored in the scholarly debates that study democratic challenges, shortcomings and possible solutions. Questions arise at every turn about how best to transpose democratic principles beyond the nation-state. The book's contributions have shed light on the previously less explored trade-offs we face when contemplating democracy in the European political order, characterised by advanced economic and legal integration with the European Union (EU) at its core. We have taken an open-ended approach to these discussions, asking the contributors to engage with different aspects of European democracy, current and past, using the exploration of particular dilemmas related to these aspects as the common thread for discussions.

The volume's focus on democratic dilemmas veers away from the grand theories of democracy and European integration as exemplified by the supranational versus intergovernmental perspectives that informed debates on the EU's democratic deficit in the 1990s and early 2000s. Several of the book's contributions venture beyond these debates to highlight other salient tensions in the emergent political order in Europe. The grand theory debates were in some sense necessary to identify the key dividing lines in early discussions on European democracy. However, they ultimately drew these lines between fundamentally different conceptions of what characterised the European political order, conceptions which then came with implications for how they understood the conditions for democracy in Europe – within as well as beyond states. The intergovernmental perspective focused on European states and the ways in which they coordinated themselves within the framework of international cooperative arrangements. Democratic representation and accountability were consequently seen as exclusively tied to the level of EU member states and focused on the representatives who negotiated the shape and form of cooperative arrangements in the EU. Thinking about European democracy beyond the state was deemed superfluous. The supranational perspective, in contrast, conceived of an emerging legal and political order centred on the EU that fundamentally challenged the system of sovereign states. EU member states had become increasingly bound up with a myriad of laws and rules, emanating not least from the jurisprudence of the European Court of Justice and the pro-integration activism of European Commission officials committed to a teleological view of an ever-deepening Union (cf. Nugent and Rhinard 2019). Seen from this perspective, the legal and political order in which EU member states now found themselves necessitated the development of supranational forms of democracy. This is not to deny that democracy remains intimately tied to individual states. However, we believe it is useful to see the European political order as an emergent political space in its own right. The tension between democracy at the level of the state and at the supranational level has served as the dominating lens through which discussions on European democracy have unfolded. As several of our contributors highlight, these tensions still carry relevance. However, they also demonstrate that the dilemma between national and supranational is both more multifaceted than has often been acknowledged and that it is only one of many dilemmas around which democracy in the European political order is constructed.

The disaggregated view of democracy that this implies has paved the way for individual contributions that collectively demonstrate that rather than dealing with a single 'democratic deficit', we are in fact faced with a range of more specific problems that become visible when we engage in discussions on particular aspects of democracy. This provides reasons to further question the usefulness of the metaphor of a general democratic deficit. It has proved to be a convenient way to indicate general shortcomings related to democracy in the EU, but it does severely underplay thorny issues brought to the fore as soon as we shift our analytical focus to ways in which we might transpose particular democratic principles and practices to the broader European political order. Our analytical focus on democratic dilemmas instead indicates that any effort to democratise the EU implies difficult trade-offs between different values and conceptions of what democracy is and can be.

Our approach should therefore caution us against relying on absolutes in the understanding of European democracy in the twenty-first century and turn our attention to the dilemmas that confront us in this complex and evolving system. In the remainder of this concluding chapter, we seek to discuss and synthesise the volume's contributions by drawing together and highlighting, first, the similarities and differences in the way they lay out Europe's democratic challenges and, second, the tentative answers that can be gleaned from these discussions. We end the chapter by looking ahead and discuss the ways in which the insights gained from this volume might be applied elsewhere and raise further questions

Multiple Democratic Dilemmas in Europe

The two reflection chapters interestingly, if not unexpectedly, identify different implications from this volume's previous contributions, and come to different conclusions in terms of where the primary challenges to democracy lie for Europe's political order. For Sheri Berman the crux of European democracy is the extent to which the political order as whole, at both the national and the European level, is able to rein in a dominant neoliberal version of capitalism. Economic inequalities provide fertile ground for the type of authoritarian politics that has taken grip in countries such as Hungary and Poland, and which fuels support more broadly for far-right political parties and movements in Western Europe. The main question to address is how to reconnect with one of the core legacies of European social democracy, finding a balance between the market and redistributive systems that operate democratically and with an eye to social equality. Applied to the level of the European political order, questions regarding this balance become even more complicated since inequalities are as pronounced across European societies as within them. Any redistributive systems at the European level places great demands on a sense of solidarity with other societies.

Daniel Kelemen's reflections tie into an important aspect of these discussions as the redistribution of EU funds are at the heart of debates on how to address one of the greatest challenges of the order, namely the autocratisation of some of its member states. Kelemen's comparative perspective emphasises the peculiar institutional set-up of the European political order. However, his comparative outlook also works to question the extent to which we should be overly concerned about the EU's democratic shortcomings when it comes to deficiencies in the functioning of its own institutions and decision-making procedures. The principal problem, instead, is that the democratic systems of individual member states, such as Hungary and Poland, are deteriorating fast, and that the way in which the European Union is set up works to exacerbate rather than alleviate these developments. Dilemmas, in Kelemen's discussion, are less about the clashing principles that emerge when we apply democratic norms to a regional quasi-federal order like the EU, and more about the failure of short-sighted and opportunistic politicians to nip autocratic developments in the bud. Here the Court of Justice of the European Union (CJEU) has recently helped to reinforce the legitimacy of attempts to hold the regimes of Hungary and Poland accountable for derogations from the principles of the rule of law. The Court has ruled that

> compliance by the Member States with the common values on which the European Union is founded – which have been identified and are shared by the Member States and which define the very identity of the European Union as a legal order common to those States – such as the rule of law and solidarity, justifies the mutual trust between those States. (CJEU 2022)

In its ruling, the Court also underlines that the EU must be able to defend those values, within the limits of its powers, since compliance is a condition for the enjoyment of all the rights derived from the application of the Treaties to an EU member state (ibid.). However, the Commission, once keen to push infringement proceedings to the Court, has taken a more passive approach to the new European autocrats (Kelemen 2022). Certainly, the actions of the governments of Hungary and Poland in seeking to dismantle fundamental aspects of the rule of law at the national level present an unmistakable challenge to the EU as the foremost expression of a common European legal and political order. However, as the contributions to our volume show, the challenges facing democratic politics in Europe are complex. Here, it is important to underline that the democratic institutions in Europe, as Berman also points out, are not under the same types of threat as those that emerged in the interwar years. A key difference is the considerable accumulation of experience with democratic rule since the defeat of fascism in Europe. In many European countries, democratic institutions are now a well-established part of the taken for granted way of doing politics.

Berman's and Kelemen's chapters, and the differences in how they diagnose the symptoms of European democracy, map on to two slightly different ways of identifying problems and solutions: one focuses primarily on institutional design, and the capacities of institutions to act forcefully to uphold the rules of the order, and the other mirrors a concern with broader social developments that could undermine or strengthen democracy. Many contributions to our volume also highlight in various ways the complex interactions between political institutions and social dynamics.

In his chapter, Joseph Lacey highlights the deeply diverse nature of the European political order and provides a discussion that counters some of the widely accepted underlying assumptions regarding what is often perceived as a key dilemma in modern societies: that between a strong element of democratic contestation and effective problem-solving. Setting up the dilemma in this way, Lacey argues, tends to lead to institutional solutions similar to those that have been prevalent in the EU up until now, creating an elite-driven and largely depoliticised project. In many ways this connects back to the functionalist analyses that underlie early discussions on postwar cooperation in Europe, informed by perceptions of democracy's inherent fragility and the need to safeguard its institutions from both the masses and opportunistic politicians. From this point of view it was only by constructing solid arrangements for European cooperation out of reach of everyday political contestation that the project could evolve. According to Lacey, however, the costs of such a project are higher than is often recognised. One often-overlooked cost is an increasing lack of communicative skills among politicians across the EU member states capable of arguing the value of the European project as a means of dealing with issues of common concern, and of helping to protect a political order based on respect for human rights and the rule of law.

The habit of treating the EU as an apolitical sphere detached from the control of voters and politicians makes it difficult to take firm positions in its defence. This is even more apparent in cases where politicians have developed a tendency to shuffle blame for political shortcomings or unpopular decisions on to an amorphous 'Brussels'. When anti-system actors enter the political arena, mainstream politicians often find themselves unable to deliver a convincing counter-message. Thus, as Lacey argues, attempts to shield politics in the EU from contestation in the name of technocratic efficiency not only tend to undermine the perceived legitimacy of the European project among EU citizens, but also leave its representatives ill-equipped to defend it. The dilemma of whether to politicise European politics is placed in a new light when considering the interactions between wider societal attitudes, the communicative skills of politicians and the institutional set-up of the European political order.

Several of the contributors to this volume make it clear that the implications for how to think about democracy when characterising the EU one way or another are far less clear-cut than the grand theory debates have made it appear. Christopher Lord addresses the question of institutional design and democratic governance in the EU and starts off from what he refers to as a 'meta-dilemma' for the EU, a political order that cannot do without democracy but which structures do not correspond well to conditions of democracy broadly defined. Lord refers to the 'indirect legitimacy dilemma' facing democracies in Europe, and vividly demonstrates that even if we are committed to the notion that democracy must be primarily based at the level of the individual states, a range of challenging questions remains about what this means for representative arrangements at the European level. In fact, as democratic states both represent and are accountable to their own citizens, EU member states together need to come up with ways of managing a range of externalities that emerge from democratic decision-making in their own as well as other member states. Lord argues that this cannot be reduced to a problem of finding optimal technocratic solutions to issues such as environmental problems, climate change and market regulation. Nor is it warranted to conclude that intergovernmental institutional arrangements are enough to deal with problems of common concern. Lord's argument is also a clear illustration of an instance where the national–supranational distinction emerges as less helpful, and his argument demonstrates how loosening the hold of this analytical lens can yield important insights. The management of externalities ultimately requires control by national democracies, but it also implies control over national democracies. The implication of the dilemma that Lord highlights is thus that the somewhat simplistic treatment of the EU as an international organisation will not be enough to adequately address the political problems that European states and their citizens now face.

The inherently political problem of how to construct, regulate and sustain the market economy is addressed head on by Kathleen McNamara in her discussion on the relation between capitalism and democracy in contemporary Europe. Her chapter also revolves around the question of how political institutions are embedded in broader social dynamics, and she shows us how concerns about inequality require us to take on a more nuanced understanding of democratic politics, including at which levels it is reasonable to expect that democratic institutions can be made to work, and to what ends. In particular, McNamara supplies us with good reasons to question the conventional notion of nationally based democracies acting as bulwarks against the inequalities resulting from unfettered capitalism. Importantly, her account instead shows how the democratic regulation of a capitalist economy can also produce and perpetuate serious inequalities. Inequality is from this perspective also the result of regulation that might take place both at the level of national democracies and at the supranational level. Berman's reflections can be said to deepen the historical aspects of McNamara's discussion as she emphasises the point that democracy in the European political order has always been deeply tied to the extent to which it can deliver the material needs of its citizens. Berman sees democracy as intimately bound up with social equality and constant work in terms of containing the harmful consequences of capitalism. Without close attendance to this balance, she argues, democracy loses its foothold in society and movements that challenge both democratic rule and the market economy as the meta-ideology of modern society become influential. The European political order, from this point of view, has been in a deteriorating state since the 1970s, accelerating in recent decades as moves towards autocratic forms of politics have accelerated and far-right populism has gained support across Europe.

However, McNamara's chapter provides us with an important contrast to the dominant story of European democracy, especially since the euro crisis. Indeed, the ability of member states to govern their own economies was seriously circumscribed as budget coordination mechanisms at the EU level were strengthened. This can be said to have diminished the influence of majoritarian institutions over the governance of European economic policy. To borrow from Lord, states are faced with externalities generated by an increasingly integrated economic space. However, McNamara's account gives us pause to take this as a clear indication that democratic mechanisms in member states, in contrast to those of the European Union, are necessarily pushing back against inequality. Rather, the problems boil down to how the dilemma between market logic and political logic is understood and acted on at various levels. Experiences from individual member states tell us that market logics have in many places become prominent aspects of its internal governance. A case in point is the marketisation of the welfare state where a case like Sweden, a former bastion of a comprehensive welfare regime governed through a strong state, has turned towards privatisation in an unprecedented way, even in a broader international comparison (Blix and Jordahl 2021).

That tensions between market and political logics are not only confined to forms of economic governance is clearly demonstrated by Sandra Seubert's discussion on the EU citizenship regime. Seubert in particular illustrates this with the dilemmas brought to the fore in the conceptualisation of European citizenship. Here she paints a picture of a 'fragmented' EU citizenship regime that draws its legitimacy from a classical conception of citizenship as safeguarding equality and the protection of substantive rights associated with democratic political orders but is in practice heavily shaped by its intimate connection to upholding the right of free movement within the common market. Political rights remain firmly ensconced within the individual member states, and EU citizenship lacks a stronger normative core that could serve to further citizens' fundamental political rights and create firm vertical lines connecting individual citizens to European institutions.

A key tension identified by Seubert is that between diversity, in terms of different constitutional traditions and ways of organising society, on the one hand, and the principle of equality, tapping into the definition of citizenship as a safeguard for the enjoyment of both social and political rights, on the other. As Seubert argues, the dilemmas between these two principles are not easily bridged. The notion of 'constitutional identity' highlights this problem. It has served to legitimise not only limits to the reach of EU law, but also the erosion of democratic rights and the rule of law with reference to the specific constitutional traditions of particular member states. It is difficult to see how discussions on European democracy can meaningfully advance without also addressing the question of what kind of European citizenship regime should be aspired to and how to reconcile diversity and equality in the context of European integration.

Michael Keating goes further in his critique of the dominant role of the unitary state in conventional understandings of democracy in the European political order. Viewing democracy in this setting requires a far-reaching problematisation of debates structured around the notion of a dilemma between politics at the national and at the supranational level. Keating mobilises the concept of rescaling to question the discussions mapped on the national/supranational binary, which he argues obfuscate important aspects of European democracy. While Christopher Lord points to the limits of this binary, and suggests ways to think about representation beyond it, Keating's argument instead suggests it is a distinction that should be more fundamentally put into question when theorising European democracy. The dilemma, Keating believes, is instead one between rescaling and democratisation. This rendition of the problem captures an increasing mismatch between the shifting loci of various forms of power, economic as well as political, on the one hand, and social and political identities, on the other. This mismatch is further reinforced by how recognition of the normative subjects of democratic politics within the European political order is limited to states. Claims for self-governance at other levels are pushed aside or ignored in favour of the nation-state and its role in the EU as the reference point in discussions on European democracy.

Keating instead argues that a broader set of subjects needs to be recognised, and that to do so we need to move beyond discussions of democracy in the EU as structured by the supposed binary of the state and supranational levels. It is thus an argument that considerably broadens the scope in which discussions on European democracy can be held, and it works to highlight underexplored democratic dilemmas hidden from view by theoretical discussions that privilege the nation-state as the natural reference point. Keating develops his argument in contrast to the concept of multilevel governance, which has been embraced by scholars as well as the European Commission since the 1990s, and has facilitated the depoliticisation of political spaces rather than addressing more difficult questions of how such spaces should be democratised (Bache and Flinders 2004). Governance from this perspective primarily refers to technocratic forms of functional adaption, and excludes emerging demands from collectives at various levels, above and below the nation-state, for recognition as legitimate sites for democratic deliberation and decision-making. Keating notes in this regard that the concept of demoicracy has not proved able to satisfactorily address the dilemma of rescaling and democratising in Europe, mostly because it tends to reproduce the idea that the relevant *demoï* correspond to unitary EU member states (Wolkenstein 2018). Plurinational states such as Belgium, Spain and the UK and others serve to illustrate the problem with such assumptions (Basta 2021). Keating makes a more general argument when he asks us to reconsider in a more far-reaching sense relevant sites of European democracy understood as 'spaces for deliberation, common purpose and compromise, and linking these to effective capacity for action in the face of other forms of power' (Keating this volume).

In her chapter, Firat Cengiz addresses the question of how to think about such spaces for deliberation in the emergent political order in Europe as she explores the extent to which insights gained from research on deliberative democracy can help to advance our thinking on the dilemmas of European democracy. While deliberative democracy should not necessarily be seen as a clear-cut alternative to representative democracy, it is nonetheless informed by the understanding that when people are given a chance to reflect on their interests and preferences together with others, this can enhance their appreciation of what actually constitutes their interests and preferences. In order to shape political outcomes, however, deliberative practices must somehow be connected to political institutions. Cengiz highlights how research on deliberative democracy has increasingly come to incorporate critical insights, not least from feminist theory, to draw attention to how social aspects influence whose voices are heard and listened to in deliberative settings. This is arguably one of the key dilemmas highlighted in the research on deliberative democracy, in the sense that it recognises that there will always be trade-offs between the quality of political deliberation and the nature of the political setting in which deliberation takes place. The point to make here is that this trade-off is not necessarily easier to handle at the national level compared to the EU level. Lacey's arguments about the costs associated with trying to insulate political processes in the EU from popular contestation, and Keating's points about the tensions that emanate from presenting the nation-state in Europe as the only legitimate space for democratic decision-making can be said to address similar problems in ways that add further nuance to our thinking on democratic dilemmas.

Addressing Europe's Democratic Dilemmas

The notion that the European political order is characterised by a range of democratic dilemmas makes widely accepted definitive solutions hard to find. At the same time, however, we should not necessarily treat as acceptable the ways these dilemmas were handled in the past. As Lacey notes, our approach challenges the conventional way of proceeding in discussions on EU democracy, whereby the normative model of democracy is outlined, and an argument is then made for the institutional arrangements that best work to operationalise that model. However, our approach, while opening new ways of shedding light on European democracy, does not absolve us from thinking about more fruitful ways in which dilemmas can be addressed. The work of the contributors to this volume to identify the trade-offs implied by particular democratic dilemmas is an important step in paving the way for meaningful discussions on such possible available alternatives.

Lord offers some answers by arguing that it is the obligations that member state representatives have to their citizens that ultimately legitimise the creation of avenues for representation that go beyond those imagined by conventional state-centric or intergovernmental theories of EU democracy. Interestingly, Lord notes that the institutions for collective decision-making devised by the EU member states have thus far not only functioned to ensure that member states deliver on their own obligations under conditions of shared externalities, but also motivated member states to search for new ways to manage externalities that have the potential to enhance their capacity to tackle common problems. In this sense then, Lord's arguments provide additional legitimation to burgeoning procedures that enable direct participation in EU affairs, for instance through the European Parliament (EP), although the basis of that legitimacy is derived from obligations that leaders of democratic states have to their citizens. Keating's argument is particularly relevant here, regarding the need for new ways to create connections between different political spaces that are not just confined to the level of the state, and to make such discussions an intrinsic part of the process of democratising the European polity. What Keating as well as other contributors demonstrate is that there are no easy fixes for the democratic dilemmas they reveal – and this, again, highlights the need to remain open with regard to which democratic subjects should be recognised.

On the notion of democratic subjects, Seubert lays out a set of more clearly articulated citizens' rights tied to and made explicit through the emergence of the EU citizenship regime. In search of a way to move beyond the current thin citizenship regime, which is essentially tied to the right of free movement rather than more substantial social rights, Seubert argues that part of the solution might be to create a more substantial core around which EU citizenship can be constructed that ties it to a 'democratic minimum', and which can also be leveraged to safeguard rights for citizens in states that are increasingly veering in an autocratic direction. However, she stresses that precisely what such a minimum should consist of must ultimately be decided by European citizens through a process of public deliberation rather than be predetermined from above.

In many ways, Seubert's reflections on democratising the EU citizenship regime come close to the case Berman makes for the historical struggle for democracy in Europe to be understood as a struggle to bring capitalism under popular control in order to instil a sense of social purpose to the market economy. Berman reminds us that this was a major historical accomplishment in those European countries where it was successfully achieved, but we need to learn the lesson that this was not an inevitable outcome and that it cannot be taken for granted. Nor does the democratisation of a given political order necessarily lead to more social equality. Indeed, there are significant differences among European democracies in the extent to which the state is tasked with compensating for economic inequalities. McNamara, like Berman, highlights the need for redistributive policies in the EU, not only to correct market failures but also to ensure broad popular support for the functioning of the common market. One question that lingers is the extent to which we could count on such outcomes from meaningful electoral contestation in the EU around the content of common economic policies, especially in a context in which political actors still seem able to exploit popular notions of creditor and debtor states in the EU.

Here it is relevant to highlight the argument Lacey makes for how democratic contestation could work to bolster confidence in the EU as a political community of EU citizens. His chapter discusses the experience thus far of three cases of institutional design intended to politicise the EU: elections to the European Parliament, national parliaments and national referendums on European integration. There are of course many potential lessons to be drawn from these cases, but it seems particularly relevant in the context of this volume to stress that in the first two cases it appears that the effects of this kind of 'top-down politicisation' have, at least in part, been increased representation of nationalist and far-right political parties at the EU level, and regained control by EU member states over the process of nominating the president of the European Commission. When it comes to the case of national referendums, however, Lacey cautions us against thinking that the most important lessons can be learned from the process that led to a UK referendum on withdrawing from the EU.

There are certainly reasons to be cautious when discussing the democratising potential of national referendums – not least due to their inbuilt tendency to reduce complex issues to binary choices. However, it seems that there is something to be learned from the Danish experience of holding a comparatively high number of national referendums on EU matters and the growing popular support for the EU in Denmark since the 1990s.

Whether this is linked to a sense among Danish citizens that their country's position within the EU is constantly improved through renegotiation, or whether they feel more accustomed and attached to an emerging European political community – or both – is of course difficult to say. The point here is that Lacey urges us to think hard about the conditions for the consolidation of this emerging transnational political community when we think about European democracy. While there are certainly reasons to be wary of the political developments currently unfolding in several member states, it is possible that the consequences of these challenges have the potential to further democratise the EU in the longer term, in that they increase awareness among larger groups of EU citizens of what is at stake at the present historical juncture (de Vries 2018).

Thus, the argument that political representatives in the EU and member states will have stronger incentives to communicate their positions on a range of political issues as a function of more contestation does not seem too far-fetched. This might be a way to ultimately protect and even deepen a political community that is not meant to supersede member states but rather embed them further in a common framework; and it certainly resonates with Cengiz's observation about the need for deliberative practices to be linked to political institutions and broader social dynamics. Keating also highlights the role of deliberation as a means not only for achieving policy outcomes, but also for having an ongoing conversation on the shape and form of European states and democracy.

The Dilemmatic Perspective and the Future of EU Democracy

Where does our dilemmatic approach to the analysis of EU democracy leave us? What are the prospects for this perspective in studying future developments in EU democracy? A first thing to note, as is also noted in our introduction, is that the themes discussed in the chapters of this volume do not exhaust the scope for discussions on European democracy. We believe that our approach opens up new avenues for the analysis of democracy in the European political order, and that the treatment of democracy in this setting as a set of multiple and overlapping tensions is indeed a fruitful one. Our contributors have shown how the application of this perspective paves the way for rethinking debates on democracy in the EU. By extension, we expect that the approach can be fruitfully applied to additional themes associated with democratic politics to help highlight other democratic dilemmas.

One such tension is that between expertise and democratic politics, that is, questions about the extent to which particular issues should be the subject of open political contestation and the extent to which experts, professionals and other types of organised interests should be allowed to become part of the democratic policy process. In the jargon of EU politics, democracy is often associated with the inclusion of 'relevant stakeholders', or organised interests of various kinds that have a stake in the specific EU policies under discussion. The dilemmas between such forms of representation and those that operate through electoral mechanisms have long been part of the conversation on EU democracy, and this has also been the object of a broad field of empirical studies (Albareda 2020; Greenwood 2007; Kohler-Koch and Rittberger 2007). It also ties in with broader debates on what benchmarks should be used to assess the quality of democratic polities, their 'input', understood as the democratic qualities of their procedures, or 'output', defined as the quality of the outcomes of those procedures. However, our volume shows that more work is needed to advance the conceptual and normative groundwork required to clearly outline the democratic trade-offs implied by this dilemma, especially as concerns what aspects of that dilemma are associated with democratic considerations and which are not.

This dilemma came to the fore in relation to the difficult balancing act between expertise and democratic procedures during the COVID-19 pandemic, and entered the public consciousness in unprecedented ways as evolving knowledge about the virus prompted far-reaching, albeit quite different, interventions in European societies. The existential threats associated with climate change raise similar dilemmas. This is not only due to the complex questions of solidarity and justice between generations and societies, which democratic politics generally struggles with, but also because the politicisation of the costs associated with a transition to a more climate friendly society are becoming increasingly tangible. It is not at all certain that popular support across European countries for policies designed to achieve carbon neutrality by 2050 or sooner will remain at current levels. Political mobilisation against the EU and European integration by nationalist and far-right parties and movements could be re-energised by populist calls to cut fuel and energy prices for 'ordinary people' and dismantle climate policies 'dictated by Brussels' (*The Economist* 2022).

However, drawing on the contributions in this volume, increased contestation around climate policies in the EU could also lead to a stronger sense of political community among citizens who are concerned about the adverse effects of climate change and are seeking effective political measures to reduce emissions of greenhouse gases. Its inherently global character means that such measures cannot reasonably be restricted to the national level. The challenges of acting against climate change are clearly not exclusively challenges in terms of expertise, but also democratic challenges.

Discussions on the subject of democratic political orders run through several of the volume's chapters. These are perhaps most clearly pronounced in Keating's discussions on rescaling – a concept that deals head-on with the question of what the legitimate reference points of European democracy should be, at which levels democratic politics can and should unfold and how the political impulses that emerge from such arenas could be acted on in a broader European context. These are also questions that appear in Seubert's discussions on citizenship, as well as Lacey's and Cengiz's suggestions for the more direct involvement of citizens in European politics. All point in some sense to a shift in emphasis to new sets of democratic subjects, and new actors actively engaging in politics.

These discussions tie into an important rationale for the dilemmatic approach: democracy requires continuous discussion of the forms and procedures best suited to realising democratic values. The challenges associated with this form of continuous meta-reflection on the shape and form of the political order itself of course generate their own challenges. This requires concerted efforts to theorise the broader implications of the inclusion of new democratic settings and actors in a political order, and a clear view of the difficult balancing act that shifting power and influence between settings might entail.

While the redistribution of influence and power in a particular political order is not always a zero-sum game, it sometimes is. Theorising democratic politics to include new settings or types of actors must therefore be accompanied by an analysis of what this means for the broader political order in which these shifts are imagined. In national settings, the possible scope for such democratic inventions is often constrained by institutionalised constitutional frameworks. The EU is an evolving political order to a much greater extent. Its democratic institutions are, as Kelemen remarks in this volume, half-baked, which leads to a set of problems not least in relation to anti-democratic member states and political parties. However, the fact that the European political order is still evolving – and, as we mentioned in our introduction, is still very much a bricolage of sometimes incoherent democratic practices – also offers opportunities in terms of allowing for democratic innovation that might be difficult to introduce in more consolidated orders.

This highlights the democratising potential of limited and piecemeal – as opposed to grand and revolutionary – political initiatives. The EU's broader institutional development of cooperative arrangements has evolved significantly between formal revisions of the fundamental treaties (Farrell and Héritier 2007). It is also important to reiterate that the treaty paragraphs outlining democratic characteristics are broad and leave considerable room for interpretation. As McNamara also notes, interesting historical parallels can be drawn with the United States, where the institutionalisation of political parties in the nineteenth century was both a result of the practices of participation and deliberation taking hold within American states, and a process that helped consolidate the US as a polity (McNamara and Musgrave 2020). There is an aspect here of the unintended consequences of practices that are not necessarily directed towards the creation of particular institutional arrangements. The emergence of a security community among sovereign states in parts of Europe after 1945 is another case in point that highlights how continued interactions among actors can help to promote practices of 'mutual attention, communication, perception of needs, and responsiveness in the process of decision-making' (Deutsch et al. 1957: 36, see also Adler and Barnett 1998; Bremberg 2018). It is possible to think of the development of democratic arrangements in similar terms. Thus, even when democratic practices are seemingly incoherent or poorly developed, they can over time have effects on the democratic character of the political order. This emphasises not only the constitutional side of democratic politics, but also its necessarily experimental nature. In a nutshell: if democratic politics were to become completely predictable, some of its democratic qualities would inevitably be lost.

The European transnational system of political parties is seen by some to hold such experimental promise (White 2014; Wolkenstein 2020). Rather than seeing party systems as dependent on a well-defined demos with a common identity, transnational political parties can be seen as a vehicle for building political coalitions and mobilising voters around issues with a distinct transnational, European character. Thus far, however, the rules that regulate this party system work to seriously circumscribe its democratic potential, especially as concerns the possibility of new political actors to enter the transnational political arena (Norman and Wolfs 2022). The lack of a deeper commitment to make the system work can to an extent be seen as a result of the difficulties associated with adding new layers to existing political arrangements. While few believe that a transnational system of political parties would seriously undermine the role of national parties, better developed European parties would shift the centre of gravity in terms of influence and power. As we mentioned in our introduction, the increased transnational mobilisation of far-right political parties in recent European elections could also make a strengthened role for Europe-wide party organisations appear less palatable (cf. Norman 2021). This highlights, once again, some of the challenges facing the increased politicisation of European institutions. As politicians identify threats to the integrity of their political order, innovations in a more democratic direction tend to become a more distant option.

Technological developments might also bring about experimental opportunities to advance European democracy. Digitalisation has in a few decades reshaped fundamental aspects of our societies and economies, as well as our daily lives. In many ways it has changed how political communication is performed and consumed. The early enthusiasm surrounding the potential to reinvigorate democratic participation and deliberation in political decision-making through digital tools and efforts to promote 'e-democracy' has faded to a large extent in the wake of digital disinformation campaigns and a growing understanding of how algorithms affect social media. Nonetheless, it could perhaps still be argued that digital tools such as electronic voting and 'e-publics' might serve to enhance opportunities for political participation and deliberation at various political levels in the EU and its member states, and thus help to better involve EU citizens in European politics (Hennen et al. 2020). The EU has also taken steps to build common capacities to counter digital disinformation (Hedling 2021). However, the extent to which the EU manages to shape and uphold distinct European policies on regulating the provision of digital services, digital interactions and transfers of digital data in the name of advancing European 'digital sovereignty' will have significant consequences for how the digitalisation of European societies unfolds in the near future. As the process of digitalisation is likely to continue to profoundly reshape European societies in the years to come, we think that it needs to be addressed as an issue that is inherent to our discussions on European democracy. A key task as we move forward will be to identify the specific dilemmas and trade-offs that emerge as a result.

Finally, we have argued in this volume that an analytical focus on democratic dilemmas represents a promising way forward for discussions on European democracy. In this concluding chapter, we have also sought to draw together contributors' suggestions on how to address these dilemmas and how this approach might further the study of democracy in the European political order. An important insight that we think can be drawn from the ways in which the contributors have used our framework is that the more we know about actual democratic dilemmas, the better equipped we become to grasp the potential resilience of democratic governance in the emergent political order in Europe. Bringing democratic dilemmas to light in the way that has been done in this book provides for a more realistic understanding of the political trade-offs that democratising the EU entail. If we accept the notion that there are multiple dilemmas, and we think that the contributions in this book suggest that we should, then it becomes analytically misplaced to focus on one overarching dilemma revolving around national and supranational levels of governance, because doing so risks concealing what is at stake when discussing European democracy today. Thus, we believe that the potential for strengthening the democratic legitimacy of the EU is helped by recognising multiple democratic dilemmas and by thoroughly discussing the different trade-offs they imply in the context of European integration. While the volume has not proposed a clear-cut model for democracy, we recognise, in line with several of our contributors, the value of creating ways for Europe's institutions to venture beyond symbolic references to democratic concepts, such as democratic contestation or citizenship. A further opening up of institutions to citizens by making more room for political participation and allowing a higher degree of politicisation might seem like perilous propositions, especially as democracy as the taken for granted framework for politics in Europe is seemingly under threat from both domestic and foreign forces. However, the alternative of further entrenchment of political institutions out of the reach of European citizens appears even more perilous.

References

Adler, Emmanuel and Barnett, Michael (eds) (1998) *Security Communities*. Cambridge: Cambridge University Press.
Albareda, Adrià (2020) Prioritizing Professionals? How the Democratic and Professionalized Nature of Interest Groups Shapes Their Degree of Access to EU Officials. *European Political Science Review*, 12(4): 485–501
Bache, Ian and Flinders, Matthew (eds) (2004) *Multi-level Governance*. Oxford: Oxford University Press.
Basta, Karlo (2021) *The Symbolic State: Minority Recognition, Majority Backlash, and Secession in Multinational Countries*. Montreal: McGill-Queen's University Press.
Blix, Mårten and Jordahl, Henrik (2021) *Privatizing Welfare Services: Lessons from the Swedish Experiment*. Oxford: Oxford University Press.
Bremberg, Niklas (2018) The EU and the European Security Community: History and Current Challenges. In Bakardjieva Engelbrekt, A., Michalski, A., Nilsson, N. and L. Oxelheim (eds) *The European Union Facing the Challenge of Multiple Security Threats*. Cheltenham: Edward Elgar Publishing.
Court of Justice of the European Union (2022) Press Release No 28/22 Judgments in Cases C-156/21 Hungary v Parliament and Council and C-157/21 Poland v Parliament and Council. Luxembourg, 16 February, <https://curia.europa.eu/jcms/upload/docs/application/pdf/2022-02/cp220028en.pdf> (last accessed 22 February 2022).
Deutsch, Karl, et al. (1957) *Political Community and the North Atlantic Area: International Organization in the Light of Historical Experience*. Princeton: Princeton University Press.
de Vries, Catherine E. (2018) *Euroscepticism and the Future of European Integration*. Oxford: Oxford University Press.

The Economist (2022) After Brexit, Nigel Farage has Net Zero in his Sights. 25 February, <https://www.economist.com/britain/2022/02/25/after-brexit-nigel-farage-has-net-zero-in-his-sights> (last accessed 3 March 2022).

Farrell, Henry and Héritier, Adrienne (2007) Conclusion: Evaluating the Forces of Interstitial Institutional Change. *West European Politics*, 30(2): 405–15.

Greenwood, Justin (2007) Organized Civil Society and Democratic Legitimacy in the European Union. *British Journal of Political Science*, 37(2): 333–57.

Hedling, Elsa (2021) Transforming Practices of Diplomacy: The European External Action Service and Digital Disinformation. *International Affairs*, 97(3): 841–59.

Hennen, Leonard, et al. (eds) (2020) *European e-Democracy in Practice*. Cham: Springer.

Kelemen, R. Daniel (2022) Appeasement, Ad Infinitum. *Maastricht Journal of European and Comparative Law*, 29(2): 177–81.

Kohler-Koch, Beate and Rittberger, Berthold (eds) (2007) *Debating the Democratic Legitimacy of the European Union*. Lanham: Rowman & Littlefield.

McNamara, Kathleen and Musgrave, Paul (2020) Democracy and Collective Identity in the EU and the USA. *JCMS: Journal of Common Market Studies*, 58(1): 172–88.

Norman, Ludvig (2021) To Democratize or to Protect? How the Response to Anti-System Parties Reshapes the EU's Transnational Party System. *JCMS: Journal of Common Market Studies*, 59(3): 721–37.

Norman, Ludvig and Wolfs, Wouter (2022) Is the Governance of Europe's Transnational Party System Contributing to EU Democracy? *JCMS: Journal of Common Market Studies*, 60(2): 463–79.

Nugent, Neill and Rhinard, Mark (2019) The 'Political' Roles of the European Commission. *Journal of European Integration*, 41(2): 203–20.

White, Jonathan (2014) Transnational Partisanship: Idea and Practice. *Critical Review of International Social and Political Philosophy*, 17(3): 377–400.

Wolkenstein, Fabio (2018) Demoicracy, Transnational Partisanship and the EU. *Journal of Common Market Studies*, 56(2): 284–99.

Wolkenstein, Fabio (2020) *Rethinking Party Reform*. Oxford: Oxford University Press.

INDEX

autocratisation
    autocratic states within the EU system, 14, 17, 191–2, 197–8
    democratic backsliding, 7, 17–18, 187–8
    Europarty alliances and, 188–90
    within federations, 188
    impact on the liberal democratic status quo, 12, 15, 18–19

Bartolini, Stefano, 150–1, 153, 156
Beck, Ulrich, 38
Brexit
    EU crisis lens and, 13, 15
    EU political deficit and, 3–4, 177
    national identity issues, 68
    the national referendum, 160
    secession and sovereignty issues, 70, 71
    United Kingdom Independence Party (UKIP), 156, 160

Cameron, David, 160
capitalism
    citizen protection from, 171–2, 173, 197, 200, 205

democratic capitalism in the EU, 137–9
    free market capitalism-democracy tensions, 121–2, 170, 171–2
    neoliberalism, 175–7, 197
    see also markets
Charter of Fundamental Rights, 112, 115
citizens
    citizen ambivalence toward international cooperation, 146, 151, 152, 199
    citizen identity as nation-based, 67–8
    in deliberative democracy, 76, 78–81
    EU engagement initiatives, 87–9
    national referendums on EU integration, 158–62
    popular (dis)satisfaction, 11, 15–17
    state obligations to, 30, 31, 51
    state protection from capitalism, 171–2, 173, 197, 200, 205
    see also deliberative democracy

citizens' assemblies, 80, 85
Citizens' Panel on the Future of
    Europe, 88, 89
citizenship
  modern conception of, 106
  multilevel citizenship, 110
  political agency, 99–100
  rights and duties of, 106–7, 201–2
  territorial boundaries and, 65
  unitary form of, 109–10
  see also EU citizenship
consensus democracies, 186–7
constitutional identity concept,
    112–13
contestation
  citizen ambivalence toward
    international cooperation,
    146, 151, 152, 199
  community integration and,
    144–6, 148, 149, 154, 199
  consociational models, 145
  as a core democratic value, 6, 11,
    147
  in deeply-divided societies,
    144–6
  empowered national parliaments
    and EU integration, 152–5, 205
  Europarty alliances and
    autocrats, 188–90
  and European integration, 11,
    149–52
  expanded democratisation of the
    EP, 155–8, 205
  minimalist democratic theory,
    148, 150–1, 160, 162–3
  national referendums on EU
    integration, 158–62, 205–6
  participatory democracy, 148–9,
    151–2
  popular (dis)satisfaction and,
    16–17
  problem-solving effectiveness,
    144–6, 148, 149, 154, 198–9
Council of Ministers
  qualified majority voting (QMV),
    42–3
  representation of member state
    governments, 8
  transparency and accountability
    of, 184–5
  voting procedures, 41–2
Court of Justice of the European
    Union (CJEU), 10, 18, 130,
    131, 136, 198
COVID-19 pandemic, 13, 16, 18,
    207

deliberation
  democratic backsliding's impact
    on, 17–18
  democratic mechanisms, 57
  equality in, 82–3
  within EU policy processes, 10
  parliamentary deliberation,
    48–9
  and representation in the
    European Parliament (EP),
    48–9
deliberative democracy
  alongside representative
    democracy, 77
  citizen involvement in
    policymaking, 76, 78–81
  citizens and the deliberative
    process, 78–9
  citizens' assemblies, 80, 85
  common identity-building
    processes, 79
  complexities of EU decision-
    making processes, 77, 78, 91
  decision-making procedures,
    83–4

dilemmas of, 77, 82–5, 203
educative power, 79
EU citizenship and engagement with EU politics, 86–7
EU initiatives for citizen engagement, 87–9
feminist critiques of, 82, 83, 85, 89, 203
institutional balance concerns and, 92, 94, 203
in long-term EU strategies, 91, 93–4
manipulation of by political institutions, 84–5, 91
meta-ethical concerns, 82
mini-publics model, 80
in ordinary legislative procedures, 91, 92–3
political design, 82
popularity of, 76
potential implementation in the EU, 76–7, 78, 90–5
practical implementation concerns, 83
reliance on expertise, 84
scholarship, 77–8
shifts in the EU-citizen relationship, 76, 87–90
size and diversity of the EU population, 77, 78, 90, 91
socio-economic location of citizen participants, 80–1, 82, 93–4
systemic approach, 77–8, 81–2, 89, 90
in Treaty amendment procedures, 91–3, 94–5
democracy
balance between expertise and democratic procedure, 206–7
collective perspective in, 57
conceptions of, 57
conditions of, 35
consensus democracy, 186–7
contested nature, 2
definition, 56, 125, 139, 144
democratic backsliding in the EU, 7, 17–18, 100, 177, 178, 183, 187–8, 191–2
democratic dilemmas, 1–3, 6–12, 56, 169, 178–9, 181–2, 195–211
in Europe, post-World War II, 169–74, 177–8
within the European political order, 1–2, 169
grand theory approaches, 3–6, 146–7, 195–6
individualist ontology, 57, 64–5
rescaling and, 64–8
tensions with capitalism, 171–2
tensions with federalism, 187
trade-offs in, 2, 5, 6, 7
democratic deficit
comparative approaches to, 181–7
deliberative democracy approaches to, 78, 95
democratic backsliding in the EU, 7, 17–18, 100, 177, 178, 183, 187–90, 191–2, 197–8
of the EU institutions, 182–3, 184–6
of the European Union (EU), 3–4, 85–6, 95, 102, 123, 174, 175, 176–7, 182–3, 196
in member state governments, 182
as a problem of democratic representation, 28–9, 32, 44, 94
underdeveloped character of EU citizenship, 190–1

democratic minimalism, 148,
   150-1, 160, 162-3
demoicracy
   definition, 67
   the demos of, 67, 203
   the EU as, 67, 109
   grand theory approaches, 5
demos
   concept of, 29
   demoicracy, 67, 203
   dilemmas of representation,
      28-9, 32
   interconnectedness of
      contemporary European states,
      29-30
   lack of, 4, 29
   potential role in European
      democracy, 4, 29
   within rescaling, 61-2, 67
   state-centric conceptions, 57-8
Denmark, 161, 205
direct legitimacy, 35

Early Warning Mechanism (EWM),
   44
EU citizenship
   democratic deficit and, 190-1
   the democratic minimum and,
      114-15, 116, 204-5
   differentiation in, 110-14,
      116-17
   and the disaggregation of
      citizenship rights, 109
   engagement with EU politics,
      86-7
   European Citizens' Initiative, 87,
      92-3
   freedom of movement, 99, 101-3,
      104, 105, 115-16, 175, 201
   intergovernmental approaches, 4
   introduction of, 9, 99, 101-2

non-discrimination principle,
   103-5, 107, 115-16
political rights, 101, 107-8, 175,
   176, 201
in relation to EU law, 9-10
rights and duties of, 9-10, 102-4,
   115
euro crisis, 15-16, 45, 150, 201
Europe of the Regions, 64
European Citizens' Initiative, 87,
   92-3
European Coal and Steel
   community (ECSC), 174-5
European Commission
   calls for a transnational political
      party system, 9
   as a democratic institution,
      185-6
   Spitzenkandidaten process, 185-6
European Court of Justice (ECJ),
   183, 196
European Parliament (EP)
   calls for a transnational political
      party system, 8-9
   coalitions, 18
   dual system of representation,
      46-7
   election process, 108, 185
   Europarties, 188-90
   Eurosceptic parties in, 156-7
   expanded democratisation and
      EU integration, 155-8, 205
   role in state management of
      externalities, 47-8
European political order
   democracy, 1-2, 169
   post-World War II democratic
      order, 169-74, 177-8
European Union (EU)
   codification of new sub-state
      spaces, 62-4

as a consensus democracy, 186–7
as a consociation, 145
crisis lens applied to, 12–14, 18, 110
democratic dilemmas, 1–3, 6–12, 56, 169, 178–9, 181–2, 195–211
democratic principles, 7–8, 17, 28
grand theory approaches to democracy in, 3–6, 146–7, 195–6
intergovernmental approaches, 3–4, 195–6
legitimacy, 123–4
national-supranational binary, 2, 3–6, 32, 88–9, 90, 100–1, 195–6, 200, 202, 210–11
north-south divides within, 15–16
as a post-sovereign political system, 9, 19, 70–1
Provisions on Democratic Principles, 7
sanctions against Russia, 13
supranational perspectives, 3–4, 5, 196
see also democratic deficit
Eurosceptic far-right parties, 15–17, 153–4, 156–7
externalities
concept of, 36–7
cooperation by states based on national systems of representation, 39, 42–6
cooperation by states supported by Union-level institutions, 39, 46–50, 51–2
cooperation by states without shared norms, 39, 40–1
the free riding problem, 37, 38, 43, 46

between interconnected democracies, 37–8, 204
managing externalities between European democracies, 30–1, 37–8, 51, 204
role of public authority, 37, 38

Farage, Nigel, 156, 160
federal democracies, 182, 183–4, 187
feminist scholarship, 82, 83, 85, 89, 203
Fligstein, Neil, 127

governance, term, 62–3

Habermas, Jürgen, 36, 45, 48, 77, 81–2, 153
Hix, Simon, 160
Hume, David, 37
Hungary, 17, 18, 24, 135, 187–8, 191, 192, 197, 198

indirect legitimacy dilemma
concept of, 30–1, 35–6, 199–200
control by national democracies, 31–2, 38–9, 200
control over national democracies, 31–2, 38–9, 200
legitimisation of the EU by the member states, 35–6, 38
managing externalities between European democracies, 38, 204
output standard, 31
institutions
within deliberative democracy, 81
the democratic deficit and, 182–3, 184–6, 198
institutional balance logic of the EU, 92, 94, 201

institutions (*cont.*)
  institutionalisation of new sub-state spaces, 62–4, 89–90
  manipulation of deliberative democracy, 84–5, 91
  see also Council of Ministers; European Parliament (EP)
integration
  citizen votes against further European integration, 11, 15
  contestation and community integration, 144–6, 148, 149, 154
  as a counter-balance to the nation state, 108–9, 169–70
  in deliberative democracy, 11
  democratic contestation and integration debates, 11, 149–52, 158–62, 205–6
  democratic representation and, 8, 17
  differentiated integration, 110–14, 116–17
  economic integration, 58–9, 174–5
  empowered national parliaments and EU integration, 152–5
  in Europe, post-World War II, 170, 173–4, 177–8
  horizontal integration, 104–5, 107–8
  market integration, 101–2, 113–14, 123–4, 134
  monetary integration, 113, 114, 123, 124, 175, 176
  national referendums on EU integration, 150–1, 158–62, 205–6
  political deficit, 174–7
  see also EU citizenship

Kelemen, R Daniel, 130
Keynes, John Maynard, 172, 173

Leyen, Ursula von der, 88, 95, 186, 189

markets
  democratic capitalism in the EU, 137–9
  democratic deficit approaches, 123
  the EU as a redistributive state, 133–6
  the EU as a regulatory state, 130–1
  free market capitalism-democracy tensions, 121–2, 170, 171–2
  Keynesianism, 172, 173
  market integration, 101–2, 113–14, 123–4, 134
  market logics-political logics relationship, 122, 126–8, 129, 132–3, 136, 181, 201
  neoliberalism, 175–7, 197
  redistribution by the nation state, 131–3
  regulation of by the nation state, 59, 127–30, 205
  relationship with democracy, 11–12, 121, 122–5, 200
  role of electoral politics, 122–3, 125–6, 136–7
  role of representation, 122–3, 125–6
  see also capitalism
Members of the European Parliament (MEPs), 5, 8
  see also European Parliament (EP)
migration flows, 15–16
multilevel governance, 60, 202–3

nation states
  borders, 13, 19, 58
  concept of, 56
  democracy as based in, 57-8
  externality management between European democracies, 30-1, 37-8, 51, 204
  free market capitalism-democracy tensions, 121-2, 170, 171-2
  impact of EU membership, 45-6
  integration as a counterbalance to, 108-9, 169-70
  market regulation function, 59, 127-30, 205
  national-supranational binary, 2, 3-6, 32, 88-9, 90, 100-1, 195-6, 200, 202, 210-11
  obligations to their own citizens, 30, 31, 51
  procedural obligations, 31
  redistributive policies, 131-3
  see also externalities; welfare state regimes
nationalism
  reflexive nationalism, 71
  at the regional level, 19, 63
neoliberalism, 175-7, 197
Next Generation EU initiative (NGEU), 133, 134-6, 138

Poland, 17, 18, 24, 135, 191, 192, 197, 198
policymaking
  citizen involvement in policymaking, 76, 78-81
  EU jurisdictional boundaries, 60, 68, 85
  rescaling challenges and, 59
  see also deliberative democracy

referendums, 150-1, 158-62, 205-6
  see also Brexit
regulation
  the EU as a regulatory state, 130-1
  market regulation by the nation-state, 59, 127-30, 205
representation
  calls for a transnational political party system, 8-9
  citizen representation, 7
  cooperation by states based on national systems of representation, 39, 42-6
  cooperation by states supported by Union-level institutions, 39, 46-50, 51-2
  cooperation by states without shared norms, 39, 40-1
  and deliberation in the European Parliament, 46-7, 48-9
  democratic deficit, 3-4, 28-9, 32, 44
  democratic representation in the EU, 33-4
  within the democratic state, 32-3
  Early Warning Mechanism (EWM), 44
  and the lack of a demos, 28-9, 32
  nation-state/supranational tensions, 8, 32
  rule-making beyond the state, 32-4
  state sovereignty and, 9, 19
rescaling
  concept of, 56, 58-9
  contested spaces of, 61-2, 202
  culture- and identity-based approaches, 66, 67-8
  democracy and, 64-8
  democracy delinked from territory, 65

rescaling (*cont.*)
  the demos within, 61–2, 67
  economic determinism, 65–6
  functionalist approaches to, 59, 65
  government responses to, 59
  individualist ontological approaches, 64–5
  institutionalisation of new sub-state spaces, 62–4, 89–90
  multilevel democracy, 68–72
  as multilevel governance, 60, 202–3
  republican association of states, 67–8
  sovereignty in a multilevel Europe, 70–1
  territorial levels of government, 63, 70

Schumpeter, Joseph, 148
Single European Act (SEA), 130
social movements, 62
sovereignty
  Brexit and secession issues, 70, 71
  the EU as post-sovereign, 9, 19, 70–1
  in a multilevel Europe, 70–1
  state-centric conceptions, 9, 15, 19, 57–8, 70
sub-state political identities, 19

Treaty amendment process, 91–2
Treaty on European Union (TEU), 3, 7

United Kingdom Independence Party (UKIP), 156, 160
United States of America (USA)
  democratic shortcomings, 183–4
  Europe's post-war democratic order, 171–4, 178

Valentini, Laura, 37
Vries, Catherine de, 151, 162, 164

welfare state regimes
  the EU as a redistributive state, 133–6
  EU citizenship and, 115
  market-correcting potential, 124, 131, 172
  Next Generation EU initiative (NGEU), 133, 134–6, 138
  redistribution by, 100, 131–3
  state protection from capitalism, 172
Wilders, Geert, 159–60